LIKE ONE
THAT DREAMED

A psalm touching genealogy

Not sole was I born, but entire genesis:
For to the fathers that begat me, this
Body is residence. Corpuscular,
They dwell in my veins, they eavesdrop at my ear,
They circle, as with Torahs, round my skull,
In exit and in entrance all day pull
The latches of my heart, descend, and rise —
And there look generations through my eyes.

LIKE ONE THAT DREAMED

a portrait of A. M. KLEIN

by Usher Caplan

foreword by Leon Edel

photographs edited by David Kaufman

McGraw-Hill Ryerson Limited
Toronto / Montreal / New York / St. Louis / San Francisco / Auckland / Bogotá
Guatemala / Hamburg / Lisbon / Madrid / London / Sydney / Johannesburg
Mexico / Panama / New Delhi / São Paulo / Paris
San Juan / Singapore / Tokyo

LIKE ONE THAT DREAMED — a portrait of A. M. Klein

ISBN 0-07-548451-X

1 2 3 4 5 6 7 8 9 10 THB 10 9 8 7 6 5 4 3 2

Printed and bound in Canada

Canadian Cataloguing in Publication Data
Caplan, Usher, date
Like one that dreamed: a portrait of A. M. Klein

Includes selections from Klein's unpublished works.
Includes index.
ISBN 0-07-548451-X

1. Klein, A. M. (Abraham Moses), 1909-1972.
2. Poets, Canadian (English) − 20th century − Biography.
I. Kaufman, David, date   II. Klein, A. M. (Abraham Moses), 1909-1972.
III. Title.

PS8521.L44Z57   C811'.52   C82-094429-7
PR9199.3.K53Z57

Designed by DAVID KAUFMAN

Contents

THE YOUNG KLEIN, AS LEON EDEL FIRST KNEW HIM.

Foreword

by Leon Edel

USHER CAPLAN'S BIOGRAPHY of the Canadian poet A.M. Klein brings into focus a remarkable if brief mid-century career, a large poetic imagination. Klein wrote in an elegiac vein — ethnic elegies of race and mind, celebrations of rites and rituals. He possessed great pride in his Judaic lore and it overflowed with empathy for his fellow ethnics, the French of Canada. His verses, in their final maturity, were fashioned out of the English tradition — the King James Bible and Shakespeare united with the racial strength of the Jews and the *Canadiens.* His early poems were romantic. These gave way in a middle period to the proletarian subjects of the 1930s Depression — pictures of life in the Montreal ghetto whose human comedy has lately been treated with the same pathos and wit by the novelist Mordecai Richler. Klein's final phase is reflected in his most "ecumenical" book of verse, *The Rocking Chair,* and its vivid feeling for French Canadian urban and rural life, taking as its principal symbol the simple article of furniture of its title that stands as if rooted on the verandahs of Quebec farmhouses all the way into the northern wilderness.

Klein's career was filled with his extraordinary energy but it was also enigmatic, in particular his falling into silence in middle life at the very moment when he seemed destined for literary fame if not literary fortune. Caplan provides the biographical evidence of Klein's inner falterings and his psychological collapse: he ceased to write, he almost ceased, like a monk who has taken a vow of silence, to speak — he who had been the most vocal and rhetorical of poets, drunk on words, and in three languages beyond his own English — Hebrew, Yiddish, and French. The biography is an admirable tribute to a mercurial and sadly truncated talent. It provides also the essential landscape that nourished the poet — the multi-lingual city of Montreal, which earlier in the century was best-known to Americans as a bountiful oasis during the Prohibition era.

Today Klein enjoys in Canada the status of a modern classic. His poetry was always exuberant and tender, solidly built, if not sufficiently worked over, on the three Montreal cultures already alluded to: the Anglos who lived on the west side, the French and their cultivated provincialisms who lived in the east end, and the ghetto Jews wedged in between. No poet has celebrated Montreal more picturesquely or more originally than Klein. He used macaronic coinages in the manner of James Joyce to sound the note of the city's grandeur — sitting as it does on the shore of a mighty river — and its Catholic austerity:

> O city metropole, isle riverain!
> Your ancient pavages and sainted routs
> Traverse my spirit's conjured avenues!
> Splendor erablic of your promenades
> Foliates there, and there your maisonry
> Of pendant balcon and escalier'd march,
> Unique midst English habitat,
> Is vivid Normandy!

Some day Montreal should name a street for this poet who managed to speak with both English and French voice in his well-wrought lines — the *érable* which patriotically evokes the Canadian national emblem, the maple leaf; the pun on masonry and species of houses in *maisonry,* followed by a description of the most characteristic features of the east-end *maisons* — the houses with their external stairways; the "pendent balcon and escalier'd march" needs a further gloss for the pun within the pun, "march" being also *marches* — the steps of the winding stair. Most important of all, "vivid Normandy" — a recall of the root-region in France from which most of the *Québecois* are descended.

Klein grew up in this city with its Mount Royal surmounted by an electric cross, its busy harbor, and its broad avenues and narrow criss-cross streets; he attended two of its universities, English McGill and the Université de Montréal, studying the humanities in one and law in the other. His emergence on the literary scene was rapid. As an undergraduate in the late twenties he attracted attention in the *Menorah Journal,* a distinguished American Jewish publication of the time. His first book came out in New York in 1940. Ludwig Lewisohn, in his foreword to it, greeted Klein as "the first contributor of authentic Jewish poetry to the English language ... He knows the Talmudic sages great and small as he knows the men and women on Saint Lawrence Street in Montreal, and into his English poetic style, even to the wild wit and sparkle of his rhymes, he has transfused their ardors, their dreams, their exquisite goodness, their storming of the very courts of God." Lewisohn recognized that it was *through* his very Jewishness that Klein reached beyond the parochial ghetto.

During the forties he continued to be productive, but he did not give his law practice the attention it needed. Instead he took on other duties: he became editor of the local Anglo-Jewish weekly, which gave him latitude to editorialize; he began to write speeches for Sam Bronfman, the whiskey magnate; he was involved in the politics of Zionism, and of Canadian socialism; he lectured on poetry at McGill. Two more books of verse appeared around the end of the war. By then he was developing as a poet and soon found his mature stride in *The Rocking Chair.*

In 1949 Klein had a profound emotional experience. He was sent by the Canadian Jewish Congress to visit the newly-founded State of Israel, and his feverish journey through the Mediterranean was rapidly embodied in a novel, *The Second Scroll.* Klein wrote this work with Joycean virtuosity, for he was immersed then in his exegetical study of *Ulysses.* Joyce's wanderer had been Leopold Bloom, a Jew in Dublin; Klein's myth of the wandering Jew was embodied in his faceless Uncle Melech, who stirs up trouble wherever he goes. The saga of the pilgrimage is dressed out in the novel with Klein's poetry, his remarkable account of the Casablanca ghetto, and a dazzling rhetorical description of Michelangelo's Sistine Chapel.

In all his writings, whether journalistic or literary, Klein embraced the ingrained wit of the human animal and showed himself master of a polyglot keyboard that yielded him endless ironies. Given other circumstances, he might have become a kind of Canadian Isaac Bashevis Singer, dealing however less with the occult and magic of Jewish fable and more with the local picturesque. His poetry, which can sometimes be faulted for looseness and for careless rhyme and the gilded lily of his rhetoric, possesses a splendid stance, a frank assertion of power. He wrote at times as if he, the little Jew (for "klein" means "little" in Yiddish or German), were speaking for a majority to an Anglo-French minority. He sowed recondite allusions, Hebrew words, biblical language in his texts, pouring his grandiose eloquence over the rooftops of Montreal and sending it into the bracing air of transcontinental Canada. But we must remember that the A.M. before the Klein stood for Abraham Moses — the father of the race and the supreme lawgiver: if he was small he embodied also legendary heroes. The nomenclature is to be taken seriously: it is a man's label and can be his identity. Klein spoke as if he were an Abraham or a Moses but at the same time he was aware of human non-sense and he possessed a becoming humility. What Caplan reveals to us in the moving pages of his book is how Klein in the end was trapped between the heroic and the mundane, plagued, like Herman Melville, with dollars. He conducted a personal five-ring circus that combined novel and poetry writing, the law, journalism, politics, and speech-making, as well as speech-writing for a corporation president. As a result, he was caught up in more conflicts than any human should ever carry. And yet in this struggle for self-assertion and livelihood he had an astonishing capacity to remain open to the world's splendors, and the splendor of words; his senses were never blocked — in the prime of his art — by his inner conflicts. He could remain in tune with an audible palpable visual world, even when he found himself out of tune with its insistences and demands.

MY EARLY MEMORIES OF KLEIN go back to our young days at McGill University in the middle 1920s. I was two years older than he was and already involved in literary and journalistic work. McGill was then a small college with a high reputation. It had had Ernest Rutherford, before he split the atom, and Sir William Osler's innovative medicine. In our time its well-known personality was Stephen Leacock, the laughing economist, whose homespun humor, very like Mark Twain's, found him audiences everywhere. The humanities tended to recruit cheap labor — young dons from Oxford and Cambridge, sometimes thorny ones like Harold Laski, who went on to the London School of Economics after a spell at Harvard, and in our time Lancelot Hogben, who later wrote *Mathematics for the Million*. McGill was lively in the 1920s and in our group we published a *Fortnightly Review* and read all the moderns that included Mencken, Cabell, Eliot, and the then still-banned Joyce.

Klein was a phenomenon at McGill, with his high forehead, his straight black hair, rimless glasses, heavy features and a curious twisted wry smile — a freshman who carried himself as if he were a senior and who was a fine orator. We both lived in the north end of the city and used to walk the length of Fletcher's Field after classes, feeling the crunch of snow underfoot and taking in fading skies of twilight that turned from pearl-white to pearl-grey. We talked of our literary enthusiasms and of my discovery of Joyce and his modernisms. One day I walked him as far as his home where he lived with his parents. It was an extended family and the house was a babble of tongues: there were numerous nephews and cousins. I recall how Klein grabbed an urchin of five with a face much in need of soap and said: "You will recite Macbeth won't you for my friend Leo." The child was set down on the dining room table and he at once tore into the soliloquy *Tomorrow and tomorrow and tomorrow* with tiny gestures and a flailing of arms. Klein had coached him well, but the childish variants were those of a juvenile comic who delivered the line about the poor player in his own special language: "That fretses and strutses his hour up-on the stage." Klein, whose own English was pure and robust, embraced the little boy for remembering so well and asked me to embrace him too.

How could we have known then that Klein himself would become that kind of player and life seem filled with the exigencies of strut and fret? And never more so than when he ran for Parliament. I lately came on a letter written to E.K. Brown, the Toronto critic, which shows how much Klein's drive to power conflicted with his self-image: "My sole regret is that every one of my political speeches — and in Cartier you have to make plenty, and in three languages — will cost me at least three poems *aere perennius*. For I certainly do not intend to stop writing. Hell, no! Not even a revolution could make me do that ..." The voters flocked to his speeches; they liked his eloquence; but they voted against him: public affairs were not for poets. Klein felt the defeat bitterly: he was fated to be a mouthpiece, a speech writer, for others, but denied a seat in Parliament.

And so bit by bit the will to achieve was eroded. It was a little like the schizophrenia of Ezra Pound, who when he discovered that none of his dreams would come true fell into a deep silence, the silence of depression. Some such stirrings of ambition were gradually undermined in Klein during the early 1950s, after the cordial reception of *The Second Scroll*; it was as if he had to continue considering himself a failure in order to feed his anger at a negligent world. Finally some fragile cord, some inner filament of his being gave way. This had been foreshadowed some years earlier in his "Portrait of the Poet as Landscape," in which he spoke with a profound self-awareness of the writer's "schizoid solitudes." He had made it the final poem in *The Rocking Chair* — the one poem in that lively book of observation and human enchantment that strikes a personal and dissonant note of anguish and terror.

I was passing through Montreal in 1957 and had a glimpse of his conscious moral defeat. I had given some lectures in Toronto and felt I should see Klein: we hadn't met in several years. He was friendly on the phone; told me he knew I was in Canada for he had seen me in a television interview. He invited me up for a drink. I came expecting a lively reunion. He opened the door, dressed in a dark suit, and wearing one of his sprightly bow-ties. He was almost too formal, considering our old friendship. He poured me a tall drink from a newly-opened bottle, gave one to his wife, but took none himself. I was invited to seat myself at one end of the room; his wife sat nearby, but Klein strangely remained at the other end and stood during the entire time, looking out of a large picture window. There was no conversation though I tried many subjects. He replied in brief phrases or with simple "yes" or "no." After a while, bewildered and sad, (as Klein continued to stand and look out into space) I politely withdrew. He seemed completely flattened out, as if in a living death. Usher Caplan has since shown me an entry in one of Klein's notebooks which illustrates poignantly the way in which the poet was seeking to become his landscape. The entry is of 1945, so it too was a foreshadowing. It reads like the record of a dream. He is attending his sister's funeral but instead of his sister in the coffin he sees himself laid out in it. And he finds he is listening to a eulogy about himself as publicist, orator, worker for Jewish causes: "From behind my tears, I watch the entire ceremony, a stranger at my own funeral. Among the dead, I am beyond pain and pity, and am unmoved by the ululation which I have so unintentionally caused.... Here my whole biography has been recounted, but nobody mentioned the fact that I was a poet." Klein adds: "I have kept the secret well. Now, no one will ever know of what I died."

This reads like a preliminary statement for the "Portrait of the Poet as Landscape," a poem that seemed to be a requiem for himself. The polished ironies describe the poet as if he were in a seascape, and he calls himself "a shelved Lycidas" — thus a drowned poet, reduced to giving off a faint phosphorescence at the bottom of the sea. But he still, at that time, could use words to describe his decision to be wordless, and his lines speak for him as his poetry does today — restores his image, his stance, his note of racial survival and melancholy. Klein still lives in his poetry even if he died of being a poet; and he comes alive in this biography almost as if he were now translated into myth and fable.

Author's Preface

I FIRST BECAME ACQUAINTED with A.M. Klein's writings fifteen years ago in a classroom at the Hebrew University in Jerusalem — a distant but fitting place for one Montreal Jew to discover another. His work excited me, in part because it arose out of the same mixture of cultures in which I had been schooled, and because it touched a nostalgic chord. The world of Montreal that he had been writing about at the end was the world of my own childhood.

During my years as a graduate student in Montreal and then at the State University of New York at Stony Brook, I often thought of writing about Klein. I never met him personally, and doubt that I ever could have, given his reclusiveness. The idea of doing a biography had not yet occurred to me then. Literature, we were taught, was separate from the author's life, and the author's life of little interest.

I am grateful to Irving Ribner and Alfred Kazin, two fine teachers at Stony Brook in the early seventies, for thinking otherwise. Ribner, who just before his untimely death was at work on a biography of Shakespeare, imparted to me some of his enthusiasm for literary detective work. Kazin, the noted American critic, conveyed a rare sense of the importance of literature to life. I recall in particular a talk he gave one evening in 1972 on the neglect of literary biography in universities and of the many missed opportunities to explore the lives of modern writers. That, I am quite sure, was the moment I decided to write this book.

Klein had died a few months before, and it seemed that some of the darkness surrounding him might finally be lifted. After an encouraging meeting with his son Sandor in the spring of 1973, I proposed to do a biography as my doctoral thesis and returned to Montreal to begin my research. By coincidence, the Public Archives of Canada in Ottawa was about to acquire the Klein papers, and that fall I had the good fortune to be hired for six months to arrange the collection and prepare a finding aid. This gave me an opportunity to study the papers very closely. Meanwhile I also pursued my search for letters and manuscripts in other collections and attempted to obtain copies of all of Klein's published writings from various libraries. In order to piece together the unrecorded facts of his life, I began corresponding with and interviewing dozens of his friends, acquaintances, and relatives. The thesis, which was completed in 1976, served as the springboard for this book. In the intervening time I was able to add to my research and to explore in greater detail the social and cultural backgrounds of Klein's life.

To round out my portrait of Klein, I have chosen to include as well a selection of excerpts from his published and unpublished writings, and an array of photographs and illustrations, some of them quite rare. Klein was very much an autobiographical writer, and the excerpts were chosen mainly for the light they cast on his life. The relationship between truth and fantasy is, of course, never simple, but a writer may reveal more about himself indirectly in a work of fiction than in factual writing. In a number of instances, excerpts have been condensed or modified slightly to suit the specific format of the book. Consequently the versions presented here should not be regarded as authoritative for purposes of quotation, and certainly not for reprinting. Since this was not intended as an academic book, it does not contain footnotes or a bibliography. Anyone interested in tracing my sources could begin by consulting the footnotes and bibliography in my doctoral thesis ("A.M. Klein: An Introduction," available through University Microfilms) as well as the finding aid to the Klein collection at the Public Archives of Canada.

For many of the pictures in this book, including all of the contemporary photographs, and for his thoughtful design work, I am indebted to my friend David Kaufman. Our collaboration began several years ago when I assisted in the making of his film portrait, *A.M. Klein: The Poet as Landscape* — a montage of interviews, readings, and images, whose success demonstrated that Klein's story was of wide human interest.

I am deeply grateful to A.M. Klein's sons, Colman and Sandor, and their wives, Alice and Mona, for allowing me to impose on them as much as I did, for facilitating my research in every way possible, and for granting permission to quote extensively from the writings of their father.

I owe a particular debt of gratitude to the staff members of the two institutions where I did most of my research — the Public Archives of Canada and the Jewish Public Library of Montreal.

Of the many people who spoke to me or wrote to me about Klein, or whose memoirs I drew upon in other ways, I am especially grateful to the following: Sam Abramson, Patrick Anderson, Harry Aronovitch, John Astbury, Charles Bender, Frances Bortz, Saidye Bronfman, Kenneth Cameron, Benjamin Caplan, Sam Chait, Marion Druker, Louis Dudek, Leon Edel, J.A. Edmison, Rachel Eisenberg, Ira Eisenstein, H.G. Files, Wynne Francis, Joe Frank, A.H. Friedgut, Leah Gaisin, Max and Sonia Garmaise, Saul Hayes, Alan Heuser, Hertz Kalles, Kalmen Kaplansky, Leo Kennedy,

Ben Lappin, James Laughlin, Irving Layton, S. Gershon Levi, David and Sophie Lewis, Florence Malus, Ellsworth Mason, P.K. Page, Melech Ravitch, David Rome, Bruce Ruddick, F.R. Scott, Regina Slatkin, A.J.M. Smith, Noah Wevrick, Dan Wolofsky, and Max Wolofsky.

The following people kindly provided me with copies of letters and manuscripts from Klein: Sam Abramson, John Astbury, Mrs. E.K. Brown, Leon Edel, Frank Flemington, Joe Frank, Leo Kennedy, James Laughlin, Shonie Levi, David Lewis, Ellsworth Mason, Melech Ravitch, and Guy Sylvestre. The Brown, Frank, and Mason collections are now in the Public Archives.

The following archives and libraries furnished me with copies of letters and manuscripts by Klein: the American Jewish Historical Society (letters to Stephen S. Wise); the Canadian Jewish Congress Archives (letters to H.M. Caiserman and Oscar Cohen); the Humanities Research Center of the University of Texas at Austin (letters to and from Alfred A. Knopf, Inc.); the Jewish Public Library (letters to Isidore Goldstick); the Philadelphia Jewish Archives Center (letters to the Jewish Publication Society); the Public Archives of Canada (papers from the Klein collection and also from the Lavy Becker, Rose Carlofsky, and Ellsworth Mason collections); Queen's University Archives (letters to Lorne Pierce and Alan Crawley); the University of Chicago Library (manuscripts and letters to *Poetry* magazine); the University of Toronto Library (letters to A.J.M. Smith); and the YIVO Archives (letters to Shmuel Niger and Jacob Glatstein).

Quotations from letters written by Leo Kennedy and Karl Shapiro are by permission of their authors. Quotations from the correspondence between Klein and Alfred A. Knopf, Inc. are courtesy of the Humanities Research Center of the University of Texas at Austin. Quotations from Klein's letters to *Poetry* magazine are courtesy of the University of Chicago Library. Selections from the *Canadian Jewish Chronicle* are by permission of the *Canadian Jewish News*.

Among other people who assisted me in various indirect ways, I especially thank Gretl Fischer, Seymour Mayne, Shulamit Nardi, and Ruth Wisse. My editors at McGraw-Hill Ryerson have been most helpful and encouraging. M.W. Steinberg, with whom I have been working for several years as co-editor of a number of volumes in the forthcoming collected works of Klein, has stimulated my thinking in countless ways. Readers who offered valuable comments on my manuscript at one stage or another, and whose names I have not already mentioned, included Sonia Caplan, Mark Finkelstein, Tom Marshall, John McLaren, Bob Taylor, and Sue Taylor. My wife, Ellen, has been of more help than I can describe.

THE CORNER OF ST. URBAIN AND VITRE, SEEN HERE IN THE EARLY THIRTIES, A BLOCK AWAY FROM KLEIN'S FIRST HOME, IN THE MIDDLE OF THE OLD "DOWNTOWN" SECTION OF JEWISH MONTREAL.

from Autobiographical

Out of the ghetto streets where a Jewboy
Dreamed pavement into pleasant bible-land,
Out of the Yiddish slums where childhood met
The friendly beard, the loutish Sabbath-goy,
Or followed, proud, the Torah-escorting band,
Out of the jargoning city I regret,
Rise memories, like sparrows rising from
The gutter-scattered oats,
Like sadness sweet of synagogal hum,
Like Hebrew violins
Sobbing delight upon their eastern notes.

(1942)

1

The Jargoning City

Fʀᴏᴍ ᴛʜᴇ ʙᴇɢɪɴɴɪɴɢ, Abraham Moses Klein was a child of two worlds. The first was the world of East European Judaism, whose ethos and lifeways his parents brought with them across the ocean from a town called Ratno, in the province of Volhynia, in the northwestern Ukraine. The other was the New World, and the particular corner of it he grew up in, itself divided into English and French, his beloved Montreal.

Klein was born in Ratno early in 1909 and was brought to Canada as an infant the following year. Though he could hardly have retained any memories of his first home, and later officially claimed Montreal as his birthplace, he always knew that Ratno was in fact and in some fatefully significant sense his true place of origin. (His parents evidently believed when he entered school that he would fare better as a native-born Canadian, and somehow the family records were altered accordingly. The truth of where he was born remained a harmless secret shared only with his close friends and relatives and with the occasional fellow-Jew from Volhynia whom he would meet in later life.)

Ratno at the turn of the century was a small Russian Jewish town, with about two thousand Jews among its three thousand inhabitants. In Yiddish parlance it was classified as a *shtetl*, that now mythical and evocative name for the hundreds of preponderantly Jewish towns that dotted the East European landscape. Life in the *shtetl* world of Volhynia was succinctly described by one of its illustrious sons, the Hebrew poet Bialik, as combining terrible poverty with a "pleasing mixture of simplicity, learning, and devoutness." The average *shtetl* Jew in the Russian Pale of Settlement eked out a meager existence and counted himself fortunate if he could earn enough in a week to set a proper meal for the Sabbath. He sought happiness not in the workday world but in the warmth of family life and in the spiritual realms of piety and Torah study.

Religious life in Ratno was colored by generations of Chassidic tradition. The town was situated in an area that had been a stronghold of Chassidism from the movement's first flowering in the middle of the eighteenth century. Although the original mystical impulses of Chassidism had waned considerably by the late nineteenth century, it remained a powerful influence in the smaller towns and a bulwark against the encroachments of secularism. A devout Jew in a typical Volhynian *shtetl* would have remained relatively untouched by the currents of enlightenment, social revolution, and Zionism that were already coursing through the more cosmopolitan centers of Russian Jewry.

Klein's parents were married in Ratno in 1897. His father, Kalman (or Koifman, as he was familiarly called), was at that time a widower, most likely in his mid-thirties, with two sons and a daughter. His mother, Yetta (or Yenta), was a widow, probably close to thirty, with two sons. In the early years of their marriage they had two daughters, Bessie and Dora, and nearly ten years later twin sons, one of whom was Abraham. The other twin took ill during early infancy and did not survive the passage from Russia to Canada.

In Ratno, Kalman Klein earned his living as a pottery merchant. The town's commercial activity centered around its single marketplace, where the Jewish merchants either sold their own craft wares or acted as middlemen between the big city manufacturers and the farmers and peasants of the surrounding villages. For parts of the year Kalman traveled with his merchandise from village to village throughout Volhynia and thus would be away from home for long stretches. According to his son's account many years later, Kalman reputedly had a flair for letter-writing and his letters home used to be read by nearly everyone in Ratno.

Isolated though he may have been from the political ferment of the large Jewish cities, Kalman could not have ignored the forces of anti-Semitism that were growing year by year and threatening the very lives of Jews everywhere in Russia. In 1881 a series of murderous pogroms had exploded across southern Russia and the Ukraine. The following year the Czar's government began enacting harshly discriminatory laws against Jews, effectively barring them from Russian society and reducing nearly half of them to abysmal poverty by the end of the century. Pogroms erupted again in 1903 and 1904, beginning at Kishinev, where scores of Jews were butchered and hundreds maimed in a police-sanctioned spree of horror that sent shock waves through all of Europe.

For many Jews there seemed no choice but to flee. A huge migration from Russia and Eastern Europe began in 1881, gathered force in the 1890s, and continued for several more decades. By the mid-1920s some four million had left, most of them for America.

Ratno itself was finally struck by devastating pogroms in 1915. But by that time the Klein family had already taken heed of the warnings and joined the exodus.

KALMAN AND YETTA KLEIN, WITH THEIR CHILDREN BESSIE, DORA, AND ABRAHAM, SEVERAL YEARS AFTER THEIR ARRIVAL IN CANADA.

KALMAN AND YETTA ARRIVED IN MONTREAL around the summer of 1910, bringing Bessie, Dora, and Abraham with them. Kalman's older children, who were already starting families of their own, also settled in Montreal during the next few years, while Yetta's older sons moved to Chicago.

Before the turn of the century many Jews had come to Canada with some vague notion that it was actually a part of the United States; others came with a clearer knowledge that Canada was a separate country and a hope that it was at least the next-best place. In the decade or so preceding the First World War the choice was simplified: entry to the United States was becoming increasingly restricted, while Canada on the other hand was actively seeking newcomers. To immigrants like the Kleins Canada seemed a promising enough destination, not only for its proximity to the "golden land" on its border but also because of its historical ties with England, which was known to be a tolerant and fair-minded democracy.

In 1881 the Jews of Canada were still a small community of twenty-five hundred, including eight hundred in Montreal, most of whom had arrived from Poland, Germany, and England around the middle of the nineteenth century. Then came the great tide of immigration from Eastern Europe; by 1910 there were already seventy-five thousand Jews in the Dominion, with close to thirty thousand in Montreal. In the next two decades these figures nearly doubled, and within Klein's lifetime the Jewish population of Montreal eventually grew to over a hundred thousand.

Montreal in the first decade of the twentieth century was the commercial heart of Canada, a thriving city of close to half a million people, two-thirds French-speaking and one-third English-speaking. The port of Montreal, despite being ice-bound five months a year, was the second-busiest in North America, surpassed only by New York. Prairie wheat moved out of the country through Montreal's massive grain elevators, and the produce of the Mediterranean was unloaded at her piers. Cheap power fueled the city's big industries — cotton and woolen goods, clothing and footwear, luxury foods, sugar, tobacco — and the factories hungered for immigrant labor.

When the Kleins arrived in Montreal they set up their first household in a small upper-storey apartment at 30 St. Charles Borromée, just south of Vitre Street. This was the lower edge of the Jewish immigrant district, which extended up the hill from Craig Street, centering on St. Lawrence Boulevard — "the Main" — and spreading several blocks east and west. The previous generations of immigrants who had already come up in the world gradually moved northward along this artery, past Dorchester Street as far as Duluth Avenue. At this time only the very rich could afford to move into the more affluent neighborhoods of Outremont and Westmount.

Concentrated in this corridor along St. Lawrence, the majority of Jews found themselves hemmed in between predominantly Protestant English Montreal to the west and Catholic French Montreal to the east. The "English," many of whom were in fact thrifty Scots, had built a solid world of commerce and struck deep roots in Canada. Montreal's great buildings and public institutions testified to their strict sense of duty as benefactors for the common good. The French Catholics opposite were generally poorer, held back by the forces of clericalism and reaction. Yet there was something to be envied in the way they guarded their heritage, its ritual splendor and holy images.

The separation of the English and French made Montreal a city of ethnic solitudes and a place where Jews could maintain their group identity more easily than perhaps anywhere else on the continent. Jewish immigrants to Canada were not drawn into anything like the American melting-pot. It was partly for this reason that Montreal Jewry in its formative years developed more along ethnic rather than religious lines. While Jews in the United States tended to preserve their identity by creating new and more liberal forms of

ST. LAWRENCE BOULEVARD NORTH OF PINE AVENUE, PHOTOGRAPHED AROUND 1930. ST. LAWRENCE WAS THE COMMERCIAL "MAIN STREET" OF MONTREAL'S JEWISH DISTRICT FOR OVER HALF A CENTURY.

synagogue life, most Jews in Canada, and particularly in Montreal, remained nostalgically attached to official orthodoxy while at the same time evolving secular Jewish institutions based on linguistic and folk-cultural bonds.

The Kleins arrived in Montreal precisely at the period when its Jewish community was beginning to flourish. Dorchester Street, just north of their first home, teemed with Jewish life. The very heart of the district was but a few blocks away at the corner of Dorchester and St. Urbain. Along the next block west was Dufferin Square, Montreal's "Jewish park." Here, on a typical Sabbath afternoon in pleasant weather, residents of the area could be seen strolling with their families, meeting other newcomers, discovering long-lost acquaintances from Europe, and exchanging the latest gossip. It was here too that older immigrants would frequently advise the recent arrivals on how to adapt to their new life and, most important, how to find a job.

Many newcomers were encouraged to look for work in the tailor shops and clothing factories clustered around Notre Dame and St. Paul Streets. Anyone could learn the trade by starting as an "under-presser" or lining maker. As in New York, Montreal's thriving garment industry was mostly Jewish-owned and thus a likelier place for a Jew to find employment. A job in the garment industry was not everyone's first choice: working conditions were notoriously unhealthy, and there were frequent layoffs during strikes

21

and slack periods. In Europe such work would have been demeaning, even for poor Jews. But here the Jewish factory-owner, who probably had started out in the same lowly circumstances, was a living symbol of the success that any ambitious laborer could dream of for himself.

Other occupations were also possible. Some Jews became peddlers, hoping eventually to open a dry goods store, perhaps even a wholesale business. Country peddlers worked the hardest, traveling with their wares for months at a time through the villages and farmland of rural Quebec. Strong young men who might have been blacksmiths or wagoners in the old country could find well-paying jobs as longshoremen at the harbor. The Canadian Pacific Railway workshops in the east end needed carpenters and metal-workers, and skilled immigrants were often recruited straight off the ships as they arrived. Foremen at the CPR shops became adept at giving instructions in sign language until the new workers acquired a smattering of French.

KALMAN KLEIN FOUND WORK in the garment industry and became a presser — not an easy job for a man of his slight build. Heavy hand-operated irons were still in common use in the stifling sweatshops of the pre-World War I era. Until the momentous tailors' strike of 1912, the workweek was officially fifty-nine hours, and even longer during the busy season.

Most immigrants quickly learned that the thing to do in "America" was to work your way up. The first English words that they acquired in the street or on the job often included expressions like "hurry up," "help yourself," "time is money." Those with the most ambition worked especially hard, attended English classes at night, and laid careful plans for setting up businesses of their own. Kalman, however, showed no interest in ever becoming more than a presser. His material ambitions in life were modest, and the peaceful haven that Canada offered him was reward enough.

True to his *shtetl* background, Kalman placed the highest value not on worldly success but on the precious hours spent in prayer and study. On moving into his first home in Montreal he found that there were already a number of *shuls*, or synagogues, nearby, such as the Chevra Kadisha on St. Urbain Street, the Chevra Shas on Lagauchetière, the Beth David, or "Rumanian *shul*," on Chenneville, and still others farther uptown. Just a few short blocks from his home was the one he probably joined, the B'nai Jacob, or "Russian *shul*," on Cadieux near Vitre. The proportion of devoutly religious Jews in Kalman's generation of immigrants was quite high, but the pervasive secularism of the New World made it difficult for them to hand down their beliefs and practices to their children. In the early years many had resigned themselves to being the last generation of religious Jews in America, and as a token defense against utter assimilation insisted only on a kosher home and bar-mitzvah lessons for their sons. In time, more rabbis and teachers began arriving from the old country, Jewish afternoon schools were established, and for those who desired it at least some form of religious tradition seemed likely to survive.

Outside the synagogues modern influences were beginning to shape the social and cultural life of the community. Russian-Jewish revolutionaries who had manned the barricades in cities like Minsk and Vilna in 1905 carried their political activism with them to Canada, joining forces with other socialists and trade unionists. In the pre-war years Montreal's Jewish socialists were radically anti-religious, anti-Zionist, and internationalist in outlook. On May Day each year a grand parade would be staged along St. Lawrence Boulevard, ending in an open-air rally at Champs de Mars, followed by a mass meeting at Prince Arthur Hall or the Labor Temple. Other nationalities began to join these mainly Jewish demonstrations, until the outbreak of the First World War undermined the ideals of internationalism. Most Jewish socialists then became increasingly concerned with the specific problems facing Jewish workers.

Simple folk like Kalman Klein hardly knew what to make of all the radical ideas that were being tossed about at work and in the Yiddish press. "My father's notions about the philosophy of Marxism were very primitive," Klein wrote many years later in an autobiographical passage of his novel *The Second Scroll*.

Occasionally on Sundays, when there was a rotogravure section, he would buy the *Jewish Daily Forward* and read with an incredulous skepticism the theoretical articles which that journal featured. Invariably he would drop his paper with the helpless comment: "*Hegel-baigal!* The way these men do stir up a stew!" Considered from the point of view of common sense, the thing was simply ludicrous.

His antipathy to the dialectic, I am afraid, stemmed also from a non-intellectual source: his gratitude to the land of his adoption. This land hadn't given him much, mainly because he hadn't been a taker, but it had given him — this was no cliché to my father — freedom. Whenever one of his Ratno compatriots took it in his mind to run down Canada and its capitalismus, my father would withdraw a coin from his pocket and point to the image thereon engraved: "See this man, this is King George V. He looks like Czar Nicholas II. They are cousins. They wear the same beards. They have similar faces. But the one is to the other like day is to night.... After Nikolaichek you shouldn't even so much as whisper a complaint against this country!"

Most Jewish laborers were practical-minded socialists. If there was a revolutionary goal that they could sympathize with, it was not the overthrow of capitalism in North America but the elimination of the anti-Semitic regime of the Czar in Russia. For themselves, the aim of socialism was essentially to ameliorate working conditions in the factories; here utopia was the forty-four-hour workweek.

A series of long and bitter strikes took place in Montreal in the years leading up to that utopia. In 1912 the well-organized tailors' union held one of the biggest strikes ever seen in the city. Factory owners resorted to hiring strikebreakers, further aggravating the class divisions among Jews. The tailors won their fight in 1912 and went from a fifty-nine-hour to a forty-nine-hour week.

Their next step was to join the Amalgamated Clothing Workers of America in 1916. The historic two-month strike organized by the Amalgamated Workers in 1917 aroused deep feelings and tensions on the picket lines. Kalman Klein, as a member of Pressers' Local 167, participated in that struggle, and the worry and excitement of it left an indelible impression on his young son. In the end the Amalgamated Workers were victorious, and by 1919 they achieved their forty-four-hour week.

Strikers were the great heroes of the day. Even housewives emulated their tactics as a form of protest each time the bakers or butchers raised their prices. In the wake of any new price increase, leaflets would quickly appear to announce a mass meeting, which usually would end up as a very homey Jewish gathering, everyone enjoying the opportunity to speak up freely and openly in Yiddish.

BESIDES SOCIALISM, other ideological currents were also beginning to flow through the community. Zionism, though still in its infancy, exerted a strong emotional appeal. Theodor Herzl, the European founder of political Zionism, had become a legendary figure in his own time; following his premature death in 1904 he had come to be worshiped by the masses as the greatest Jew of the modern era. As if in answer to the ubiquitous visage of Marx, Herzl's aristocratic-looking portrait, with its piercing visionary gleam and patriarchal black beard, became a fixture in many Jewish homes and gathering-places. In practical terms, Zion was still only a beautiful distant dream, a place where pious Jews were buried, not where modern Jews lived. But the hope of re-establishing the ancient national home was alive in Jewish hearts. Zionist songs were sung at local gatherings and Zionist politics were followed with keen interest.

The gulf separating the socialists and the Zionists was partly bridged by the Po'alei Zion, the Labor Zionists, who struggled to make Jewish nationalism an acceptable part of socialism. Two of their leading orators, Chaim Zhitlowsky and Nachman Syrkin, frequently visited Montreal and stirred audiences there. Zhitlowsky would fire the imaginations of his listeners with his socialist-revolutionary view of Jewish history, drawing comparisons between Isaiah and Marx.

The center for nearly all philanthropic and communal activity was the Baron de Hirsch Institute on Bleury Street. Here help was extended to widows and orphans, the poor and the unemployed, the sick and the abandoned. The Institute's night classes were attended mostly by young immigrants eager to learn English. For many of the students, the Baron de Hirsch soon became their social center as well — classroom romances blossomed into marriages, intellectuals and artists discovered one another and formed clubs, and business partnerships were started in casual conversations. The Institute's library offered books and newspapers in English and Yiddish. Newcomers had the highest regard for the teachers at the Institute, and for anyone, in fact, who could read English; to have learned English meant that one was already coming up in the world. The wealthy Montreal Jews who maintained the Baron de Hirsch Institute also earned the respect of the new immigrants, even though these were usually the same Jews who exploited them by day in their factories.

Yiddish drama was the favorite mainstay of the community's cultural life. Most of the Yiddish plays and occasional operas staged in Montreal were imported from New York. Audiences loved the familiar atmosphere of the Yiddish theater, its nostalgic evocation of old-world emotions, its gushing sentimentality, its idealization of the poor workers. Until the first movies came to Montreal, Jewish audiences learned a good deal of popular history, as well as fashions and manners, from the famous Yiddish actors of the period. During some seasons there would be a play performed just about every night, either at the Monument National Theater on St. Lawrence or at one of the various other halls. The Monument National became one of the landmarks of Montreal's Jewish district; it was also used for indoor rallies, and every Rosh Hashanah and Yom Kippur, to the perennial dismay of rabbis and communal leaders, it would be converted into a makeshift synagogue.

The city's own Yiddish daily, the *Kanader Adler*, had gotten off to a shaky start in 1907 but soon emerged as a guiding force in the life of the community. The newspaper's editors brought the vital issues of the day to public attention, supported Zionism, and gave many communal agencies and projects their first boost. It was through the *Kanader Adler* that immigrants still unable to read English first learned about the wide, unknown city beyond their neighborhood, and about Canadian history and politics. International events and movements were treated no less seriously; some of the paper's first columnists were recently-arrived members of the Russian-Jewish intelligentsia — highly educated, literate, and politically sophisticated.

Canadian politics did not provide this immigrant generation of Jews with a field for the playing out of its ideological passions. Besides the language barrier, no socialist party yet existed around which the workers might rally. Basically, Jewish involvement in the local political scene grew out of the practical need to counter anti-Semitism by ensuring the presence of a Jewish voice at every level of government.

Anti-Semitism in the province of Quebec emanated from intellectual and ecclesiastical quarters far removed from the average citizen. Individual relations between Jewish and French Montrealers were normally quite friendly — much warmer, at any rate, than relations either group had with the aloof and paternalistic English. Nevertheless there were occasional outbursts of rowdy hooliganism. In the wake of such happenings, which evoked dreadful memories of pogroms in Europe, mass meetings would invariably be called, at which invited politicians and representatives of the Citizens' League would try to allay fears and encourage more active participation by Jews in local politics.

The first generation of Montreal Jewish representatives emerged out of the established uptown community. Abraham Blumenthal became the city's first Jewish alderman in 1912, and in 1916 Peter Bercovitch was elected to Quebec's legislative assembly. On the federal level, S. W. Jacobs represented Montreal's "Jewish riding" of Cartier for the Liberals from 1917 until his death in 1938. Jacobs had previously distinguished himself as one of the first leaders of the Baron de Hirsch Institute and as a co-founder of the English-language *Jewish Times* of Montreal. As a lawyer, he had pleaded brilliantly in a famous anti-Semitic libel case in Quebec City. His success as the eloquent, aristocratic spokesman of his people made him a model for the coming generation of educated young Jews who might be drawn to politics.

It was amidst all of these social and intellectual crosscurrents that A. M. Klein's character was initially formed. The world of Jewish Montreal in which he grew up underwent great changes during his lifetime, and in certain respects even disappeared. Yet, in his mind and imagination, it was to remain a constant reality.

from Montreal

Grand port of navigations, multiple
The lexicons uncargo'd at your quays,
Sonnant though strange to me; but chiefest, I,
Auditor of your music, cherish the
Joined double-melodied vocabulaire
Where English vocable and roll Ecossic,
Mollified by the parle of French
Bilinguefact your air!...

Never do I sojourn in alien place
But I do languish for your scenes and sounds,
City of reverie, nostalgic isle,
Pendant most brilliant on Laurentian cord!
The coigns of your boulevards — my signiory —
Your suburbs are my exile's verdure fresh,
Your parks, your fountain'd parks —
Pasture of memory!

City, O city, you are vision'd as
A parchemin roll of saecular exploit
Inked with the script of eterne souvenir!
You are in sound, chanson and instrument!
Mental, you rest forever edified
With tower and dome; and in these beating valves,
Here in these beating valves, you will
For all my mortal time reside!

(1944)

from Stranger and Afraid

...Nor have the days of my childhood really passed; I am still that child who with patriarchs and prophets peopled St. Lawrence Boulevard, and City Hall Avenue; the big tree on the corner was the Oak of Mamre to me, and any day I expected an Angel to stop at my door, to leave some happy message for my father, away at work. Over the street where I played my childhood games, hiding under the legs of staircases when it rained, it was Noah's Rainbow which shone for me, like the wrapper of some new chocolate bar. And O the days when I bore the heavy folio of the Talmud through the streets. I walked with Tannaim, my head full of the subtleties of its most clever rabbis, and of the romance of Resh Lakish, gladiator turned scholar, and of Rabbi Akiva, poor, and sitting on the window-sill of the academy, hearkening Torah, and Rabbi bar bar Hunah. Time, and the advent of worthies from other spheres, speaking other accents, has not banished them. They still escort me, like good wishes, on my way.

(mid-1940s)

2

Out of the Ghetto Streets

KLEIN ALWAYS HAD happy memories of his early upbringing. As the youngest child, with two doting sisters hovering over him, he received more than his share of nurturing attention. The children of his older half-siblings were his first playmates; he was in fact their uncle, but most of them were about his own age. His father's brother, Mayer, who boarded with the Kleins for several years, became almost a second father to the boy. And since the home served as the focal point for the extended family, young Klein regularly found himself amidst the bustle of visiting relatives, particularly on Saturday nights such as the one described in his nostalgic poem "Autobiographical."

Kalman Klein was a kind and gentle father. His greying beard and slow, quiet gait seemed to confer on him a measure of humble dignity. His many children and grandchildren trusted his wisdom and would turn to him regularly for counsel or to resolve a domestic quarrel. Being a God-fearing and learned Jew, he was frequently called upon to serve as a *dayan*, a member of a rabbinical court. It became almost a legend in the family that because of his religious principles he had once remained unemployed for over a year until he could find a job that did not require working on the Sabbath. Kalman's mildness was philosophical. Fighting was for goyim, he would say; better to flee from trouble, as he had from czarist Russia, and let the Almighty settle scores. To his youngest child, this passive stoicism would long remain a mystery — was it really a kind of inner strength, or was it simply faintheartedness?

Yetta Klein was no less pious than her husband, though hers was rather the housewifely religion of folklore and superstition. In temperament she was quite different from Kalman. If her son's semi-fictional sketches of her serve as evidence, she was a demonstrative and excitable woman, very proud, and in her later years given to melancholy. She was always fiercely protective of her Abram. Her ambitions for him were those she could understand — success, tangible rewards, popular esteem.

As a young boy in a religious home, Klein was taught to observe all the customs and rituals of orthodox Judaism. Life followed the rhythm of the Jewish calendar. Every Friday evening and Saturday morning — all "starched up," as he later recalled — he would accompany his father to the synagogue. On Saturday afternoons father and son would review together the weekly Torah reading. The festivals in their seasons were especially exciting times, rich in symbolism and in pleasant sensory associations.

In 1914 the family moved northward to what is today 4071 Hôtel de Ville, between Duluth and Rachel. Klein was five years old and began attending Mount Royal School, several short blocks west on Clarke near Rachel. (Like all Jewish children in Montreal, he was enrolled in the Protestant rather than the Catholic educational system.) In 1918 his parents decided to move again, this time to an upper duplex at 4267 Clarke, close to the school, and it was here that they lived for the next twelve years.

Klein's parents must have noticed very early his sharp intelligence and lively imagination. Much as he liked playing with friends on the street and in the parks nearby, he valued the times he could spend alone, reading and daydreaming. When he was ten, he was given a set of the *Book of Knowledge*, which he pored over in fascination. His parents had little time for reading and owned no books other than the usual collection of holy tomes and prayerbooks customarily found in a religious household. At the age of eleven he joined the Jewish Public Library, then located in a rented house on St. Urbain Street, and immediately became known to the staff as the boy who had asked to borrow Darwin's *Origin of Species*.

At Mount Royal School he stood out as the model pupil to whom everyone else would be disparagingly compared, and led his class every year. An early schoolmate recalled how "each time the teacher would ask a question, up would shoot this boy's hand. We were sort of annoyed with him at first, because he would always be the enthusiastic student, the one who knows all the answers." He fitted the image of the shy, sensitive bookworm, moody at times, slightly awkward in manner, not at all athletic. His friends would tease him for years about his first swimming lesson at the YMCA pool, where he nearly drowned in four feet of water and had to be fished out with a pole.

One winter he broke a leg while trying to learn to skate and had to be hospitalized at the nearby Hôtel Dieu. This and other visits to the Hôtel Dieu were probably his nearest childhood encounters with Catholic Quebec — experiences in which fear and love were unforgettably mingled. Once, after returning home from a stay at the hospital, he mischievously shocked his parents by showing how he had learned to cross himself and recite a small

from The Mountain

In layers of mountains the history of mankind,
and in Mount Royal
which daily in a streetcar I surround
my youth, my childhood —
the pissabed dandelion, the coolie acorn,
green prickly husk of chestnut beneath mat of grass —
O all the amber afternoons
are still to be found.

There is a meadow, near the pebbly brook,
where buttercups, like once on the under of my chin
upon my heart still throw their rounds of yellow....

And all my Aprils there are marked and spotted
upon the adder's tongue, darting in light,
upon the easy threes of trilliums, dark green, green, and white,
threaded with earth, and rooted
beside the bloodroots near the leaning fence —
corms and corollas of childhood,
a teacher's presents.

(1947)

prayer in French. Years later he paid fond tribute to the hospital sisters in their black robes and white hoods

> who fluttered to me in my childhood illnesses
> — me little, afraid, ill, not of your race, —
> the cool wing for my fever, the hovering solace,
> the sense of angels...

Klein's fondest memories of early childhood all had to do with his initiation into the world of Hebrew language and learning. His Jewish education began at home, under his father's guidance, and then under a series of tutors, first among them the old Rabbi Tannenbaum, pictured in *The Second Scroll* as a "round little pygmy of eighty, bearded to the breastbone." At six or seven he began attending the nearby *Talmud Torah*, the Kerem Israel Hebrew Free School on St. Dominique near Marie Anne, where classes were held Sunday mornings and weekdays in the late afternoon.

The most revered of Klein's religious mentors was Rabbi Simcha Garber, the same Reb Simcha memorialized as "Sophist" in "Portraits of a Minyan." Rabbi Garber was for young Klein the rationalist, Mitnagdic counterbalance to his father's Chassidism. Having noticed the boy's cleverness one Saturday at synagogue, he began tutoring him privately for a number of years and nearly persuaded him to enter the rabbinate.

Garber was a Talmudist in the Lithuanian tradition, which meant, first of all, that he insisted on a high standard of analytic argument. Apart from his great gift of memory, he had an agile, athletic mind, and an ease with his own learning that opened onto humor. In later years, Klein often enjoyed recalling Garber's dazzling intellectual feats and the swift dialectic skill with which he could construct extraordinary edifices of logic.

> One placed a pin upon a page
> Of Talmud print, whereat the sage
> Declared what holy word was writ
> Two hundred pages under it!
>
> The skull replete with logic's tricks
> Is long returned to that matrix
> Where it's the worm that splits the hair
> As the last fallacy's made bare.
>
> But I think that in Paradise
> Reb Simcha, with his twinkling eyes,
> Interprets, in some song-spared nook,
> To God the meaning of His book.

Klein was about thirteen years old when he stopped going to Garber's home for private lessons. During the next few years he continued his Talmud

KLEIN IN EARLY ADOLESCENCE, PROBABLY AROUND THE TIME OF HIS BAR MITZVAH. HIS CHILDHOOD FRIEND SAM ABRAMSON LATER RECALLED HOW KLEIN'S SOMEWHAT SHELTERED UPBRINGING "PREVENTED HIM FROM PARTICIPATING IN THE NORMAL BOISTEROUS ACTIVITIES OF BOYHOOD. HE WAS KNOWN IN THOSE EARLY YEARS AS A BOOKWORM AND 'SISSY'."

studies under several other very capable tutors, but by then he had already entered high school where new influences were beginning to steer him in other directions.

SECONDARY SCHOOLING was by no means universal in Klein's generation. For many Jewish immigrants, sending a child to high school rather than to work was more than they could afford. Those families that were able to make the financial sacrifice were motivated by an ingrained respect for learning and the belief that education was the key to all worldly success. In Klein's case, given his father's studiousness and his mother's practical-mindedness, there was never any question that he would receive as much education as possible.

The high school Klein attended, Baron Byng, was on St. Urbain Street near Rachel, with its back entrance on Clarke almost directly across from his home. The school had just been built and Klein's class was the first to enter, in September 1922. Reflecting the neighborhood, the student body was almost entirely Jewish; the school itself, however, had a noticeably English atmosphere in that era, many of the teachers having come from overseas.

Life and Eternity

I

This wrist
Is tied
With twist
Of hide
The which
Is bound
My watch
Around.

II

I list
To catch
Of wrist
And watch
The beat.
Their rhyme
Doth meet
In time ...

III

Wrist-pulse
Marks strife,
Impulse
Of life.
Watch-tick
Is Time's
Chronic
Gasped rhymes ...

IV

I hate
Watch-tick.
'Tis Fate's
Sharp prick ...
I love
Life-pulse
Above
All else ...

V

Some day
I fear
You may
Not hear
The throe
Of vein
For lo!
No strain ...

VI

Death-kissed
The throb
Of wrist
Will stop ...
But watch
Will still
Tick-scratch
Its will ...

written as an exercise for John Astbury (April 1926)

Baron Byng was to serve as the first important gateway to success for several generations of young Montreal Jews, most of them the children of poor immigrants. Its graduates, comprising a rather remarkable who's who of Canadian Jewry, would gradually create an almost mythical aura around their fondly-remembered alma mater.

The teacher who left the greatest impression on Klein was a Canadian from Nova Scotia, John Astbury, who taught him Latin and English in grades ten and eleven. As a Latin teacher, Astbury was best remembered by his students for the enthusiasm with which he brought to life the poetry of Virgil, making his subject far more than a dry study of declensions and conjugations. In his English classes he frequently drew comparisons between English and Latin poets. Many years later Klein paid tribute to him as the teacher "who in the high company of the man from Mantua first opened for

34

me the magic casements of English literature." It was under Astbury's influence that he acquired his early liking for Keats, Shelley, and Browning, and his aversion to Wordsworth. Astbury tended to take a personal interest in his most promising students. He expected great things of Klein, and was the first adult to recognize his poetic talent and to encourage him in that direction.

Klein grew increasingly bookish in high school. His hunger for knowledge was all-consuming, a striving for perfection. Regardless of how interested or uninterested he might actually be in a subject, if it seemed to him part of what a cultured person ought to know, he was determined to know it. He forced himself, for example, to listen to music so that he could discuss it intelligently, but frankly admitted that it gave him no pleasure.

His close school friends were impressed with his braininess and his precocious command of English. Doing homework together at the Jewish Library, they would sometimes notice in amazement that he would be reading a dictionary from cover to cover as if it were a novel. His leaning towards English poetry seemed odd to them at first; certainly it was an unusual interest for a bright Jewish youngster of that time and place. Nevertheless they found his witty phrases and rhymes amusing. A few of the girls in his class memorized his off-the-cuff lines of doggerel so well that they could still recite some of them fifty years later.

In 1924 Klein and several of his friends formed a small intellectual circle they called the "Sholom Aleichem Club," named after the famous Yiddish storywriter. Meeting from time to time at a Jewish school in the neighborhood, the group devoted itself mainly to discussions of modern Yiddish literature. It was at one of these sessions that Klein first met David Lewis, who was to become one of his closest friends through high school and college.

Lewis was almost Klein's age, but being a recent immigrant from Poland, with Yiddish as his mother-tongue, he had at first been placed two grades behind. Klein was among those who helped him learn English, and later Lewis skipped one grade. Their friendship developed out of a common intellectual bent and a passion for debate. Klein by this time was already moving away from his strict observance of orthodox religion towards an equally devout commitment to Zionism. Lewis came from the very opposite end of the Jewish spectrum; his father was a doctrinaire Bundist, dedicated to socialism and secular Yiddish culture, and firmly opposed to Zionism. Yet Klein, in his openness to all varieties of Jewish feeling and expression, took great delight in visiting Lewis at his home and being drawn into heated discussions in Yiddish with both father and son. The two young men naturally influenced each other over the years of their friendship. Lewis acquired from Klein a sensitivity to poetry and the arts and a respect for at least the cultural side of Jewish nationalism. Klein on the other hand gained a serious interest in political theory and began leaning towards Lewis's brand of democratic socialism.

Klein's drift away from orthodox Judaism was perhaps inevitable. Yet in Lewis's recollection of this stage in Klein's intellectual development there is a slight hint of self-reproach:

Partly because of new friends he had made, friends like myself, but mainly because of his reading and thinking, he veered away from religion. He did an immense amount of reading; he began to read philosophy when we were still at high school. He began to think about the world in general a little more deeply, and to question, not so much the existence of God and the background in Jewish religion, as the observance, the habits, the rituals. I remember we talked about it a great deal.

In the first years of their friendship, Lewis's calmly expressed objections to religion evoked strident arguments from Klein, but by the time he was about to enter university Klein had not only given up his earlier ambition of studying for the rabbinate but had abandoned virtually all religious practice.

IT WAS THROUGH LEWIS that Klein came to know Bessie Kozlov, the girl he was eventually to marry. In June 1925 Lewis met and fell in love with his future wife, Sophie Carson, a classmate of Klein's from early childhood. Sophie immediately set out to introduce her very close friend Bessie to Lewis's circle and to Klein in particular. Sophie Lewis would always have warm memories of Bessie and of this romantic season in both their lives:

Bessie was a very sweet, sensitive, and kind person, with a generosity of spirit that was most unusual. She had a very beautiful face, and a character that reflected itself in everything she said. We loved each other very much and spent wonderful times together, at dancing, choir practice, playing the piano. She used to dabble a bit in writing poetry then, but stopped after she met Klein.

I didn't like the boyfriends she had at the time — they were older but less refined. When I suggested she might like to meet the group of young men I had met recently, she scoffed at first. But one Friday evening in August I persuaded her to come along with me. We were gathered around the bandstand on Fletcher's Field, and the moon was shining. That was the night Klein was first introduced to her, and one could see the look on his face — he was so enraptured, so thrilled. He was — for him — speechless. He fell in love with her at once.

But to begin with she didn't feel the same way about him. When we returned home — we lived right next door to each other and used to converse across adjoining balconies — I asked her, what do you think of Klein? "Oh," she replied, "he's cocky! He's arrogant! I'm not interested in him!" I said, "Give him a chance. He's so .brilliant." "Well," she answered, "I don't like some of the things he says, and he makes us all feel very inferior." I said, "He doesn't make *me* feel inferior; just answer him back!" But this wasn't in Bessie's nature at the time. Not that she was ever a willy-nilly sort of person, but she didn't really assert herself.

BESSIE KOZLOV, KLEIN'S HIGH SCHOOL SWEETHEART AND FUTURE WIFE.

KLEIN POSING NEAR THE ENTRANCE TO HIS HOME ON CLARKE STREET IN THE LATE TWENTIES.

Bessie was not alone in being put off by Klein's condescending manner. Several other female classmates were also to remember him as unpredictable in his moods — usually friendly and gregarious, but then suddenly sarcastic or utterly aloof.

Klein in fact was a typically bashful adolescent who often tried to hide his awkwardness behind a facade of cleverness and indifference. He was painfully aware of his own social clumsiness and struggled to control it. One way he sought to win Bessie over was through his poetry, and in the early years of their long courtship he composed scores of love poems and sonnets to her, many of which he later published. In one sonnet he seems to allude to their first meeting and relates his shyness to his Jewishness.

> Upon a time there lived a dwarf, a Jew.
> His shelter was a thatch, a beard his clothes.
> He loved God, and feared women. When he knew
> A girl was at his hut, he thumbed his nose.
> One night the moon turned Shadchen. In its glow
> The dwarf beheld a girl, a maid, a lass...

The image of the "dwarf" — a punning reference in Yiddish to his own name, Klein — is part of his playful self-denigration before Bessie. In another sonnet, he is

Sonnet Semitic

Would that three centuries past had seen us born!
When gallants brought a continent on a chart
To turreted ladies waiting their return.
Then had my gifts in truth declared my heart!
From foreign coasts, over tempestuous seas,
I would have brought a gold-caged parrakeet;
Gems from some painted tribe; the Sultan's keys;
Bright coronets; and placed them at your feet.
Yea, on the high seas raised a somber flag,
And singed unwelcome beards, and made for shore
With precious stones, and coins in many a bag
To proffer you. These deeds accomplished, or
I would have been a humble thin-voiced Jew
Hawking old clo'es in ghetto lanes, for you.

(late 1920s)

> No handsome Greek nor even wealthy Jew,
> But only a poor scribbling Abraham.
> Behold this brow is not smooth stone; this nose —
> Well, smaller noses grow on bigger men ...

Gradually he won Bessie's affection and love. Sophie Lewis noticed the surprising change all this made in his character.

After meeting Bessie he seemed to be transformed. Before, he had been so sure of himself, so assertive. Suddenly he was very humble and submissive. ... She exuded a feeling of patience and tolerance, she was so simple and unassuming, and this impressed him very much. I think, too, that it took a long time before he got over the wonder of this beautiful young woman having fallen in love with him.

During the years to follow, the four friends would often go walking together on evenings and weekends, usually in Fletcher's Field or Lafontaine Park, stopping to sit and read or talk about events of the day. Klein sometimes continued to exhibit a certain lack of ease at social gatherings, as Sophie Lewis was later to recall:

When the weather wasn't that good we would go either to Bessie's home or to mine. The girls would play piano, David would play the fiddle, and we would sing songs — Yiddish songs, popular songs of the day, songs from school — and invariably we noticed that Klein never joined in. He was quite self-conscious that way — we also could never teach him to dance. Once we questioned him about it: the poet, the man of rhythm, unable to sing? "Oh no," he said, "I can't keep a tune." I said, "You *do* sing, I've heard you humming something." "Oh," he said, "there's only one tune, people know what it is — *Yes sir, that's my baby. No sir, don't say maybe...*" And at the end of every one of our singing sessions, up would pop his voice with *Yes sir, that's my baby.*

Klein and Bessie shared the stage as class valedictorians at their graduation ceremonies in October 1926. Klein's valedictory address was nearly censored at the last moment by Principal Campbell. In his text, Klein recalled the official opening of the school four years earlier and remarked how strange it had seemed then that among all the many flags that bedecked the new building the only one missing was the banner of the people who made up ninety percent of the student body. Reviewing a draft of the speech beforehand, Campbell was taken aback by its candor and consulted Astbury, who replied simply, "It's true, isn't it?" Klein was permitted to go ahead, and, when speaking, concluded his thought with words to the effect that "it wasn't so bad, after all, because a wind came up and parted the clouds, and there overhead was the blue-and-white of the Jewish flag." Klein's outspoken pride, conveyed in this simple image, remained impressed in the memories of all his fellow graduates from Baron Byng High School.

from STRANGER AND AFRAID

In a passage from one of his unfinished novels, Klein points to the early influences on him of his father's meekness and his mother's vituperative temper.

A million million watts of sun shone down upon the street, and in the distance padded my Hebrew teacher, bearing his curled umbrella. On the corner, in the windows of the big cafeteria, philosophers sat stirring the livelong tea. At the door, old man Ungar as usual took up his stance, his tzitzith dangling from his fly, in his outstretched hand pamphlets — the miracles of the Baal Shem Tov, the Jewish calendar in a twelve-page book. Across the street, a dog was leashed by a bitch's tail.

My friends played in the street the game of frogs, the game of running sheep, the game of ball and mitt. The staircases stretched their legs down from the buildings, so good, so warm.

A water wagon passed with its crystal broom of water, and the asphalt changed color, and the air changed odor. But the sun was still shining, licking the barber's candy-pole, warming the hot-house garden in the grocery window. And I, on a stoop watching the players, watching a horse nuzzling his oats from a bag, and the lady on the balcony who didn't wear any pants, and the passers-by, and the standing baby-carriages. I was munching on an unpeeled cucumber, salting it with salt from a paper, and making it last with bites from a heel of bread. The little cucumber-seeds were good, the smell was fresh and watering, and I was thinking of the always bitter taste of the last cucumber-bite. Would I bite that bite, or would I have the strength to forego it?

Suddenly someone shouted *Look out!* and I got the feeling that a ball had maliciously been aimed at me, either because I was standing there, innocent and smaller, or because I looked happy eating my cucumber, or because I seemed to be engrossed in myself and in my doings and the ball would shock me out of my daze. I turned my head in time, and dropping my food — I wouldn't have the last bitter bite, after all — caught the ball in my hand. I flung it up the street. They would have to run for it. It might even roll into a drain.

Hey, whadaya tink yer doin'? The ball-thrower was running up towards me, all fight and indignation. It was Simki, whose mother kept going to the Juvenile Court to plead for him.

Gawon! he said, Gawon and get't!

Yah, the gang chimed in, you threw it, you get it.

You threw it first, I said, and you threw it at me, you get it.

Simki turned to his henchmen, with a look which said Leave this to me, boys.

We'll see who'll get it, he said. He heaved his body against mine. I staggered and almost fell. I regained my balance. I made myself look bold and brave.

Who d'ya think you're pushing? I said.

Nobody, he said, nobody at all. Just a little runt. C'mon, get a move on.

You fucken bastard! That gave me status. Take this!

A fight! A fight!

I flailed into him with both my hands, and we were at it, for a long tiring time, fists and elbows, puffings and bumpings, clinches and withdrawals. An uppercut, the kids were shouting. Hit him in the muscles! Hit him in the kishkas!

Simki landed a blow plop on my nose. It began to bleed.

Blood, the boys shouted.

I was frantic, and full of pity for myself. I wanted to cry, but held back my tears. Then he rushed me again. My arms whirled, my heart pounded, my head bobbed up and down, and my legs were very tired. I lost count of the blows I was receiving.

Cheese it — someone said — his old man!

It was so good to hear that. They scattered. Simki looked around and saw that it wasn't his old man. He took to his heels. Someone went for the ball.

And there coming up the street was my father, walking quickly toward me.

Even on Sunday I can't rest, he said. What happened? Why did they do this?

Now I could weep.

They started up, I said. They threw a ball to hit me, and then wanted me to go and get it!

And if you had gotten it for them what would have been? You would have lost something?

Sure, they would have called me coward.

So they'd call you coward. Fighting is for goyim. A big thing — to show a fist!

But I gave him good, too. I'm sure he's going to have a bump on his forehead.

Alright, come in the house. How many times have I told you not to go near those bums and tramps. They're not your equals. Truckdrivers, that's what they're going to be, truckdrivers and icemen. America! Only fighting! Heathen! Jewish heathen!

I walked meekly beside him. It was so good to be near him, he so protective, and knowing all about the true things in life, and what God really esteemed. Moreover, he never made any great fusses. Everything, he felt, would pass. Nothing that happened to him or his was unbearably tragical. But not so my mother.

Woe is me! she cried, a calamity, a misfortune! She wiped my nose with the hem of her apron. My fighter! she ironized. Look who stands up to maintain his dignity. A word goes, remain the blows! But look, his eye is swelling! O, all the evil dreams that I dreamed yesterday, and the day before yesterday, on *their* life and limbs may they settle! The bandits!

(mid-1940s)

from Hapaxlegomenon

In this excerpt from another unpublished piece of fiction, Klein projects onto the hero, Wolf Pimontel, his own autobiographical portrait of the artist as a young Hebrew-school lad. The character of Rabbi Glazer is undoubtedly based on Simcha Garber.

... He was in the Bible class of the Kerem Israel Talmud Torah, the class of the twelve-year-olds. It was Sunday morning, and the venerable Rabbi Glazer, followed by a retinue of school trustees, scholars, men busy in the communal interest, has come from his sacred preoccupations as head of the rabbinate to give ear to the sucklings of Torah. Mr. Herscovitch, the teacher, is very excited; his thin home-made cigarette, set between the hairs of his beard and his mustache, glows bright, like Moses' bush. Burnt down, he drops it to the floor and stamps it down, wisp of tobacco and leprous stain of ricepaper. Mr. Herscovitch finds the presence of the honored company extremely disturbing; he keeps moving his skullcap back and forth over his head; he smiles, ingratiating; he is apologetic; and, finally, he proceeds with the text in Genesis. The word *tzohorayim* is reached.

"Is there any boy here who can tell us why *tzohorayim* means noon?"

It is Rabbi Glazer himself who puts the question. The worthies who have escorted him smile benignly one to the other. Even Mr. Nathan Gordon, the distinguished lawyer of whom it is said that he is "learned in the jots and tittles" and that it is this very erudition which has made him the brilliant jurisconsult that he is — all gentiles, it seemed, were foredoomed before so irresistible a Talmudist — even he appears to be impressed. A good question: one will see whether the little heads are of the true line, whether the apples do indeed fall not far from the tree.

There is silence. Some of the boys demonstratively knit their brows in concentration. Suddenly the boy recently arrived from Europe — he enjoys in Holy Writ, therefore, an unfair advantage — is waving his hand frantically. His palmful of knowledge will not be contained.

"From *tzoroh* — trouble? Because at noon it is very hot?"

From the expression on the faces of the elders it is clear that the answer is wrong. The immigrant boy falls back crestfallen ...

And he — Pimontel remembered this distinctly — he had rejoiced at his rival's discomfiture; so early had displayed itself his avidity for intellectual pre-eminence, his corrupting cursed pride of mind. But no one had noticed it then, not that day in the classroom; later, a year later, his father was to suspect it, as he did that Simchas Torah when his son, in the arrogant piety of his confirmed thirteen years, had come home, after having visited five synagogues in each of which he had been accorded an aliyah *and* the ritual glass of wine, and in his drunkenness and with a very wide gesture had declared to his father that he, Wolf the son of Kalman, designate Pimontel, was the Messiah. He could not but smile at his father's response to this annunciation. "Yenta," he had said, addressing his wife, "give him a sour pickle, and let him go to bed!" ...

His mind reverted back to philology in the Kerem Israel where Mr. Gordon was asserting that this last had been a good try, but that in *tzoroh* the *hai* followed the *resh*, while in *tzohorayim* it was the other way round. This, then, was the clew: one must look for a word in which the *hai* was before the *resh*. *Tza'ar*? No, that was with an *ayin*. *Tzir*? That was with a *yud*. Ah, *tzohar*!

He was a young boy again, raising his hand in triumph.

"From *tzohar* — a window. Because at noon it is very bright."

The countenances of the old men light up like shining fenestrations.

"And how do you know that *tzohar* is a window?"

"Because it is written: *Tzohar ta'aseh latevoh* — Make a window in the ark."

They glow with racial pride, these elders, looking down at the shoots and sproutings in their garden. Rabbi Glazer advances and strokes affectionately the prodigy's cheek. Mr. Gordon, too, praises an ingenious derivation, nor can he resist an excursus of his own. There are other words, he says, which might have been adduced: *zohar*, splendor, *sohar*, the moon; and in Mr. Herscovitch's Pentateuch he seeks examples. The boy's mind wanders off in a rumination of possible English parallels — window, noon-do, moon-dawn — while Mr. Gordon continues to wet his finger to turn the pages to find the quotation to show the hues and uses of the chatoyant word.

"But who," exclaims the lawyer suddenly, interrupting his spittled researches, his finger in mid air, "who will give me the derivation of *apiryon*? ... And what does the word mean?"

There is a depressing silence. Mr. Herscovitch frowns.

"Does nobody remember," Mr. Gordon hints, "King Solomon's *apiryon*? From the Song of Songs?"

The Song of Songs? This he, Pimontel, knows. Does he not recite it every Friday night, in the company of his father, to usher in the queenly Sabbath? *Apiryon*. Murmuring to himself the introductory verses, he at last recites out loud:

"*King Solomon made himself an apiryon of the wood of Lebanon. He made the pillars thereof of silver, the bottom thereof of gold, the covering of it of purple, the midst thereof paved with love, for the daughters of Jerusalem.*"

"Very good! Very good!" Mr. Gordon praises. "Now what is an *apiryon*?" He pauses. "But the question isn't really fair. Nobody knows for certain. *Apiryon* belongs to that class of words in the Scriptures known as *millot bodedot*. Isolated words. Lonesome words. They occur but once in the whole Torah, and are related to no other word. In English, or rather in Greek, they are called hapaxlegomena, words of single occurrence. Once, only once, do they appear in the Bible, and then are not heard from again...."

Throughout the years he had remembered that word, and remembered also, sometimes with pride and often with embarrassment, the use which Rabbi Glazer that day had made of it. Always there was, the Rabbi had said, in every group, or congregation, or community, some one person who, too, might be called a hapaxlegomenon — a man who for learning, or piety, or good works, was single of his generation. These of mankind were God's especial gems, even as were gem-like the unique words set in the crown of Torah. Towards such singularity to strive was a good and meritorious thing; he hoped that in this classroom there was one who was destined for such distinction. And here it was that there had been made personal for Pimontel the reverberating word, for the Rabbi, seeking through flattery to set the boy athirst for Torah, had then turned his homily about the bright answers that Pimontel had made and had prophesied that if he kept along the path which he seemed to be taking then he might one day be a great one in Israel, a scholar, a rabbi, an eminence of The Law. There were no heights which couldn't be scaled....

(late 1940s)

McGill University's Arts Building, appearing today much as it did in Klein's college days.

from Hapaxlegomenon

The rabbinic discipline appealed to his mind, but his spirit revolted at it; they were too many and too onerous, the prohibitions and behests heaped upon the man who would be religious mentor to his people. The fact was that he was not good enough, not godly enough, not godly at all. Worldly doctrine, moreover, had come to seduce him away from the arbitrary rigors of tradition.

It had been at about this time — his zeal for ordination abated, he was following now a course in Arts at McGill — that he had begun his at first careless and later systematic breaking, not of The Commandments (God forbid!), but of those proliferative other un-thundered precepts of the Law....

His religion, he had realized, was no longer his mother's religion, with its tabus and superstitions, its cherishing of bottles of healing holy water sold by saints, its hanging of talismans in the rooms of parturitive women, its tearing of grass from graveyards, its shun-me scarecrows and its kiss-me fetishes; but still it was something which to him was valid, important. He wanted, even now, to justify — perhaps in a secular way? — the high hopes that Rabbi Glazer had entertained for him, to fulfill through a variant thereof the prophecy with which he had blessed him.

And a way had indeed suggested itself: it would be with words, themselves a kind of deed, that he would serve his Author. With little verbal fiats of his own would he pay his tribute to him Who had uttered the fiat, first and all-creative....

(late 1940s)

44

3
Green Celebrants

KLEIN ENTERED MCGILL UNIVERSITY in the fall of 1926. McGill at this time was an academy of international repute and a venerable institution of English culture in Canada. Jewish students were already beginning to make a distinctive mark on campus life, for as Montreal's immigrant community grew and prospered in the twenties, more families were able to send their children to university. When Klein was at McGill fully a quarter of the students in the Arts Faculty were Jewish.

McGill's attitude towards its Jews was in some ways typical of how Montreal's English establishment in general regarded this eager element in its midst — as privileged guests, who were welcome to enter but barred from ownership, and who were expected to learn all they could but not forget their place. Certain faculties, such as Law and Medicine, instituted unofficial quotas to keep back the ever-increasing number of Jewish students seeking admission. An academic career, which a bright Jewish student like Klein might otherwise have embarked upon, was simply out of the question.

The McGill students of Klein's generation were somewhat of an élite group. Many of the twenty-seven hundred or so men and women who formed this close-knit community saw themselves as part of an avant-garde that would shape the world's future, and they approached the social and political problems of their day with earnestness and optimism. At the same time there was a certain lightheartedness about university life, a sheer enjoyment of the camaraderie, the humor, and the buoyant mood of the late twenties.

Klein's daily walk from his home on Clarke to the campus downtown carried him out of the familiar lower-class streets of his childhood and on to the stately wide thoroughfare of Sherbrooke Street. The gray, solid, Victorian houses surrounding McGill spoke with mute dignity of wealth and establishment. Though he may not have felt completely at ease in this alien environment, Klein eagerly absorbed from it the best that could be had. McGill's attraction for him lay not so much in the social vistas it opened, or seemed to open, as in the intellectual and creative stimulation it offered. In this respect, he was fully in his element at McGill. It was the school that finally shaped his mature sense of tolerance and fairness, his deep feeling for English civilization, his commitment to the improvement of society, and above all his respect for serious learning and for reasoned argument finely expressed.

During his freshman year he enrolled in general courses in English, French, Latin, Greek, European history, mathematics, botany, and zoology. His favorite subject from the outset was Latin, which he chose as one of his two majors. W. D. Woodhead of the Classics Department took a special interest in Klein and nominated him at the end of the year for the Barbara Scott Scholarship, which gave $115 to the freshman student excelling in classics. "Woody," as he was known, remained friendly with Klein for many years after. His urbane wit and pedantically literate puns, and the ready quips and quotations with which he spiced his talk, always delighted Klein.

In second year he took advanced courses in Latin prose and poetry, an introductory course in philosophy, and introductory courses in economics and political science, both given jointly by J. C. Hemmeon and Stephen Leacock. Of the two, Hemmeon was the real economist and the greater teacher. He called himself a communist; some called him an anarchist, though nobody could imagine this shy, eccentric old bachelor ever espousing violence. Hemmeon's fine skeptical mind impressed only the most serious of his students, among them Klein's friend David Lewis.

Stephen Leacock, on the other hand, attracted a following not so much for his intellectual qualities as for the outlandish character he played, with his shaggy mustache, crushed suit and fedora, tattered lecture gown, and his long, unbuttoned coonskin coat. He was already widely renowned as a humorist and had an infectious habit of chuckling at his own cracks. Klein, in reminiscing about McGill, would remark that in Leacock's classes the dismal science of economics had truly been made into a gay art. Leacock loved to make fun of mathematical economists and properly speaking was not himself an economist at all. His most enthusiastic students responded to his earthy humanity and were stimulated by his sense of the sweep of history and the interconnectedness of human thought and action.

By the time he was in second year, Klein had already made up his mind to go into law, which was one of the main reasons he chose economics and political science (joined then in a single department) as his second major. Law was an extremely popular career choice among Jews at McGill; in fact, during the late twenties Jewish students made up about forty percent of the Law Faculty. As Klein noted with some concern: "Every Moishele, Shloimele, and Berele of the bourgeois immigrant aspires to a forensic career. Nincompoops, mediocrities, and Litvaks vie with each other in the soliciting of trade. The roll-calls of colleges rhyme monotonously with bergs and vitches.... Only enigmatic examinations and birth control can remedy the situation." But if the field was crowded, Klein's budding talents as a debater and public speaker seemed to give him an edge.

In third year he registered in two more of Leacock's courses, in addition to Latin, half-courses in botany and education, and a course on Chaucer, Spenser, and Milton given by George Latham. It was from Latham that he acquired his life-long fascination with slang expressions and their roots. He took no other English courses at McGill, since he was already reading all he wanted and had no plans to pursue graduate studies in literature.

In his senior year he took advanced courses in Latin, political economy, history, and philosophy. For his major paper in political economy he wrote on the history and development of the Amalgamated Clothing Workers of America in Montreal, drawing partly on his childhood memories of the two-month Amalgamated Workers strike of 1917, in which his father had participated. His interest in labor history was prompted as well by his increased involvement during his senior year in the McGill Labor Club.

Though conscientious about his studies, Klein also managed to devote a great deal of time to extracurricular pursuits — as a Zionist, a public debater, and an aspiring poet. Off campus, he joined Young Judaea, a popular Zionist youth organization with branches in many North American cities. Klein was initially attracted to Young Judaea because of its emphasis on Hebrew culture and education. He agreed with the "cultural Zionist" Achad Ha'am that the land of Israel was not to be just a political haven for Jews, but rather a spiritual center for the renaissance of Jewish creativity around the world. At the same time he was hardheadedly realistic about the struggle for the Jewish homeland, to which he was passionately committed all his life. In the final analysis Zionism for him was infinitely more than a political plan, an economic solution, or a cultural way of life; it was, in his words, "also a faith," no less than orthodox Judaism had been for his father.

In the fall of 1928 Klein became the editor of the *Judaean,* a small monthly magazine published by the organization's national office in Montreal and distributed to members across Canada. He remained at this job until 1932. Simultaneously, as Young Judaea's educational director, he supervised evening courses in Jewish studies, prepared teaching materials on Zionism, Hebrew literature, and Jewish history, and frequently gave lectures himself, not only in Montreal but in many other Canadian cities to which he was sent. An annual activity of Young Judaeans was the re-enactment of an international Zionist Congress, in the style of the mock parliaments that were popular at McGill. Klein loved to participate in these events and on several occasions played the role of the fiery orator Vladimir Jabotinsky. He would always identify strongly with the literary figures in the Zionist movement — Herzl, Nordau, Jabotinsky — and would project onto them an idealized image of the poet-statesman that he found inspiring.

Herzl in particular would be Klein's great model of the litterateur who, with dramatic flair and messianic zeal, chooses to consecrate his life to his people.

Herzl had been a literary dabbler, a typically cultured gentleman of Paris and Vienna, the dilettante citizen of the world. He frittered away his energies in the concocting of epigrams, he wasted his time in preparing dialogues for contemporary plays. Suddenly he realized that the monologue of woe which was his people was of far greater consequence than the scintillating dialogues of his ephemeral plays; suddenly he realized that he did not have to write dramas — a drama was before him; suddenly he was aware that a volcano should not spend itself in festival fireworks, and that a Jew should not write feuilletons when tragedy stalks before him.

To Klein, Herzl was a poet in the highest sense: a maker, a creator, who with the spell of his language brought to life, out of nothing, the vision of a Jewish state.

Few of Klein's classmates knew very much about his work for Young Judaea. On campus he was probably best known for his activities in the university's Debating Society. When Lewis entered McGill in the fall of 1927, the two friends began debating together in many forums, usually as a team, sometimes as opponents. The performances of Klein and Lewis were high entertainment, always attracting large appreciative crowds of young people. Their debating styles were complementary: Lewis calm and logical, speaking as from the heart; Klein flamboyant, quick-witted, often hilarious. They came to be known around McGill as the poet and the politician, though it was not always clear at first who was which.

Klein and Lewis often performed for McGill's Jewish student club, the Maccabean Circle, in debates which seemed to carry forward their intense adolescent discussions begun in high school: Could orthodox Judaism withstand the forces of assimilation in America? Was Zionism or socialism the better path for Jews to follow? Had religion or science contributed more to the welfare of humanity?

In public debate, as in private conversation, Klein never let go of an opportunity to raise a laugh, even if it contributed little of substance to his argument. Whether in the form of a sparkling epigram or an impromptu retort, wit was his strongest weapon, ingratiating him with his audience and unnerving his opposition. As Lewis noted:

When he came out with something really witty, his whole face would light up in a broad grin and his eyes would sparkle. Often he would laugh at his own one-liners with great hilarity, shaking his broad shoulders up and down in a manner that reminded me of Leacock.

He was oratorical when he debated, standing firmly, using his hands and arms —

DELEGATES TO THE EIGHTH NATIONAL CONVENTION OF CANADIAN YOUNG JUDAEA, MONTREAL, 1931.
KLEIN IS SEATED SIXTH FROM RIGHT. SEATED TWO AND FOUR SEATS TO HIS LEFT RESPECTIVELY ARE HIS
FRIENDS MAX GARMAISE AND JOE FRANK. AT HIS RIGHT IS SAM CHAIT.

not excessively, but sometimes jabbing the air with his index finger for emphasis. He
had a somewhat musical voice, a bit harsh-sounding on occasion, but even the
harshness was not unmusical. His tone, his enunciation, had a bit of the lilt of the
Jewish district. And of course you could tell he loved words just by the way he rolled
them out. He didn't just toss off his good lines, he savored them.

Another fellow-debater at McGill, Alexander Edmison, described how
Klein would sometimes start off in a quiet voice and then suddenly boom
forth. "He was very forceful, and people who didn't know him would be
scared stiff.... If any opponents had the temerity to quote from the Old
Testament, he would simply slay them, because he would always have four or
five other quotes to rebut!"

His public speaking and debating skills, and then his membership in the
McGill Labor Club, already seemed to point him towards a life in politics. To
a few of his more cynical classmates it appeared likely that after completing
law school he would outgrow his radicalism and then settle into a
comfortable career in the Liberal party, in the line of other Liberal
representatives of Montreal Jewry like S. W. Jacobs and Peter Bercovitch.
Klein's socialist sympathies, however, were to remain strong and would
ultimately preclude such a course.

HIS REAL AMBITIONS, in any case, did not seem to lie in politics; the higher calling that he truly wished to follow was poetry. For someone with Klein's literary ambitions, McGill in the late twenties provided an ideal point of departure. In 1925 a group of enterprising students had come together to create a literary magazine, the *McGill Fortnightly Review,* which in its mere two years' existence was to usher in the "modern movement" in Canadian literature. The magazine's poetry editors and brightest literary lights were A. J. M. Smith and F. R. Scott. Another poet, Leo Kennedy, was not a McGill student but was invited to join the publication in its second and final year. Leon Edel, whose reminiscences of the *Fortnightly* group were later to make him its unofficial chronicler, started out as managing editor.

Klein, a mere freshman, was evidently too young at first to break into the *Fortnightly* circle. In the spring of 1927 the magazine announced that it would cease publication after one more issue. Klein had not dared to submit anything all year, but seeing his last chance he decided to bring one of his poems to the poetry editors, Scott and Smith. Edel was present at the meeting, and later often had occasion to recall it:

Klein turned up one day at the McGill Union and timidly offered — as timidly as was possible for so ebullient a freshman — a fine sonnet for the *Fortnightly*. Smith read it with feeling and emotion. He liked it. Scott liked it. But, they said, what about the word "soul" in one of the lines? — romantic, old-hat, an intrusion in an otherwise admirable piece of poetic declamation. I sat watching the emotions in Klein's face: pride of authorship mingled with eagerness to be printed. He was in conflict. He wavered. He almost said yes — and then suddenly pride of authorship won. It would have been a delight for him, a freshman, to make the *Fortnightly*. But he couldn't square revision with his pride. He took the poem back; and Scott and Smith, with their insistence on tone and modernity, didn't change their minds. Thus the *Fortnightly* never printed him.

Smith and Scott went on to keep alive the spirit of the *Fortnightly* and to advance the modernist influence in Canadian poetry. Klein, in his remaining years at McGill, formed close and lasting friendships with most of the group's members.

Arthur Smith, when Klein first met him, was no longer actually a student at McGill. He had completed his B.Sc. in 1925, and then switched to English and wrote his M.A. thesis on the poetry of Yeats the following year. When the *Fortnightly* was in its last season, he was employed as a teacher at Montreal High School and was about to depart for the University of Edinburgh to begin his Ph.D. studies. Edel recalled him as

a slim youth of medium height, with fine dark brown hair which he combed back; usually a few strands fell over his forehead and his gold-rimmed spectacles, so that he looked like the young Yeats. He carried himself with an excess of politeness that was in his English breeding, but he was a tempest of revolt against Establishment hypocrisies. He was the son of English immigrants and lived in bourgeois comfort in Westmount; he invited his friends to tea in formal English fashion.

Smith had already been published in the prestigious *Dial* and now took it upon himself to be the champion and herald of modern poetry at McGill. He gave his friends T. S. Eliot to read and inspired them with his accurate feeling for the symbolist idiom.

Frank Scott was several years older than Smith and had recently returned from Oxford to study law at McGill. "He was highly verbal," Edel noted. "He had a genius for deflating pomposity, for capturing the sense of the ridiculous in everyday utterance — it is written large in his satirical verses." He conveyed a sense of maturity, a combativeness for just causes, and a powerful feeling of Canadian rootedness. "He was Canada, he was Quebec,

his father was a verse-writing padre. Tall, endlessly energetic, with a piercing humorous gleam in his eye and suppleness of spirit, Scott was a kind of father figure to us all."

Klein was especially drawn to Leo Kennedy, whose lively, mischievous sense of humor was not unlike his own. Kennedy, an aspiring journalist and poet, lived in one of Montreal's other lower-class ghettos, Verdun. He was of Irish-Catholic background, entirely self-taught, the cheerful survivor of a tempestuous Dickensian sort of childhood. In the late twenties he was still a devout Catholic and imparted to Klein some of his overflowing enthusiasm for the writings of G. K. Chesterton. Klein always believed in some mystical affinity between the Jews and the Irish. Kennedy was a living example of this — he even began peppering his speech with Yiddish idioms, for which he had a fine ear. When he dropped in one night at a Young Judaea meeting, Klein, tongue in cheek, solemnly nominated him for the presidency of the organization. In 1929 Kennedy took a Jewish girl, Miriam Carpin, for his wife. Klein wrote a prothalamium for them, "Christian Poet and Hebrew Maid," in which he celebrated their marriage as a symbolic commingling of their two religions.

Leon Edel was a senior at McGill during the *Fortnightly*'s last season and was preparing to take his M.A. in literature there the following year. Though quite cut off from his own Jewish heritage, Edel admired Klein's intense pride of race. He sensed in the young man a deep-rooted strength and a largeness of imagination that foretold of great things. Never had he known anyone so brimming with poetry, who could spew forth the Bible and sayings of the Talmud in the same breath as Shakespeare and Keats. Klein was a most congenial audience for Edel's own enthusiasms as well. It was probably at Edel's urging that he first read James Joyce's *Ulysses,* a book that was to haunt his mind forever. During the winter of Klein's sophomore year the two

LEFT TO RIGHT:

F. R. SCOTT, WHO OVER HIS LONG CAREER WAS TO DISTINGUISH HIMSELF AS A POET, LAW PROFESSOR, AND FOUNDING MEMBER OF THE CCF.
LEON EDEL, WHO WAS TO EMBARK ON A CAREER IN JOURNALISM AND THEN TEACHING, BECOMING BEST KNOWN FOR HIS LIFEWORK ON HENRY JAMES.
A. J. M. SMITH, THE LEADING POET OF THE *FORTNIGHTLY* GROUP, AND LATER THE MOST INFLUENTIAL ANTHOLOGIST OF CANADIAN POETRY IN HIS GENERATION.
LEO KENNEDY, THE FIRST OF THE "MONTREAL GROUP" OF POETS TO PUBLISH A COLLECTION OF VERSE — *THE SHROUDING*, IN 1932.

friends spent countless hours analyzing the novel's intricacies as they trudged homeward in the snow after classes.

Joyce's notorious masterpiece was banned in North America but underground copies were available and Klein had managed to borrow one. Another copy, mailed directly from Paris in a plain wrapper, and undetected by customs officers, turned up at the McGill library one day as a result of Edel's nonchalant recommendation to an innocent librarian. Klein was attracted by many qualities in Joyce — his poetic use of language, his blending of modernism with classical sources, his humor, his urban sensibility. Unlike Eliot, Joyce was clearly a Judeophile. His amiable hero, Bloom, the isolated wandering Jew in Dublin, touched Klein deeply. The love between parent and child that shines through *Ulysses* revealed a sympathetic understanding of the close family ties that Klein valued. Above all, perhaps, it was the novel's vindication of decency and intelligence over coarseness and brute force that endeared this Irishman to this Jew.

Klein often thought of writing a monumental poem or novel that would capture the Montreal of his youth just as *Ulysses* had memorialized Joyce's Dublin. He first approached the execution of such a plan in his poem of the early thirties "Diary of Abraham Segal, Poet." In the forties he made several starts at a novel set in Montreal, using himself as the model for its Jewish hero and drawing up elaborate schematic outlines in clear imitation of Joyce. In the end he was daunted by the challenge and abandoned the idea of writing the Canadian *Ulysses*.

Meanwhile, though, as if in preparation for this formidable task, he set about observing the city he had come to love, storing away images that were later to appear in his poetry. During his summers off from McGill he worked as a "spieler" on sightseeing buses that ferried tourists around old and new Montreal. Spielers thrived mainly on tips, and Klein was often well remunerated for his entertaining patter. The various city tours usually took at least two hours, and a long day might include four excursions. Starting from Dominion Square, the different routes would take in locations such as Notre Dame Cathedral, the City Hall area, Lafontaine Park and the nearby French neighborhoods, Westmount and Sherbrooke Street, Mount Royal with its new steel girder cross, the southern lookout from the mountaintop, and St. Joseph's Oratory with its massive dome still under construction. One of the longer trips out of the city went to the Indian reservation at Caughnawaga. All of these scenes were to remain etched in Klein's mind for nearly two decades before emerging in his last book of verse, *The Rocking Chair*.

His flair as a spieler was noticed by the operators of a special bus chartered by Seagrams that featured a stop at its distilling plant in the suburb of Lasalle — a destination of interest to American tourists in the days of Prohibition. Klein was soon hired to work on the Seagrams bus and became so popular that the president of the company, a young Jewish business tycoon by the name of Sam Bronfman, asked to meet him. Bronfman was immediately drawn to Klein and may already have imagined how he might make greater use of his talents in the future.

DURING HIS FOUR YEARS at McGill Klein succeeded in laying the foundations of a promising literary career. Having missed his chance to appear in the *Fortnightly* as a freshman, he decided as a sophomore to take matters into his own hands. In the fall of 1927 he persuaded the editors of the *McGill Daily* to allot him space for eight consecutive weekly columns consisting of light verse, parodies, and humorous essays. Most of the pieces were his own, though several, including a take-off on *Ulysses* signed Joyous James, were contributed by friends. Out of a last remaining trace of diffidence he never signed his full name, but simply A.M.K., or in sillier moments pseudonyms such as A. M. Keats or Antonius Mentholatum Kochleffel. He called his column "The McGilliad," a title which no doubt appealed to him for its Homeric allusion, its hint of *megillah*, and its barely concealed "McGill-yid."

In his opening column he launched into a half-serious attack against free verse. "Free verse is merely prose in the hands of an insane compositor," he declared. "True poetry is a dream; free verse is a nightmare." In a similarly satiric vein he went on in another column to denounce cubist painting. A few of his columns reveal an interest in Chesterton, whose paradox-strewn prose he consciously imitated. On one occasion he boldly made fun of his own polysyllabic verbosity: "Johnson incorporated his opinions in his dictionary; AMK incorporates his dictionary in his opinions.... It is evident that AMK, with malice aforethought, is attempting to conceal lubricity in his thesaurus, to wrap concupiscence in verbiage." To which AMK, in dialogue with himself, replies: "I will persist in amazing with maziness; I will continue to make myself clear through an enlightened obscurantism; and still shall I puncture morons with oxymorons — my preciosity is precious...."

One reason for Klein's high spirits was the appearance of his sonnet sequence "Five Characters" in the November 1927 issue of the *Menorah Journal,* published in New York. At the age of eighteen, he had "made it" into the liveliest and most distinguished journal of Jewish culture in America. Over the next several years he became a frequent contributor, slowly building his reputation among a select readership that could truly appreciate the intellectual artistry of his Jewish poems.

In May 1928 Klein was elated over the news that *Poetry* magazine of Chicago had accepted his "Sequence of Songs," the only condition being that he agree to a number of corrections and omissions suggested by the editor, Harriet Monroe. In his grateful reply to Miss Monroe his usual obstinacy melted away. "I have re-read my copy of the Sequence," he humbly wrote, "and have seen that it contains a good number of bad lines... which you have not overlooked. It is because I am heartily in accord with all the suggestions that you have made that I do not enclose a re-typed copy but do rather rely on you making the necessary corrections in your own." Rarely in his life did Klein stand for red-penciling, but this chance to appear in one of the world's most illustrious "little magazines" of modern poetry was worth everything to him.

In 1929 he began publishing in the short-lived *Canadian Mercury,* and then in the *Canadian Forum,* where the first of his poems to be accepted was the very sonnet that Scott and Smith had rejected for the *Fortnightly* two years earlier. Klein continued publishing in the *Forum* through the thirties and forties. He always respected its fostering of high critical standards and its opposition to the naive "boosterism" of the more parochial organs of Canadian culture. The spirit of Canadianism encouraged by the *Forum* was progressive, independent, and open to intellectual currents from abroad. Strangely, almost none of Klein's Jewish writing ever found its way into the *Forum*. In time this tended to create for him two distinct audiences, which he had constantly to choose between — general readers mostly in Canada, and Jewish readers mostly in the United States.

Klein's last and most satisfying literary success at McGill came in March 1930 when, with the help of David Lewis, he launched a new campus magazine, the *McGilliad,* to fill the void left by the demise of the *Fortnightly.* Klein graduated after the first two issues appeared, and Lewis took over the magazine in its second and final year, until his own graduation.

Klein and Lewis were already well known around McGill as a fairly radical pair, but the spirit of their magazine was emphatically non-partisan.

Klein in particular seemed to revel in the diversity of conflicting opinions. "The editorial policy," the *McGilliad* announced in its opening issue, "is simply that there be no policy."

There are in our midst conservatives, liberals, and laborites, idolaters and iconoclasts, traditionalists and ultra-modernists, religious adherents and religious skeptics, idealists and materialists, patriots and cosmopolites. Every opinion and class is represented in our university population, and every opinion and class will obtain equal and unprejudiced consideration from the editors. All that the editorial board requires of a contribution is that it have literary excellence, and be devoid of any willful offensiveness.

The *McGilliad* aspired to an elevated, British-sounding tone, typical in some ways of the journalism of the period. It published a broad range of essays on politics, philosophy, and the arts, as well as poems and book reviews.

By the end of his senior year, Klein had become one of the best known characters on the McGill campus. His growing self-confidence showed itself in his firm bearing and purposeful stride, which had, as Lewis noted, a certain swagger about it. Kennedy recalled how

at that time young bucks who attended McGill thought they were very fashionable if

HUMOROUS ILLUSTRATIONS IN THE 1930 YEARBOOK ATTEST TO KLEIN'S POPULARITY ON THE McGILL CAMPUS.

they walked with a cane. They all did it; it was a most outrageous affectation. I remember Abe Klein and Dave Lewis walking home from McGill one day, going up Clarke Street, swinging their canes. As they got up towards Mt. Royal Avenue, back on their own turf, they stuck the canes up their sleeves. On their own territory, it was too much.

Some of Klein's college acquaintances found that behind his cleverness and sparkling humor was a moody aloofness that made him difficult to approach. His aggressiveness in argument often seemed abrasive and ill-mannered. Even one of his close colleagues on the *McGilliad* remembered him as an extremely self-contained young man: "His wit was a fence around his emotions." Over a lifetime, this ambiguity in Klein's nature, the mixture of geniality and guardedness, would persistently give rise to widely divergent impressions of his character.

A SCENE FROM THE EARLY THIRTIES OF PILGRIMS ON THEIR KNEES ASCENDING THE HUNDRED STEPS OF ST. JOSEPH'S ORATORY, ONE OF THE DOMINANT LANDMARKS OF MONTREAL. THE CHURCH CONTAINS A SHRINE IN MEMORY OF ITS FOUNDER, BROTHER ANDRÉ, WHOSE REPUTED HEALING POWERS ATTRACTED THOUSANDS OF SICK AND CRIPPLED WORSHIPPERS.

The Cripples

(Oratoire de St. Joseph)

Bundled their bones, upon the ninety-nine stairs —
St. Joseph's ladder — the knobs of penance come;
the folded cripples counting up their prayers.

How rich, how plumped with blessing is that dome!
The gourd of Brother André! His sweet days
rounded! Fulfilled! Honeyed to honeycomb!

whither the heads, upon the ninety-nine trays,
the palsied, who double their aspen selves, the lame,
the unsymmetrical, the dead-limbed, raise

their look, their hope, and the *idée fixe* of their maim, —
knowing the surgery's in the heart. Are not
the ransomed crutches worshippers? And the fame

of the brother sanatorial to this plot? —
God mindful of the sparrows on the stairs?
Yes, to their faith this mountain of stairs, is not!

They know, they know, that suddenly their cares
and orthopedics will fall from them, and they
stand whole again.

      Roll empty away, wheelchairs,
and crutches, without armpits, hop away!

And I who in my own faith once had faith like this,
but have not now, am crippled more than they.

(1946)

DETAIL OF A STATUE IN FRONT OF THE
ORATORY.

KLEIN'S MCGILL GRADUATION PHOTO, 1930. ALONGSIDE IT IN THE MCGILL YEARBOOK ARE LINES PARAPHRASED FROM BLAKE, "AND WE WILL BUILD JERUSALEM AGAIN/IN ENGLAND'S FAIR AND PLEASANT LAND." KLEIN GAVE AS HIS FAVORITE EXPRESSION, "IT'S THE POOR WHAT GETS THE BLYME."

from Université de Montréal

Gaily they wind and stagger towards their own
and through the maze already see themselves
silken and serious, a gownèd guild
a portrait painter will one day make traditional
beneath the Sign of the *Code Napoléon.*

This, then, their last permitted juvenal mood
kicked up by adolescence before it dons
the crown and dignity of adulthood.
Today, the grinning circle on the *Place d'Armes,*
mock trial, thumbdown'd verdict, and, singsong,
the joyous sentence of death; tomorrow, the
good of the state, the law, the dean
parting deliberate his beard
silvered and sabled with rampant right and wrong.

Thus will they note in notebooks, and will con
the numbers and their truths, and from green raw
celebrants of the Latin Quarter, duly
warp and wrinkle into *avocats.*
The solid men. Now innocence and fun.
O let them have their day, it soon will go!

(1947)

4

No Wide Estates

Leaving McGill in a flush of optimism, Klein embarked on his law studies at the Université de Montréal in the fall of 1930. Like many other Jewish students he had chosen the Université de Montréal over McGill's law school in order to become more fluent in French and thus be better prepared for practice in Quebec. The campus environment reinforced his warm feelings towards French Canadians and awakened a lifelong interest in French literature. Nevertheless his social contacts at law school were few, and he turned increasingly to Young Judaea for comradeship and intellectual stimulation.

It was at the Université de Montréal that he became friendly with another law student and fellow member of Young Judaea, Max Garmaise. Together they made plans to go into partnership immediately after graduation. Classes at the university were held early in the morning and late in the afternoon. Officially, Klein was at work the rest of the day articling in the firm of another of his Young Judaea colleagues, Sam Chait, fulfilling an academic requirement that neither of them took too seriously. With Chait's blessings, Klein in fact spent as much time as he wanted at Young Judaea headquarters, editing the *Judaean,* reading, and preparing lectures on Jewish topics.

He missed the intellectual and literary stimulation of life at McGill, but kept on writing and produced a steady stream of poems, short stories, translations, articles, and reviews, mostly for the *Judaean.* The flow abated somewhat after he gave up his editorship of the magazine in 1932 to concentrate more on his law studies and on his articling duties for Chait.

In the spring of 1932 Leon Edel returned to Montreal from Paris after four years of study and writing at the Sorbonne. He was surprised and moved when he found Klein waiting to greet him on his arrival at the train station. Both young men were eager to recapture the spark of youthful imagination that had enlivened their days at McGill. The carefree twenties now seemed to them like some fool's paradise. Many old friends had already left for other cities and countries, all hoping to ride out the Depression and somehow find the futures they had dreamed of in those better times.

Klein spoke to Edel of his ambition to combine a law career with a life of writing. He felt confident that he could have both; in any event, he would not allow himself to starve in a garret like some bohemian poet. By the strictest self-discipline he had already begun to divide his time among a multitude of activities and obligations, yet always setting aside regular hours for specific literary projects he intended to carry through.

He showed Edel some of the poems he had written over the previous four years. Edel was instantly struck by the maturing of Klein's talent and arranged to write an article on him for the *Canadian Forum*. For this purpose Klein lent him a thick bundle of over 150 poems, all neatly typed by Bessie and about to be gathered into a pair of custom-bound volumes labeled *Gestures Hebraic* and *Poems*.

Gestures Hebraic brought together virtually all of Klein's Jewish poems, published and unpublished, from the mid-twenties to 1932. The earliest of these deal with biblical subjects; martyrdom and death are their frequent themes. By the late twenties Klein's interests, as a poet, had shifted entirely away from the Bible to the world of East European Jewish life. Here satire and sentimentality are balanced in quaint, richly-observed depictions of religion and folk culture: portraits of a minyan, joyful chassidim, a preacher, a scribe, the Passover seder, wedding festivities. Historical and legendary figures abound — Spinoza, the Baal Shem Tov, Levi Yitschok of Berditchev, the Golem of Prague.

In several longer poems and ballads he evoked the terrors of pogroms. Klein's poetic reaction to Jewish suffering alternated between philosophical stoicism and angry defiance at God. Although the militant Zionist response to persecution was a major element in his political thinking, it played only a small role in his poetry. Klein seemed to sense that the Jewish literary tradition out of which he was writing could not easily accommodate a fierce militancy; if the Jew is ever spared from evil, it is only by a divine miracle.

Edel, in his article for the *Canadian Forum*, judged Klein's Jewish poems to be his most important writings to date. Biblical and Talmudic learning, the romance of medieval Jewish history, and all manner of exotic Hebrew lore clearly constituted the vital fount of this endless stream of verse. Edel remarked in these poems "a strong race consciousness, a feeling for the past, a *hardiness* of thought and of feeling which singles them out as, undoubtedly, the most original of all the poetry which is being written in Canada today."

Klein's non-Jewish poems, gathered under the simple title *Poems,* impressed Edel for their lyricism. The best of these were the early love poems and sonnets written for Bessie. Phases of their courtship are discernible — in one group of poems he temporarily renounces his love; in another he addresses her longingly from a distance. Several poems are occasioned by Bessie's sorrow at her father's death in 1928. The collection also contains a

cycle of poems on the seasons, several short verses in the imagist manner, and a series of poems on the theme of poetry itself.

Edel detected a new phase in Klein's most recent work. "He has become a poet of the proletariat. The Marxian influence is beginning to show itself. ... His 'industrial' poems, as he calls them, bearing the imprint of that arch-realist Eliot, combine his interest in Judaism with contemporary economic problems." Like many other writers in the thirties, Klein was indeed beginning to dabble in socialist themes. The Jewish working-class district in which he lived was hit especially hard by the Depression. From very early on there was widespread unemployment in Montreal's garment factories, and painful cases of poverty and hunger were often visible. Along the streets of the neighborhood, small groups of laid-off workers would often cluster together to discuss social problems in the same spirit of radicalism that had characterized the struggles of the union movement twenty years earlier.

Though Klein could hardly have avoided the pervasive sense of crisis and ideological debate, the Depression never really politicized him as it did some of his closest friends. During the thirties Scott and Lewis were already well on their way to helping found Canada's first major socialist party. Kennedy, by now a lapsed Catholic, had become a doctrinaire communist — a position which to Klein was, and always would be, anathema. As Lewis sensed from the outset, Klein's was strictly a "mild kind of socialism."

He would not be interested in anything violent because he was essentially a humanitarian, a lover of humanity and a moralist. He could not accept the notion that the end justified the means, and he would therefore be very careful about the means. He also wasn't the kind of socialist who is concerned about structures — about the nationalization of industry, or planning boards, and so on. His socialism was the socialism of social justice, of human equality and human dignity.

As a poet, Klein was particularly wary of the corrupting influence of politics on literature. The exploitation and abuse of the artist under communism agitated him deeply all his life. "Although it must be admitted," he wrote in 1932, "that one of the functions of art, though certainly not the only one, is to rouse the reader to a realization of existing injustice and current oppression, it still is to be doubted whether this need be achieved only through the perversion of letters into a series of political phrases and economic clichés." What offended him was not merely the reduction of art to ideology but the frightening prospect of the poet becoming the servant of the politician. Stalin is wiser than Plato, he noted sarcastically, for "Plato banished poets from his republic; but Stalin uses them." Klein never could decide who was the more pitiable: the poet neglected or the poet used.

The "industrial poems" that had caught Edel's interest, principally "Soirée of Velvel Kleinburger" and "Diary of Abraham Segal, Poet," are satirically anti-capitalist and impassioned in their depiction of the squalor of the poor worker's life, with its "days in dusty factories, among machines that manufacture madness." "Diary of Abraham Segal, Poet" is the more ambiguous for its cynically apolitical undertone.

> My friends? My bitter friends, at loggerheads,
> The blackshirts, the bluestockings, and the reds,
> Evoke from me the vast abysmal yawn...
>
> All, in the end, despite their savage feuds, —
> Italic voices uttering platitudes...

Only under the stars, in the pastoral meadows of Mount Royal, does Abe Segal finally escape the anguished weariness of his workday world.

> They see again, his eyes which once were blear.
> His heart gets speech, and is no longer dumb.
> Before the glass o' the moon, no longer high,
> Abe Segal nattily adjusts his tie.
> Gone the insistence of inveterate clocks;
> The heart at last can flutter from its bars.
> Upon the mountain top, Abe Segal walks,
> Hums old-time songs, of old-time poets talks,
> Brilliant his shoes with dew, his hair with stars...

Closer to Klein's heart than proletarian poetry was a collection of Jewish children's verses that he had started writing in the early thirties. These fanciful poems contained an unusual blending of the English nursery rhyme and the Yiddish folk song, with forest and barnyard creatures, town fools, fairytale monarchs, and folk figures of the messiah and his herald Elijah populating a dreamlike childhood paradise. Klein evidently conceived them as amusements for his nieces and nephews and for younger readers of the *Judaean.* Many of the poems, in fact, seem far too richly allusive to be appreciated by children and might better be regarded as expressions of the child in Klein, verses in which his lyricism and playfulness are perfectly matched.

The completion and gathering together of these children's poems in 1934 marked the end of a prolific period of about eight years in Klein's life. It is true that in terms of technique his later poems, written mainly in the forties, would far surpass most of these early efforts, but rarely again would Klein write with such openness, youthful passion, and overflowing high spirits.

Though poetry was his first love, Klein also had begun to experiment with fiction in his student years. Virtually all of his short stories from this period deal with Jewish subjects and show the influence of his constant reading in modern Hebrew and Yiddish literature. Two of the more notable early stories are "The Meed of the Minnesinger" and "The Seventh Scroll." The former tells of a medieval Jewish troubadour who turns his back on his people to sing at a Christian court. His pious father fails to persuade him to return to the fold, but when the young troubadour is mocked by Jew-baiters at the court, he regrets his decision and burns all his manuscripts.

"The Seventh Scroll" is a studiously crafted tale revealing the influence of the modern master of symbolist fiction in Hebrew, S. Y. Agnon. In Klein's story, a scribe named Yekuthiel Geller is completing his seventh and last Torah scroll, to be dedicated to the memory of his late wife, whom he loved deeply though she bore him no children. Geller remarries but his second wife turns out to be a jealous shrew who impedes his work and indirectly causes his death from pneumonia just as he succeeds in finishing the scroll. After Geller's death the scroll is discovered to contain a scribal flaw, rendering it invalid. Accordingly it is buried in the ground along with its maker. Klein's tale resonates with the mystical symbolism of the Torah scroll as wife-lover and as offspring. On an allegorical level it speaks of the sad fate of the artist; Klein often seemed to regard the scribe as a figure of the poet in Jewish ritual.

WITH THE ADVENT OF THE DEPRESSION, Klein faced new responsibilities at home. In 1930 his sister Dora separated from her husband and returned, with two young children, to live with her parents. To make room, the Kleins moved to larger quarters at 4455 St. Urbain. In the next few years Kalman's

KALMAN KLEIN, AS SKETCHED BY THE MONTREAL ARTIST ERNST NEUMANN, PROBABLY IN THE EARLY THIRTIES.

Heirloom

My father bequeathed me no wide estates;
No keys and ledgers were my heritage;
Only some holy books with *yahrzeit* dates
Writ mournfully upon a blank front page —

Books of the Baal Shem Tov, and of his wonders;
Pamphlets upon the devil and his crew;
Prayers against road demons, witches, thunders;
And sundry other tomes for a good Jew.

Beautiful: though no pictures on them, save
The scorpion crawling on a printed track;
The Virgin floating on a scriptural wave,
Square letters twinkling in the Zodiac.

The snuff left on this page, now brown and old,
The tallow stains of midnight liturgy —
These are my coat of arms, and these unfold
My noble lineage, my proud ancestry!

And my tears, too, have stained this heirloomed ground,
When reading in these treatises some weird
Miracle, I turned a leaf and found
A white hair fallen from my father's beard.

(1933)

health began to fail, and after a prolonged illness he died in November 1933. Klein was now in effect the male head of a household consisting of his mother, his sister, and a niece and nephew.

His father's death induced him to take stock of his spiritual as well as material legacy. In an unfinished elegiac poem he idealized his father's piety, confessing himself an unworthy heir, a breaker of Sabbaths, "a withered limb upon a sacred tree." Kalman had left his wife and children no financial inheritance. In the forties Klein would sometimes joke about this, with a touch of bitterness, as the great misfortune of his life. On an unspoken level, he seems actually to have resented his father's extreme simplicity and resigned lack of worldly ambition. From the moment of his father's death, he assumed the solemn burden of responsibility for his various dependents, and guarded against ever failing them and succumbing to the shame of poverty.

After Kalman's death the family moved again, this time to 4353 St. Urbain. It was into this home that Bessie would arrive following her marriage to Klein on his twenty-sixth birthday — February 14, 1935.

Upon graduating from law school in 1933, Klein continued working with Sam Chait for one more year. Then in 1934, after Max Garmaise had graduated, the two friends joined forces and opened their first office in the Dominion Bank building at the corner of Bleury and St. Catherine Streets.

The Depression was at its very worst when Klein and Garmaise were trying to establish themselves. Days passed in idleness, the two young lawyers whiling away the hours in conversation and eagerly awaiting a knock at their door. Having as much free time as he did, and noting that certain American magazines still paid rather handsomely for popular fiction, Klein began writing more short stories. A fair portion of the office expenses now went into stationery and postage as he sent his manuscripts off to editors and anthologists. To his great dismay, hardly any were ever accepted for publication.

The very emptiness of those days in the law office kept appealing to him as the opening for a story:

As he leaned back in his swivel-chair, his hands behind his neck, and his feet like two leather-bound codes reposing upon his desk, the mind of Timothy P. Thorne contemplated his clientele, and the mind of Timothy P. Thorne was a blank. For days now, not a soul had entered his office, not a one, save the landlord, and to a tenant a landlord was technically not a soul. Neither plaintiff insistent on redress, nor debtor imploring delays beyond delays, had this many a week set foot beyond the threshold of his door. Such unwelcome and compulsory leisure had not been utterly a loss...

Over ten years later the same scene would still haunt his memory:

Just to have a face to look at was exciting. Any face, as long as it was halfway human, and might have business. I was tired of looking at the wall in front of me, a green like mild poison, with the hanging Daumier where the judge addressed the wretch at the bar: *But, prisoner, look at me! When I'm hungry I don't steal!* I was beginning to find the thing less and less funny. Definitely, my sympathies were with the wretch at the bar.

For three months now I had sat in that cubicle, waiting for the rush. What rush? There wasn't even a wrong number. And three months had passed since I had sent out my card, embossed and glowing with formality and hope . . .

The practice of law was frustrating and disappointing to Klein. Most of the legal work he could find was tedious and dry. He dreamed at first of specializing as a criminal lawyer, but the fierce competition in this area and the unpleasantness of actually having to deal with hardened criminals slowly eroded his enthusiasm.

The rough-and-tumble of the legal profession destroyed any illusions he may still have had about the nobility of his calling. Litigation, he perceived, was "of the act of war rather than of the abstract science of spiritual truth." Judges, particularly when their decisions were not in his favor, were merely "humans permitted divinely to err." He could not avoid being cynical when noting the discrepancy between high-principled Justice on the one hand and the day-to-day interpretation of the legal code on the other. "The heart said one thing, the code as a rule echoed it, and then, when these sounds were coursed through a courtroom — with circumstance distorting them, and the human voice recording them in prejudiced fortissimo, in self-protective pianissimo — how strange, how unrecognizable, the original high principle issued!"

Yet he was meticulously thorough and conscientious in preparing his cases, and often brilliant at arguing them. He was proud of his forensic skills, and it galled him to lose in court to an opponent whom he could easily have trounced in his old debating days at McGill. Nothing infuriated him more than to see injustice win out over his eloquent appeals. From the point of view of the average successful lawyer, Klein's problem was that he was too dogmatic and unyielding, too unwilling to play the game of compromise.

During the early years of his practice he derived some personal satisfaction out of defending indigent clients referred to him by the Prisoners' Aid and Welfare Association. His friend Alexander Edmison, who served as legal counsel to the Association during the thirties, was struck by the keen interest Klein took in his legal aid clients, most notably one young man whom he counseled for several years to help in his rehabilitation. In another characteristic gesture, when an accused man he was defending died before being sentenced, Klein took up a collection among his fellow lawyers to assure a proper burial.

The melodramas of crime and punishment that he sometimes encountered in his legal work titillated his imagination. It was about this time that he

After a courtship of ten years, Klein married Bessie Kozlov in 1935. The day of the wedding, chosen to coincide with Klein's birthday in mid-February, was unseasonably mild and rainy. After their honeymoon in New York, Bessie moved into the Klein household on St. Urbain Street.

acquired his keen appetite for mystery novels and became studiously engrossed in the slang and rituals of the underworld. His droll interest in the macabre often led him to seek out intimate knowledge of life's extreme situations. In 1936 he arranged to meet Canada's itinerant hangman, a personal legal client of Edmison's who went by the official name of Arthur Ellis. Based on his interview with Ellis he wrote a short article that he evidently hoped to sell to some popular magazine. Ellis typified the peculiar

KLEIN AND BESSIE, AROUND THE TIME OF THEIR MARRIAGE, TOGETHER WITH OTHER MEMBERS OF THE FAMILY. BELOW HIM ARE HIS SISTER BESSIE WOOLF AND HIS MOTHER, YETTA. AT THE LEFT IS BESSIE WOOLF'S HUSBAND, DANNY, AND ON THE RIGHT IS BEN WEINPER, ONE OF YETTA'S SONS FROM HER FIRST MARRIAGE. THE PICTURE WAS PROBABLY TAKEN BY KLEIN'S SISTER DORA, WHOSE YOUNG SON IS STANDING NEXT TO DANNY AND BESSIE'S DAUGHTER.

sort of personality to whom Klein was sometimes drawn, in this case a pathetically lonely and depressed man, feared and hated for his profession, "friendless and childless, compelled to an alias."

THROUGH THESE LEAN YEARS, Klein's work as a Zionist turned out to be an important source of additional income for him. Though he had ceased editing the *Judaean* after 1932, he continued to lecture frequently on Jewish cultural and political topics. In September 1934 he accepted the position of national president of Canadian Young Judaea. By this time he was already becoming active in Young Judaea's parent body, the Zionist Organization of Canada, helping to establish its monthly magazine, the *Canadian Zionist*, and becoming one of its regular contributors. In September 1936 he took on the editorship of the magazine and was appointed by the Zionist Organization to serve as its director of publicity.

In his work for the Zionist Organization, Klein saw part of his role to be a disseminator of modern Hebrew culture. He took the time to read and translate many of the important authors of the literary renaissance in Palestine and was especially taken with the writing of the Hebrew poet laureate, Chaim Nachman Bialik. Next to Joyce, Bialik was his greatest literary hero. Klein saw in him the ideal model of the Jewish national poet, a twentieth-century biblical prophet, an elevated genius who nevertheless remained a true man of the people. He began publishing English versions of Bialik's work shortly after the poet's death in 1934 and hoped one day to translate the complete poems.

Klein had little inclination to write poetry during the mid-thirties but was eager to have a collection of his early work published. In the spring of 1934 he sent a manuscript, probably containing selections from *Gestures Hebraic* and his recent children's verse, to the Jewish Publication Society in Philadelphia. In his official response to Klein the following April, Isaac Husik reported that the members of the Society's editorial committee "all thought highly of your work, but objected to the gloomy atmosphere pervading most of the poems, and to certain words like 'spittle' and others which you used rather more frequently than they liked."

Such philistine carping might have turned him away from an American Jewish audience altogether, were it not for the warm support and praise he received from the editors of *Opinion* and the *Menorah Journal*. Through these influential periodicals, in which he was featured regularly, he came into contact with an American circle of highly literate, well-educated Zionists and liberal Jews. Two of the leading figures in this group, Ludwig Lewisohn and Maurice Samuel, became his devoted admirers and friends.

Lewisohn, in his fifties, was one of the deans of American Jewish letters, an accomplished novelist and essayist, steeped in modern European literature, and a passionate late convert to Zionism. He had first noticed Klein's poetry at the beginning of the decade and felt a certain kinship, mingled perhaps with envy, on seeing how remarkably at ease Klein was with the natural fact of his Jewishness. Lewisohn was then living in Burlington, Vermont, not far from the Canadian border-crossing south of Montreal, and Klein paid him several visits there. In 1936 Lewisohn wrote a short preface for Klein's manuscript of poems, in which he proclaimed him "the first contributor of authentic Jewish poetry to the English language." It was this "authenticity" that Lewisohn valued most highly in the young poet. "We need not," he argued, "blindly accept our heritage; we may legitimately rebel against it. But he who blankly 'represses' it, denies it, flees from it cannot evidently be a poet. Deep and strong poetry as deep and strong imaginative literature of any kind is not written, to use the common phrase, from the neck up."

Another good friend during these years was the American Jewish author and editor Leo W. Schwarz, who printed some of Klein's poems and translations in his widely-read *Golden Treasury of Jewish Literature*. After Klein had been turned down by the Jewish Publication Society, Schwarz put him in touch with Jacob Behrman, a New York publisher who specialized in Jewish books. Behrman accepted Klein's manuscript in 1936, hastily obtained Lewisohn's preface, and scheduled the publication of a volume tentatively entitled *Selected Poems* for 1937. At the last moment, however, financial difficulties arose and Behrman was forced to delay the book's appearance for several more years.

Klein would also have liked to see a collection of his early non-Jewish verse published in Canada, but the Depression years proved to be a difficult time for such hopes. His status among contemporary Canadian poets was confirmed in 1936 with his appearance in *New Provinces*, a significant albeit slender anthology that also included poems by F. R. Scott, A. J. M. Smith, Leo Kennedy, E. J. Pratt, and Robert Finch. *New Provinces* went beyond celebrating the modernist breakthrough of the twenties and implicitly called on Canadian poets to deal ever more vigorously in their works with the social upheavals and economic injustices of the thirties. Klein was among the few actually to heed this summons, though his handful of Depression poems and stories, published in the *Canadian Forum* and elsewhere, generally lacked the controlled intensity of feeling characteristic of his best writing.

MUCH OF KLEIN'S ATTENTION during the mid-thirties was taken up with the personal problem of earning a living. One plan that he discussed with Garmaise was to move out of Montreal and set up practice in a less depressed area of the province. Early in 1936, during one of his periodic speaking tours on behalf of the United Palestine Appeal, he visited a number of remote Jewish communities in northeastern Ontario and northwestern Quebec. A stop on his itinerary brought him to the relatively prosperous Quebec mining town of Rouyn. Sensing that the opportunities for a lawyer were better here than in Montreal, he persuaded Garmaise to go to Rouyn and test the situation by opening a branch office. Garmaise left in May, and the experiment proved successful. After a year Klein decided to follow and arrived with Bessie and their newborn son Colman in October 1937.

At first he was pleased with his new life in Rouyn. Work was readily available, and the fact that he was at last able to earn a respectable living at law gave him a precious feeling of security. The Kleins and Garmaises kept each other company in a small two-storey home that they shared in the residential town of Noranda, adjoining Rouyn. Klein seemed to enjoy the relaxed atmosphere and devoted his long leisure hours to reading and writing.

His feelings of contentment and hopefulness were conveyed in a letter to his Montreal friend Joe Frank in January 1938:

I would have written you long ere this, but acclimatizing myself to this Nordic environment has left its mark upon my correspondence....

From these quarters you know that no great intellectual news can be forthcoming. As for financial apocalypses, underground mining, like overground nature, begins to blossom only in the spring.

As for ourselves, we are getting along nicely, doing justice unto others and unto ourselves. We are getting a little but not too much of the sacred ore of our ancestors. And when the day's clients, confident and at ease (and in no way patronizing, like the Montreal ones), leave our offices, we return to our homes, Max to work on some abstruse bridge problem, and I to play with my little boy, and write some lines of a play in verse that I am writing — on industrial strife — dubbed "Barricade Smith."

From the remoteness of rural Quebec he followed news of the civil war in Spain and dedicated a poem to his boyhood friend Sam Abramson, who had volunteered with other Canadians in the battle against Franco.

How you have shamed me, me the noble talker...

'Tis you who do confound the lupine jaw
    And stand protective of my days and works,
As in the street-fight you maintain the law
    And I in an armchair — weigh and measure Marx.

Sending a copy of the poem across the sea to Abramson, he added:

Confessionally speaking, I was once of the opinion that I didn't give a hoot in hell about civil war in Spain. I felt a sort of postponed vicarious feeling of revenge for the Spanish Inquisition. Let them decimate themselves, I said, to the greater rejoicing of us marranos. But 'tis not so. You are fighting the Torquemadas and Don Pedros of today.

Of yet greater concern to Klein than the war in Spain was the fatal conflict looming between Hitler and the Jews of Europe. The refusal of the supposedly civilized nations of the world to receive the many thousands of Jews seeking refuge from Germany prompted him in the spring of 1938 to write his impassioned dramatic monologue "Childe Harold's Pilgrimage." He proudly regarded the poem for some time after as "one of the best things that I have done in the past few years." Its reliance on a dramatic archetypal figure to personify the entire Jewish people was to become a recurring device in his writings. The cyclical view of history on which the poem's philosophical stoicism rests would also continue to occupy a central place in his thought.

Writing to Joe Frank again in August, Klein described with satisfaction the various poems and translations that he was working on, and lamented the fact that Behrman had still not brought out his book. "May my publisher be drowned in ink," he cried, "may he be crushed between presses, may the printer's devil take him — he is giving me the runaround. The contract is signed. The manuscript has been made up, but the publisher stands, like life, between me and immortality." While publication was being delayed, he took the opportunity to add "Childe Harold's Pilgrimage" to the manuscript and to change the book's title to *Hath Not a Jew.*

In the same letter he confided to his friend that after less than a year in Rouyn he already found himself longing for his old haunts.

I do frequently miss my Montreal friends, and the Montreal scene. It is only my work which saves me from becoming provincialized in an atmosphere of bridge and boorish- ness. If it were not for the fact that I am getting my due share of the world's goods here, with sure prospects of more to come, I would have abandoned my exile long ago. Why, I sometimes, like a worm nostalgic for its horse-radish, get lonesome even for some of the metropolitan shtunks you mention.

Added to the growing sense of isolation that Klein experienced was the fact that his mother was utterly heartbroken over his absence. To appease her he would journey alone to Montreal almost every month, traveling eighteen hours each way by train. Her tearful displays and accounts of how she prayed incessantly to be reunited with him made his visits to her unbearably painful. In the early fall of 1938 he came back from the last of these trips, haggard and distraught as always, and reported to Garmaise that his mother simply would not allow him to stay away any longer. With few major regrets but consid- erable worry over his financial future, he hastily began planning his return to Montreal.

from STRANGER AND AFRAID

... It is true that, here in my native city, I have not suffered much from this Jew-baiting. Certainly not from its violent forms, its forest-ferocities. Only a pin-prick of prejudice here, a rub of racialism there. But nothing that required medical attention, not unless one wanted to go pamper the psyche. Trivialities, things that never, or only seldom got reported in the papers. Nothings.

I am returning from school with my friend. Today we have been taught the meaning of unity, for today our teacher told us the fable about the sticks that could be broken, one by one, but could not be broken if held in a handful altogether. She said that the sticks meant the people of Canada. On our way home, we have to pass the streets where the Frenchies live. At the corner a group of boys, somewhat older than ourselves, stands scrutinizing us. Suddenly, as if in a prearranged chorus, they burst out in sing-song: Meestah with da wheeskahs! Meestah with the wheeskahs! We hurry on, afraid; we are two, and they are many. Safely away from them, on the other side of the ghetto boundary, we turn back, and yell: Pea-soup! Pea-soup! French pea-soup!

The streetcar is rumbling along. I hang on a strap, listening to the talk of the overalled laborers, their tin-cans on their laps. They have worked hard. The car stops, and an old Jew, bearded and sweaty, puffs up the steps. He is hauling two huge bolts of cloth. The conductor gives him an argument, he is taking up too much room, he says, for his seven cents; he should have used a taxi. The Jew smiles ingratiatingly: "What you care?" he says, "Is it, then, your car? It's the company's car. The black year won't take them." Nonetheless he tries to constrict himself into a corner, and he and his bolts become one. The laborers, amused, have watched the argument. They have stopped talking about their hard lot. "Did you hear," says one to the other, loudly, so that the whole streetcar may listen, "the story of Ikie and the fingerbowl? Oi," he mimics, "is that a story!" Then they oi it right and they oi it left. Everybody titters, particularly the women. Even their bosoms seem to part and grin. Disguised by my clean shave and my nondescript appearance — I have been taken for

both a Russian and a French Canadian, depending upon the recency of my haircut —
I swing on the strap, reading the ads, swallowing hard.

An incident; nothing; harmless fun.

At the corner of St. Denis and Ste. Catherine, I have just bought at the French
bookstore *Les Fleurs du Mal*. I am waiting for the streetcar home, and in the
meantime I read the large type in the newspapers suspended outside the corner
kiosk. Whether because annoyed that I am nibbling his headlines without buying a
paper, or whether out of a desire to share important intelligence, the newspaper
vendor draws my attention to a new hebdomad, *Le Chameau*. On its cover there is
displayed an ugly cartoon — a frightened female, scrolled Quebec, and a leering Jew
hovering over her, all nose and lechery. *La verité*, he says, *pour cinq sous*. I give him
his nickel for the truth. I will read this before the poetry.

It is election time, and the orators are out. I have a free evening, and I decide to go
to the Salaberry School where a meeting is to be addressed by Camillien Houde. He
is a brilliant speaker, colorful, witty, histrionic, a character, and I love to hear him
talk. But Camillien has not yet arrived. A lesser worthy is called upon to mark time
until his arrival. He speaks from a working man's point of view, he says. He is also a
wag. He makes jokes, not pertinent, but laughable in their own right. And he also
has his serious side, — a theory. The theory is that all of the world's ills are caused by
international finance, and that all Jews are international financiers. I do not know
whether to laugh or to spit. Unconsciously, I feel for the several coins in my pocket. I
leave the hall, Camillien unheard.

Or the signs on the summer resorts, *Restricted Clientele*, at which I inwardly
sneer, telling myself that I don't care to go anyway and childishly content myself by
calling down upon their owners the detailed imprecations of Deuteronomy. Or my
friend the poet and the radical who tells me that he is scrupulously careful about
the race-question. Why should he feel that he has to be scrupulously careful? Or the
Marxist who is of the opinion that important party resolutions should not be moved
by Jews — bad publicity. But really these things are nothing; they can be endured;
they sting, but they do not devastate. Trivialities. Things to be ignored.

But no matter how much I try to ignore them, I cannot, I cannot ignore them —
these nothings. I shut my eyes to them, I please myself into believing that these things
are merely signs of an absence of breeding, vestiges of old prejudice, frivolities, not
really important. I make myself the statuary monkey: I won't see, I won't hear, I
won't even mention what I haven't seen or heard. It has happened, it is gone, it has
passed through consciousness as through a sieve. I am, I assure myself, living in a
country that is free and civilized. These things are anomalies, and ought not to
bother me. And then, as I pause to consider my Self, myself, the focus taken from off
my environment, I am amazed to discover that these things have never passed
through my consciousness, as through a sieve, at all, at all. They cling to my mind,
and at the most unwelcome moments reveal themselves in the strangest forms. I meet
a casual acquaintance on the street, engage in conversation, and am soon
embarrassingly aware that he is talking too loud, his thoughtways, his inflections are
objectionably Jewish. Objectionable to whom? I shudder at the revelation:
objectionable to me. I consider the behavior of my fellow-Jews, and find myself

Le Juif lance la plus grave insulte à la langue française

THIS ANTI-SEMITIC CARTOON WAS PUBLISHED IN THE DECEMBER 11, 1937 ISSUE OF *LE PATRIOTE*, A FASCIST TABLOID. THE CAPTION READS: "THE JEW HEAPS INSULT UPON THE FRENCH LANGUAGE."

passing judgement upon them, not according to the general social code, but according to some unwritten laws which I apply to Jews only. It is I who am now passing discriminatory legislation. I come to a gathering to which the general public has been invited, and soon realize that I am counting the number of Jewish faces present — it is I who am proceeding according to a *numerus clausus*. I walk into a room, and unintentionally and unknowing gravitate towards my own — it is I who make the ghetto bench. A horrible dialectics has taken place. The hater has converted the hated. . . .

(mid-1940s)

HITLER AT A NAZI YOUTH RALLY, NUREMBERG, 1934.

A psalm of Abraham, when he hearkened to a voice, and there was none

Since prophecy has vanished out of Israel,
And since the open vision is no more,
Neither a word on the high places, nor the Urim and Thummim,
Nor even a witch, foretelling, at En-dor, —
Where in these dubious days shall one take counsel?
Who is there to resolve the dark, the doubt?

O these are the days of scorpions and of whips!
And all the seers have had their eyes put out,
And all the prophets burned upon the lips!

There is noise only in the groves of Baal.
Only the painted heathen dance and sing
With frenzied clamoring.
Among the holy ones, however, is no sound at all.

(early 1940s)

5

The Harnessed Heart

IN PLANNING HIS MOVE BACK to Montreal in the fall of 1938, Klein's first concern was to secure a livelihood. He knew that he would be able to resume his law practice — the Montreal office of Klein and Garmaise had never officially been closed — but, fearing the worst, he wished to be sure of other sources of income as well. The Zionist Organization, which had provided him part-time employment since 1928, evidently had no interesting position for him at this moment. His next approach was to Hirsch Wolofsky, whose Eagle Publishing Company printed the Yiddish daily *Kanader Adler* and its English weekly counterpart, the *Canadian Jewish Chronicle*. Klein had occasionally contributed articles and editorials to the *Chronicle* from as early as 1930 and had developed a warm relationship with Wolofsky. Now he offered his services as a regular columnist and editor. Discussions ensued, and in October Wolofsky sent word to him in Rouyn: the paper's current editor was due to step down and Klein could take over immediately.

Within a month the Kleins returned to Montreal and took a small apartment at 117 Mount Royal Street West, where they remained for just over two years. Klein opened a law office at 20 St. James Street East, at first under the old firm name of Klein and Garmaise. It soon became apparent, however, that Klein would be staying in Montreal, while Garmaise had no intention of leaving Rouyn. By the spring of 1940 their partnership had been amicably dissolved, and shortly afterwards Klein joined his former colleague Sam Chait at 276 St. James Street West, establishing the firm of Chait and Klein.

Despite the gradual improvement in business conditions during the forties, Klein grew increasingly disenchanted with his law career. The editorship of the *Chronicle,* while taking very little of his time, provided a most pleasant distraction. The paper was issued every Friday, for weekend reading. Klein usually wrote his columns at home, bringing them into the Eagle office on Wednesday night or Thursday morning. Sometimes he would dictate them to Bessie from a set of notes such as he used for speeches, which accounts not only for the rough finish of many of the editorials but also for

their pronounced oratorical style. Often he would simply write them out in
haste at the last moment, leaving no time for typing or revision. His
high-flown language made it all the more difficult for the Eagle typesetters to
decipher his handwriting. When one of the staff suggested that he tone down
his vocabulary out of consideration for his less educated readers, Klein
replied with some annoyance: "Let them go to a dictionary and rise to my
level, I'm not going down to theirs." The very rhythm of his sentences echoed
this assertive tone of pedagogical authority.

He was to continue writing for the *Chronicle* almost without interruption
from the time of his return to Montreal until his retirement in the spring of
1955. His first initialed editorial appeared on November 18, 1938, the week
following Germany's infamous *Kristallnacht*. The war in Europe, imminent
and then actual, became his main topic over the next seven years. His other
regular subjects included local and international anti-Semitism, the Jewish
refugee problem, and Zionism. Around each Jewish festival he would, like
the rabbi he was once intended to become, sermonize on the parallels between
ancient and contemporary events. As well there would be the usual editorials
of congratulation, or *in memoriam,* or in support of various charities.

That his journalism might have been viewed by some as hackwork did not seem to bother Klein. Leo Kennedy, himself harnessed in a Toronto advertising agency, wrote warningly in 1940: "Those editorials in the *Chronicle*, Abe, are even lower than my copywriting." Klein did not agree, and in fact over the years the *Chronicle* was to become his most important creative outlet. Besides writing on current events, he published in its pages a large number of poems, stories, book reviews, literary essays, and translations. As editor, he was free to write almost anything at all for the paper, and thus was able to experiment and to follow his interests wherever they might lead.

He enjoyed his routine visits to the Eagle office and would sometimes linger there for hours to exchange gossip and discuss politics with Wolofsky or with Israel Rabinovitch, the editor of the *Kanader Adler*. Klein's personal opinions were generally compatible with Wolofsky's editorial policies. The only time that Wolofsky explicitly dissociated himself from Klein's position was in July 1937 when Klein (as a substitute editor that month) contributed a signed column strongly opposing the recommendation of Britain's Peel Commission that Palestine be partitioned. A different type of conflict would arise whenever there was a federal election in Canada: Klein supported and campaigned for the socialist CCF party, but his publisher traditionally backed the Liberals. During election periods Klein would simply refrain from comment, and the newspaper would publish an editorial endorsement of the Liberal candidate, signed by Rabinovitch or Wolofsky.

Read as a whole, Klein's weekly columns in the *Chronicle* present a fascinating image of their times and of their author. Quite by chance, Klein's term of editorship coincided with the most terrible and most glorious years in modern Jewish history. In his empathic sensitivity to the events of those years, Klein spoke personally for a nation, thereby revealing the complete range of his own emotions — his fears, his pain and despair, his quixotic outrage in the face of injustice, his sardonic wittiness, even his sometimes ghoulish attraction to the humorous side of tragedy, and his rare moments of jubilation.

The swift approach of war in Europe at the end of the thirties did not take Klein by surprise, but rather confirmed his longstanding conviction, shared by only a small number of other prescient observers, that Hitler needed to be taken seriously. His particular sense of foreboding for his own people was informed by a close attention to news from Europe and by an ingrained historical awareness of Jewish vulnerability to barbarous attack. As early as 1928 he had been alerting readers of the *Judaean* to the anti-Jewish demonstrations of the Hitlerites in Germany. In the summer of 1932 he noted the increasing strength of the Nazis in the German Reichstag. "The deluded mobs who voted for the Brown Shirts now know where to find a scapegoat ... It is a scapegoat with a beard; it is a Jewish scapegoat." It still seemed unlikely to Klein that anti-Semitism would ever prove to be more than an "extra-curricular activity" of the Hitlerites, though he warned that "it is a well known failing of human nature that man spends more energy on his hobbies than on his vocations."

As the decade unfolded, his worst fears were borne out. Reacting to the organized attacks upon Jews throughout Germany in November 1938, he wrote:

There is a lunatic abroad in Europe; and the world had better give heed.... A conquering nation does not treat its prisoners of war with that ruthlessness with which the German Reich has treated its Jewish citizens. Decency is exiled from that land; honor has been expelled from it; civilization has been placed in a ghetto. If ever there was a case of violent insanity which merited segregation, it is the case of the German leaders, mad with Hitlerics; if ever there was a source of pestilence which deserved quarantine, it is that of the German pirate ship of state.

Klein worried about the attitude of French Canadians to the impending war and about their response to the plight of European Jewry. When the French Montreal daily *Le Devoir* advised against the admission of German Jewish refugees to Canada, he questioned the Christian piety of the paper's editor. "Let him remember what is written in the New Testament about that man who, when he beheld a fellow-man beset by thieves and murderers, bleeding and sore afflicted, turned his head and crossed to the other side of the street. For that is precisely what Pelletier has done."

In February 1939 Montreal's much-loved mayor, Camillien Houde, addressing a Young Businessmen's Club at the YMCA, declared that in the event of a war between England and Italy, French Canadian sympathies would rest with Italy: "The French Canadians are Fascists, not by name, but by blood." Houde was to be interned from 1940 to 1944 for his open defiance of military conscription; as in the First World War, French Canadians had no wish to risk their lives and their sons' lives in what they deemed to be a purely English affair. Klein had always looked upon Houde with affection as the quintessential French Canadian folk hero, a leader with the common touch, a born raconteur and wily orator whose speeches he frequently enjoyed attending. Now Houde's appeal to the blood brotherhood of his people pained and baffled Klein, who knew very well the emotional tug of racial kinship, yet feared its explosive power.

On the eve of war, Russia's last-minute pact with Germany came as final proof to him that Nazism and Stalinism were indeed "two sides of the same drum.... The red dictator has found his soul-mate, the brown one; the totalitarian color-scheme is complete." His patience with Leo Kennedy's Marxism was now at an end. A few months earlier, Kennedy had asked him to contribute one of his "proletarian poems" to an anthology he was planning to assemble. When Klein insisted on submitting "Childe Harold's Pilgrimage" instead, Kennedy pressed him to delete or rewrite a passage in the poem that accused Soviet Russia of religious intolerance towards Jews. Klein now chastised his old friend angrily: "I am disappointed to discover that your naiveté knows no bounds and your evangelical Marxism no limits this side of heaven. With particular reference to my poem, you ought to know me well enough to know that I will not under any circumstances submit to red-penciling. This is true even if my opinions are wrong, but *a fortiori* when I am right as I am in this case."

At the end of August 1939 Klein foresaw with stark clarity that three and a half million Polish Jews would imminently be "handed over en masse for the further delectation of Nazi savagery. It will mean the debacle of that fifth of the world Jewish population which has made some of the most outstanding contributions to our national and religious life, and the elimination of that group which more than any other in recent times has been the preserver and guardian of our traditions. We do not — we need not — dwell upon what it will mean in destruction, human misery, and death."

In September, war broke out. "The issue is clear!" Klein wrote. "It is purely and simply the conflict between day and night, between light and darkness ... between civilization and barbarism!" Hitler's special war against the Jews was already in its seventh year. His objective, Klein stressed, "has been shouted from the roof-tops, and has been echoed across the world — the utter destruction, the complete annihilation of Jewry.... Should the gangster of Germany emerge victorious — may the Lord forfend! — then that victory spells the end of our people, its culture, its religion, its individual lives."

EVENTS IN EUROPE had by this time galvanized many Canadian Jews, including the man who was to become their most prominent spokesman, the wealthy distiller and philanthropist Sam Bronfman. The vehicle for Bronfman's leadership of the community was the Canadian Jewish Congress, an organization that had originally been founded in 1919 to aid Jewish victims in the aftermath of the First World War. The Congress remained dormant for two decades and then was revived in the late thirties to deal with the problem of Jewish refugees from Germany. In 1937 and 1938 Bronfman served as chairman of the Congress's Refugee Committee. In January 1939, at a national convention in Toronto, he was elected to the presidency of the Congress, a position he was to retain for the next twenty-three years.

Bronfman and Klein had known each other distantly from the time that Klein, in his college days, had worked as a spieler on the Seagrams tourist bus. Early in 1939 Bronfman began to take note of Klein's eloquent columns in the *Canadian Jewish Chronicle* and decided to hire his talent. He invited Klein to work personally for him as a public relations advisor and as the principal writer of his speeches, public messages, and official correspondence. Klein readily accepted the offer and remained at this job almost to the very end of Bronfman's tenure of the presidency.

In addition to the financial rewards, which at times must have meant a great deal to him, Klein derived a certain amount of genuine satisfaction from his work for Bronfman. He instinctively shared the great concerns of the Congress and appreciated the important role that a person of Bronfman's stature was likely to play not only in Canada but also in the broader arena of international Jewish affairs.

At the outset Klein's writing for the "maestro," as he liked to call him, was limited to Jewish community matters, but after a few years it began to encompass a good deal of Bronfman's business and personal activities as well. Among the more interesting projects for Klein were a number of literary and public relations ventures undertaken by Seagrams. In 1941, for example, the company sponsored the writing and publication of Stephen Leacock's *Canada: The Foundations of Its Future,* a handsomely produced volume issued at first in a series of limited editions that were distributed free to a select group of influential citizens, mostly in government and financial circles. It was Klein who anonymously authored Bronfman's preface to the book as well as the scores of personalized inscriptions that needed to be written to many of the recipients. With tongue in cheek Klein went on to review the book in the *Chronicle,* lavishly praising Bronfman's "eloquent and well-thought-out preface" as "one of the finest credos for Canadians that has ever been published."

It was no doubt thanks to his sense of humor that Klein found it possible to play to Bronfman's inflated ego as he did. Bronfman's fiftieth birthday in March 1941 evoked a long, fawning editorial from Klein in the *Chronicle,* capped by the following sonnet in acrostic form:

> Sincere, laborious for the common weal,
> Able, of heart capacious, broad of mind,
> Militant for his country, of great zeal
> Unto the human of earth's humankind,
> Excellent in most wise philanthropy,
> Leader well-chosen for his people's need,
>
> Bringing where union was not, unity,
> Resolving acts to implement the creed —
> Out with it, Sonneteer, reveal his fame,
> Name him, that all may know this kingly man,
> Fervent of purpose, lofty in his aim!
> Merit reveals him! His achievements scan
> And thus acknowledge him by deed and name,
> Name that does honor both to chief and clan!

SAMUEL BRONFMAN.

from Journal, 1942

Rejoicing and drinks — the maestro's — at the planning of the final banquet of the annual philanthropic campaign. Everybody complimented by everybody, even me, who am only the author of its slogans — the proxy of the poor — the compiler of its sob-letters. Particular backslap for an anonymous poem about the grace of charity — Ah, the charm of gilded platitude — printed on the banquet souvenir-program. Poor me! poet parsleyate to a menu. Actually the sonnet was written only to avoid writing the sickening prose called for… But that I should write it at all. It is a humiliation only a philanthropic world makes possible.

The gloating talk — objective reached, we'll show them, etc. — not a whisper about the hundred aspects of social distress, about the milk of human kindness from which this campaign sundae is dished up. All froth.

The campaign poem which was not written:

My dear plutophilanthropist,
Unclench your tight white-knuckled fist,
And give, as others of the tribe,
The annual philanthropic bribe:
From ancien and from nouveau-riche
The unimpeachable baksheesh!
It shuts the big mouth of the poor
From seeking and from getting more,
Narcoticizing with crumb'd bread
Rebellion in the pauper-head
And it costs nothing; for returned
Is merely part the pauper earned —
The sweetest saw-off to be had:

Two cents the dollar — Is that bad? —
And even these two paltry cents,
Being tax-exempt, are Government's.
For us the cake, — the poor a *maka*.
Great is the Hebrew ideal: *zdaka*!
Can better business deal be made
Than this most double-dealing trade
Which here below, preserves your own
And up above, takes to the Throne
The blessing of the synagogue:
This overlord helped underdog.
Can better profit come to you —
All this, all this, and heaven, too?

(September 1942)

To my dear friend Abe Klein

In whose soul there is Poetry —
in whose mind there is truth —
in whose heart there is Loyalty
Who helped me so much with
my thoughts and immortalized
them with his golden pen
Sam Bronfman
Dec 7/42

FOUND AMONG KLEIN'S HAND-WRITTEN DRAFTS FOR THE PERSONAL INSCRIPTIONS THAT SAM BRONFMAN WAS TO WRITE IN HIS GIFT COPIES OF STEPHEN LEACOCK'S HISTORY OF CANADA.

Outwardly, Klein rarely displayed any great sense of unease or embarrassment about being Bronfman's ghostwriter. "He always seemed to treat this chore as a game," one member of the Congress staff observed.

No one expected Bronfman to write his own speeches any more than they expected him to prepare the financial reports of the Canadian Jewish Congress. Besides, Bronfman never tried to conceal the fact that the addresses he delivered were written for him. There was the odd occasion when Klein got carried away in the writing, so that Bronfman's rhetorical flights would exceed what was normally expected from a captain of high finance. At such times, people would look at each other and at Klein sitting in the audience, in an exchange of knowing glances that asked who was whose ghost.

WHEN HIS FIRST COLLECTION of verse, *Hath Not a Jew*, appeared at last in April 1940, Klein proudly mailed out inscribed copies to dozens of friends and colleagues. He received many congratulatory letters from his long-time admirers, but was disappointed at the small amount of attention his book received from serious reviewers of poetry. As he himself recalled several years later, in a fictionalized memoir:

For the most part the reaction to the book was motivated not by its style or manner, its technical achievement, or passionate sincerity, but by its theme; thus Jewish periodicals who recognized in its pages the specter of their own plight or the image of their own hopes hailed it with hyperbole, at last a poet writing in English who spoke the authentic voice of his biblic ancestors, at last the Semite naturalized into Saxondom, etc., etc., while the English journals saw only what they suspected was a narrow chauvinism, a retrogressive nostalgia for outmoded traditions, a too-zealous remembrance of things past. They ignored the volume.

Klein's literary dilemma was most acutely perceived by the New York Yiddish critic Shmuel Niger, who posed the basic problem of whether the culture of one race could ever in fact be united with the language of another race. Niger elaborated on this question in his correspondence with Klein:

Won't your English readers need a Yiddish and Hebrew dictionary, just as I need an English one? Even more — for me the dictionary is sufficient; I doubt if it would be enough for them.... In order to really penetrate most of your poetry, it isn't enough to have the explanation of a particular word or name; it is necessary to have lived in the atmosphere which nurtures your outlook and gives it life. Here no dictionaries will help. One needs to have breathed the air of learning Gemara, of Chassidism, of Jewish folklore...

Niger's remarks evoked a thoughtful response from Klein:

I have just received your very serious letter and I hasten to reply to it because it raises questions not noted by anyone else in relationship to my poetry, except yourself — and myself. It is, in a word, the problem of synthesis between cultures.

First, as to the question of language. Today English is my daily tongue. I speak it everywhere and always, except to my mother, who understands only Yiddish...

If I wrote to you in Yiddish you would observe immediately that I think — insofar as sentence structure is concerned — not contents — in English.

Naturally, therefore, if I had to write poetry — and the compulsion thereto I shall not now discuss — it had to be in English. What does, what should, a poet write about? Only about what he feels and what he knows. Borrowed emotions will not do. Unassimilated knowledge will not do. Rilke once made a very pertinent and indeed profound remark when he said that all poetry is an attempt to recapture one's youth and even one's childhood. For me that means recapturing the nostalgia and the beauty of my childhood, which was a Yiddish-speaking and Hebrew-thinking one, Mitnagid from my teachers, Chassidic from my father. The theology, I may say, has vanished but the tradition has remained.

English being the language, it is its technique which is applied to the Hebrew theme. This is not any stranger than Yehuda Halevi writing *l'havdil* Hebrew poetry in Arabic meters or Immanuel of Rome borrowing the sonnet form from Dante. It would be a static literature indeed, which confined itself solely to the parallel construction of the Bible — our own original contribution to literary forms. As for the difficulty of the English, believe me I did not make it so on purpose. One of the chief factors in the creation of poetry is language; my mind is full of linguistic echoes from Chaucer and Shakespeare, even as it is of the thought-forms of the prophets; and if these creep into the text it is further to fulfill the definition of poetry, which suggests but does not say.

You are right when you say my book presupposes on the part of the reader a knowledge of Hebrew tradition. Apart from being written because I wished to write it, the book is addressed precisely to those who have that knowledge or those who may acquire it. In English literature references to a so-called alien culture is not a novelty. Milton's *Paradise Lost* presupposes great biblical knowledge. A better

KLEIN INTRODUCING THE PRO-ZIONIST AUTHOR AND JOURNALIST PIERRE VAN PAASSEN (SEATED NEXT TO HIM) AT A GATHERING AT THE JEWISH PUBLIC LIBRARY.

example, — large tracts of English poetry assume on the part of the reader an intimate knowledge of Greek mythology and the close relationships between the various Gods and Goddesses of Greek lore. To amalgamate factors, therefore, of two cultures does not to me appear to be an impossibility... Joyce's *Ulysses,* where every chapter has its counterpart in a similar chapter of Homer's *Odyssey,* is to my mind a completely successful literary merger of the values of two cultures.

Klein believed strongly that the principle of cultural synthesis was central to all Jewish literature. He was careful to reject the insinuation that he had "set out of purpose to accomplish a tour de force: to show that Hebrew values could be translated into English terms." Yet the very deliberateness of this protest seemed to betray his own suspicion that much of his Jewish poetry was, indeed, just such a tour de force.

KLEIN PROBABLY ACHIEVED his most effective merging of Hebraic and English literary modes in a sequence of short lyrics that he composed mainly during the first year of the war. Having in mind the centuries-old custom among pious Jews to recite psalms in times of suffering and distress, he began in 1939 to write a modern sequel or appendix to the 150 psalms of the Bible, beginning at number 151 and ending at 200. By the fall of 1940 he was able to report to Leo Kennedy that "more than half is already done, the rest outlined, awaiting only the moving spirit." The spirit evidently moved him no further, for in the end he managed to produce only thirty of the projected fifty psalms. In order to bring the sequence to its intended length, he later resorted to adding a number of his early unpublished poems under new titles.

The psalms that Klein composed in 1940 are generally distinguishable in tone and diction from his early poems. A good number of them are startlingly personal, even confessional. Several years later, at the time of their publication in book form, he admitted to having had misgivings at first about their directness. "I am beginning to realize, however, more and more, that to say what you mean so that you are understood is not necessarily an aesthetic liability."

Klein's psalms are modeled outwardly on the psalms of the Bible. Strictly speaking, there is only one, "A Song of Degrees," which is actually written in the manner of biblical poetry. Many, though, are cast in the form of prayers of petition or thanksgiving and make subtle use of biblical images and expressions. Klein is closest to the spirit of the Scriptures in those rare instances where, despite adversity, he avows a childlike faith in Providence. More often it is the modern voice we hear — challenging God, cynically misanthropic, finally doubting and resigned.

In a number of psalms Klein finds solace in the innocence of nature and simple creaturehood. The dumb, "more-than-human" beasts of the field are more companionable to him than arrogant, treacherous man. Inspired by a passage in the Jewish morning prayers, he sings a "psalm to teach humility" from the wisdom of the rooster.

> O creature marvelous — and O blessed Creator,
> Who givest to the rooster wit
> to know the movements of the turning day,
> to understand, to herald it,
> better than I, who neither sing nor crow
> and of the sun's goings and comings nothing know.

The rooster, the dove, and the sacrificial scapegoat of Azazel are all angelic figures; the eagle of death, in contrast, symbolizes for Klein man's demonic side.

The intricate workings of the human organism and its harmony with nature are also subjects for praise: the miracle of sleep, the five senses, the blessing of a "green old age," the healing power of drugs, and poisons.

> And sweet white flower of thy breath, O Lord,
> Juice of the poppy, conjuror of timeless twilights,
> Eternities of peace in which the fretful world
> Like a tame tiger at the feet lies curled.

In fine Jewish tradition, Klein easily calls God to task for the suffering of humanity and dreams of breaking the "abominable scales on which the heavenly justice is mis-weighed." In a humbler mood, he begs forgiveness for his blasphemies. He imagines himself scoffed by his faithless neighbors as a "babbling pious woman" and begs God "justify my ways to them." Skeptic himself, he discovers God in His very absence.

> I have no title for your glorious throne,
> and for your presence not a golden word, —
> only that wanting you, by that alone
> I do evoke you, knowing I am heard.

Though outwardly gregarious, Klein usually concealed his private feelings. In his more personal psalms, however, he unburdens himself and alludes to his fears and disappointments with unusual candor.

> I would not tell this to the man met on the street,
> The casual acquaintance, even the intimate friend,
> Stopping to speak of the news, complain about the heat:
> Him would I tell my triumphs mount, and have no end,
> The times are good, thank you, and never were they better.
> But to tell you, O Lord, it is a different matter—
> I would not have you pity my cheap lies.
> You know the truth, the ache I have and had,
> The blind alleys, the frustrations, and the sighs.
> O Lord, the times they are not good at all,
> And one might even say that they are bad.

Klein's psalms formed the core of his next collection of verse, which he began assembling in the fall of 1941. The manuscript that he submitted to the Jewish Publication Society the following February consisted of fifty psalms, grouped under the heading "Psalter of Avram Haktani"; three long poems, *"In Re* Solomon Warshawer," "Murals for a House of God," and "Yehuda Halevi, His Pilgrimage"; five short war ballads; and six love sonnets. The "Psalter of Avram Haktani" (in Hebrew, Abraham the Little, or "Klein") differed significantly in contents and arrangement from the earlier projected series of Psalms 151 to 200. Among the items that Klein had now added to the sequence were six wedding poems composed in the early thirties, before his own marriage, and five "Bratzlaver" poems based on Rabbi Nachman of Bratzlav's "Tale of the Seven Beggars," which he had started working on in Rouyn in 1938.

For two exasperating years Klein and his editors at the Jewish Publication Society haggled over the revision or exclusion of numerous poems in his manuscript. The editors, in their prudishness, objected to Klein's use of words such as "gutter," "privy," "filth," and "grovel." The collection in its entirety seemed to them objectionably depressing, gruesome, and at times blasphemous. In the end Klein consented to many of the changes that they insisted upon. Where he could not give in to their demands he had no choice but to withdraw complete poems, including several psalms that he considered to be among his best.

By the time the book was finally set for publication at the end of 1944, Klein had been forced to delete, substitute, or amend approximately half the poems in the collection. As a result, his fifty psalms were reduced to thirty-six, only one section of "Murals for a House of God" was published, three of the five ballads were left out, and none of the sonnets were included.

Klein's frustrating arguments with the Jewish Publication Society could only have reinforced his growing doubts about the wisdom of writing principally for Jews. The Jewish audience that he had attracted was generally unsophisticated in its aesthetic responses and now threatened to impede his creativity and block his path to wider acclaim. Leo Kennedy's disturbing challenge to him in 1940 must have often echoed in his mind: "You are a writer of propaganda poems, and the propaganda appeals only to a small group, the middle-class Jews. If you're content to be another Ludwig Lewisohn, it's all right.... if you want a wide audience, you have to write more widely.... you're endangering your talent, selling it for an easy success in a narrow confinement."

Such advice, which he had tended to shrug off at first, gradually had its effect on Klein's natural pride and yearning for recognition. If he was to be serious about poetry, he could not afford to be regarded as just another Jewish versifier. It became more and more evident to him that to achieve any literary standing at all in the world he would have to be judged in the company of the very best English-speaking poets of his generation.

MAYOR CAMILLIEN HOUDE ADDRESSING AN ANTI-CONSCRIPTION RALLY IN MONTREAL. HOUDE WAS ARRESTED FOR HIS ANTI-CONSCRIPTION ACTIVITIES IN 1940 AND INTERNED FOR FOUR YEARS.

Political Meeting

(For Camillien Houde)

On the school platform, draping the folding seats,
they wait the chairman's praise and glass of water.
Upon the wall the agonized Y initials their faith.

Here all are laic; the skirted brothers have gone.
Still, their equivocal absence is felt, like a breeze
that gives curtains the sounds of surplices.

The hall is yellow with light, and jocular;
suddenly some one lets loose upon the air
the ritual bird which the crowd in snares of singing

catches and plucks, throat, wings, and little limbs.
Fall the feathers of sound, like *alouette's*.
The chairman, now, is charming, full of asides and wit,

building his orators, and chipping off
the heckling gargoyles popping in the hall.
(Outside, in the dark, the street is body-tall,

flowered with faces intent on the scarecrow thing
that shouts to thousands the echoing
of their own wishes.) The Orator has risen!

Worshiped and loved, their favorite visitor,
a country uncle with sunflower seeds in his pockets,
full of wonderful moods, tricks, imitative talk,

he is their idol: like themselves, not handsome,
not snobbish, not of the Grande Allée! *Un homme!*
Intimate, informal, he makes bear's compliments

to the ladies; is gallant; and grins;
goes for the balloon, his opposition, with pins;
jokes also on himself, speaks of himself

in the third person, slings slang, and winks with folklore;
and knows now that he has them, kith and kin.
Calmly, therefore, he begins to speak of war,

praises the virtue of being *canadien*,
of being at peace, of faith, of family,
and suddenly his other voice: *Where are your sons?*

He is tearful, choking tears; but not he
would blame the clever English; in their place
he'd do the same; maybe.

Where *are* your sons?
               The whole street wears one face,
shadowed and grim; and in the darkness rises
the body-odor of race.

(early 1940s)

A 1942 SKETCH OF KLEIN BY HIS FRIEND
ERNST NEUMANN. KLEIN WROTE OF
IT IN HIS JOURNAL: "MOST
UNSATISFACTORY. SHOWED ME GRIM
AND MEAN. WHICH I AM NOT ALWAYS
... I TOLD HIM THAT THE FACE HE DID
HAD ITS GEOGRAPHY CORRECT, BUT ITS
CLIMATE WAS ALL WRONG."

from Portrait of the Poet as Landscape

Himself he has his moods, just like a poet.
Sometimes, depressed to nadir, he will think all lost,
will see himself as throwback, relict, freak,
his mother's miscarriage, his great-grandfather's ghost,
and he will curse his quintuplet senses, and their tutors
in whom he put, as he should not have put, his trust.

Then he will remember his travels over that body —
the torso verb, the beautiful face of the noun,
and all those shaped and warm auxiliaries!
A first love it was, the recognition of his own.
Dear limbs adverbial, complexion of adjective,
dimple and dip of conjugation!

And then remember how this made a change in him
affecting for always the glow and growth of his being;
how suddenly was aware of the air, like shaken tinfoil,
of the patents of nature, the shock of belated seeing,
the lonelinesses peering from the eyes of crowds;
the integers of thought; the cube-roots of feeling.

(1945)

6

A Rich Garland

Through the forties, Klein's high ambitions as a writer were sustained in part by the encouragement and stimulation he received from a dynamic community of young poets that had suddenly cropped up in Montreal. "There is quite a literary 'renaissance' taking place in the old town," he informed Leo Kennedy in 1945. "It reminds one of the good old days of '28 and '29; you would like the goings-on, too, if only for its juvenescent effect." The "goings-on" in Montreal revolved around two modestly produced literary magazines, *Preview* and *First Statement,* which were published by two separate groups of poets between 1942 and 1945.

Klein was most closely associated with the *Preview* poets, whose principal members included Patrick Anderson, Frank Scott, P. K. Page, Neufville Shaw, and Bruce Ruddick. For Scott, *Preview* represented a revival of the modernist spirit that he and A. J. M. Smith had originally brought to Canadian poetry in the twenties at McGill. Smith's personal involvement in *Preview* was quite limited, for he was now teaching at a college in Michigan and spending only his summers in Canada. He might otherwise have emerged as the dominant figure in the group, but instead it was Anderson, a young writer recently arrived from Oxford, via New York, who wielded the greatest influence.

Klein was reluctant at first to accept Scott's invitation and become a full member of *Preview.* He occasionally submitted some of his new poems, and from time to time joined the group in its social gatherings at Scott's home. It was not until March 1944 that his name actually appeared in the magazine's masthead. From then on he began showing up regularly at editorial meetings, usually at Anderson's flat, where the group would gather twice a month to read aloud from new work and select material for each coming issue.

Klein and Anderson enjoyed each other's company, although their friendship was not particularly warm. Anderson's communist loyalties and somewhat bohemian private life stood as an invisible barrier between them. Anderson always sensed a "dangerous sparkle" in Klein's readiness to

quarrel, and later remembered him as a "prickly man . . . who magnetized any trace of anti-Semitism one might have in oneself." Neither cared very much for the other's poetry, and to make matters worse Klein also had a low regard for Anderson's idol, Dylan Thomas, whose poems he dismissed as nothing but a series of images strung together on a thread. Anderson thought that as a poet Klein "tended too much to rhetoric" and that he "led his poems by the nose . . . you could see the way they were going too easily." Despite these differences Klein learned from Anderson's work and also managed to be helpfully honest in his criticism of it. In 1944 Anderson noted in his diary that though Klein was "scarcely up my emotional alley" there was nobody else in Montreal at the time with whom he could seriously discuss his poetry.

Perhaps the most pleasant friendship that Klein formed in *Preview* was with Patricia Page. Their relationship, though never really intimate, was a very relaxed one, based on a genuine mutual admiration. Page responded especially to Klein's bubbling sense of humor and also to what she felt was "a certain reverence in his nature, a sense of the mystery of the world." Klein was seven years her senior but she would always think of him as much older, for he was already a relatively established poet, a partner in a law firm, a husband and father, whose orderly life contrasted sharply with her own hand-to-mouth existence.

Page's vivid recollections of Klein in the mid-forties attest to the wonderful sense of exhilaration he seemed to experience in the company of other poets:

PATRICK ANDERSON AND P.K. PAGE, MEMBERS OF THE *PREVIEW* GROUP OF POETS. KLEIN ENJOYED AN EASY-GOING FRIENDSHIP WITH PAGE BUT SHOWED A CERTAIN TOUCHINESS IN HIS DEALINGS WITH ANDERSON.

I remember the time he'd just written his "Montreal" poem. He was so excited about it. He said, "I've written a poem, and anyone who can only speak French or anyone who can only speak English will be able to understand this poem. Listen." And then, eyes twinkling behind ice-cube glasses, he began reading "O city metropole, isle riverain!" in a robust baritone. We were in Patrick Anderson's kitchen, I think, crammed around the table, Abe pleased with his "bilingual" poem, savoring its words as he read it with relish. And *we* were excited too, because it seemed such an extraordinary feat.

We were drinking tea — or Anderson was. Tea was rationed still in 1944. Scott would have been drinking the bottle of beer he had brought for himself. We were modest in our needs and self-sufficient, often going on to Murray's for hot chocolate, or, if too late for Murray's, then to Bowles' with its rubby-dubs and overnight sleepers. We were light-hearted, "crazy" people at that point in our lives, and very relaxed with each other.

Abe was much loved in the group. He was such fun to be with, for one thing. Despite his formal appearance — and he did look formal in his navy blue suit — he was an informal, easy person.

Sometimes he would phone on a summer night and say "what about a drink at the Mount Royal?" and I would meet him there. He always wanted to read his poems. He had this extraordinary rhetorical way of reading, and this very Jewish voice, really. It was a rich, lovely voice, with a thick, guttural sort of pronunciation. He would start reading, and in those days there weren't many poets around and the waiters would look at him as if he were out of his mind. Then I would read, we'd discuss things, and we would laugh a tremendous amount together.

His puns were unbelievable — he just couldn't resist them. Language was marvelously flexible on his tongue, he could bend it any way at all, make it do anything. Klein had that sense of the child in him, to delight in language and play with it. His joyfulness, his delight in things — he was so alive to the world.

I never saw him moody or angry. He was the last of the *Preview* people whom I could have imagined having a breakdown. Any of us, I could have thought, might have had before Klein.

Along with all the *Preview* poets, Klein was more or less condescending in his attitude to *First Statement,* whose leading members were John Sutherland, Irving Layton, and Louis Dudek. From the very outset there existed a friendly rivalry between the more established, cosmopolitan poets of *Preview* and the rough young iconoclasts of *First Statement.* Yet Klein more than anyone else managed to straddle both groups and happily contributed his poems to both magazines. When *First Statement* acquired its own printing press on Craig Street and set up its headquarters there, Klein would sometimes walk over from his nearby law office to sit in on editorial meetings and offer his ideas. Dudek scorned the more snobbish members of *Preview,* but was touched by Klein's amiable warmth and kindness, and was struck by how very much at home he seemed to feel among the *First Statement* group. "There is," he wrote some years after they had first met, "a shyness about him, and a simplicity which he makes an effort to conceal; something, one feels, that might be easily bruised."

Klein had somewhat less of a rapport with John Sutherland, a headstrong Irishman whose shrewd, uninhibited criticism may have prevented any close friendship. Sutherland consistently argued that Klein's youthful lyrics in *Hath Not a Jew* were far superior to his more solemn and serious poems of the early forties, which suffered from a "flabbiness of thought" and a style indicative of the "belief that rhetoric can be passed off as poetry." In an article published in 1946 he attacked Klein's use of convoluted syntax, the reliance on abstractions, the endless catalogues relieved only by pedantic variations — "a funeral procession of iambic pentameters, calculated geometrics, and ponderous stanzas that seem carved from stone." It was only at the end of the decade that he was willing to grant that the "dull and direction-less" poems of the early forties had constituted part of a necessary maturing process leading, in Klein's final collection of verse, to "a new, more intense lyricism fortified by sophistication and a tough logic."

Klein's contact with *First Statement* came mainly through his friendship with Irving Layton. The two had first met in 1930, introduced by their mutual friend David Lewis. Layton, a bright but already obstreperous young man, had been expelled from Baron Byng in his last year and needed help in preparing for his final examinations. At Lewis's request Klein agreed to coach him in Latin poetry at no charge. Layton passed in the end, though what he was to retain was not the Latin, but the sonority of Klein's reading of Book II of the *Aeneid* and the infectious excitement with which his young tutor described the beauties of Virgil's rhetoric and prosody. Layton would never forget their first meeting at a corner of Fletcher's Field,

sitting on a bench, hearing Klein roll off the Virgilian hexameters in a beautiful oro-tund voice that rose above the roaring traffic. I think it was then that I realized how very, very lovely and very moving the *sound* of poetry could be. I must confess my Latin wasn't sufficient to enable me to appreciate the sense that Virgil was making with his marvelous musical hexameters, but Klein's zeal and enthusiasm, his forceful delivery, his very genuine love of language, of poetry, all came through to me at the time. And I think that was most fortunate for me.

In the thirties their paths continued to cross. Layton moved in left-wing circles and spent his best hours in vociferous arguments over socialism and communism at public meetings and debates, or more informally at Horn's Cafeteria on St. Lawrence, next door to the Eagle. Klein, though more moderate in his politics, also gravitated to these forums.

At the same time Layton began writing and brought some of his first poems and stories to Klein for comment. But it was not until the early forties that their friendship really blossomed. Layton would come calling for Klein at his law office as often as two or three times a week and accompany him to the nearest Murray's Lunch where they would sit and spend several hours in conversation. Klein was only too happy to leave his legal business for a while and satisfy Layton's hunger for intellectual talk by discoursing on whatever books or ideas happened then to be on his mind. He would always be glad to read any new poems Layton might bring him, and eventually started showing Layton some of his own recent work as well. "In those days poetry was a secret vice," Layton recalled.

To know there was a poet living in Montreal, a living poet, meant a great deal. Not only was he kind, looking over my first efforts, but the fact that I talked to him, saw him breathe, drink a cup of coffee, established a world of reality for me. I very much doubt that I would have become a poet if there had not been somebody like Klein in Montreal at the time.

IRVING LAYTON AT BAT, 1952. LAYTON, AN OUTSPOKEN AND CONTROVERSIAL FIGURE, WAS VERY POPULAR WITH HIS STUDENTS AT HERZLIAH HIGH SCHOOL, WHERE HE TAUGHT FOR MANY YEARS.

Klein commanded a properly reverential attitude from the normally brash and pugnacious Layton. He felt certain, too, that Layton was a genuine poet and spoke favorably of his work to editors and publishers. In reviewing Layton's first collection of poems in 1945, Klein hailed him as an unmistakably powerful talent and regretted only that his Jewish heritage was not as prominent as it might have been. "Perhaps," he conceded, "Layton's Jewishness manifests itself more in his approach to a subject than in the subject itself ... the neat cerebration with which he fashions his epigrams, the pilpulistic antitheses, the wit double-jointed."

Though Klein was merely three years older than Layton, there seemed to be a generational gulf between them. When Layton once spoke to Klein about his imminent marriage break-up and his plans to marry John Sutherland's sister, Betty, Klein reacted with deep dismay and in rather fatherly tones took him to task for leaving a Jewish wife to marry a Christian. To Layton, Klein's concerns over such matters were so outmoded as to appear almost comical. At times, he thought, Klein was positively "proud of his squareness ... He sneered at poets who were, according to his lights, immoral."

Though most of the *Preview* and *First Statement* poets respected Klein as a senior and established writer in their midst, they never felt overshadowed by him, and in fact tended to think that he learned more from them, by way of example and criticism, than they learned from him. Perhaps the greatest benefit for Klein during this all-too-brief period in his life was a sense of validation, a feeling that poetry somehow mattered, even if only to a small number of others like himself. It was also becoming increasingly possible for someone like Klein finally to take pride in the fact that he was a Canadian poet and to look forward to the continued growth of a vital literary community in his own country.

Already in the early forties Klein enjoyed an enviable reputation among his own colleagues in Canada, although in such a small society of writers as existed then it was often hard to distinguish honest praise from mutual backscratching. In 1941 E. J. Pratt wrote to Klein to thank him for a laudatory review of one of his recent books and took the opportunity to express his own admiration for Klein's work, remarking on how very high his literary stock was in Toronto circles. "E. K. Brown, Leo Kennedy, A. J. M. Smith and I are united in our praise of you. Certainly you have given this country so absolutely original a product that you have become a national discovery." Brown, who was probably Canada's premier literary critic at the time, felt no hesitation in naming Klein the best Canadian poet of his generation. Klein's own vote in this unofficial contest went for A. J. M. Smith, whom he always liked to address as *il miglior fabbro* — the better smith, the superior craftsman — echoing Eliot's famous tribute to Pound. Smith, in his landmark *Book of Canadian Poetry* in 1943, magnanimously ranked Klein as "the greatest poet living today in Canada."

All this mutual admiration may have bolstered a few egos, but it also inhibited the possibility of frank, open criticism. Klein was both too prudent and too tender-hearted to write derogatorily about anyone who happened to be among his acquaintances. "Friendship," he once noted, "corrupts my judgement and cramps my style." Adroitly backing out of a commitment to review a book by the Vancouver poet Earle Birney, for fear that he might not find anything favorable to say, he pleaded: "It is not I who would want to hurt his feelings." In fairness, though, it should be remembered that the praise of friends was all that even the best Canadian poets could count on to sustain them in the forties.

Without doubt, this unexpected flowering of poetry in Canada had an exhilarating effect on Klein. Probably for the first time in his life, and to a degree that would never be repeated, he felt that he had found his true vocation. In the summer of 1943 he wrote to a friend with uncharacteristic candor and assurance: "All I am *really* interested in, above everything, is writing poetry. Everything else in my life is mere adjunct, a means to that end."

As HE MOVED INTO THE MAINSTREAM of English Canadian poetry, hoping in this way to launch himself into the world of English-language poetry in general, Klein grew increasingly uncomfortable with his well-deserved reputation as a specifically Jewish poet. He knew, of course, that his intense Jewishness had been, so far, the very lifeblood of his best poetry. But now he worried that he would be categorized in narrow terms as no more than a parochial ethnic poet, isolated from the general literary culture. Writing to Smith in 1943, he complained bitterly about how the Canadian critics E. K. Brown and W. E. Collin tended to define him in terms of his Jewishness. "Lord, O Lord," he cried, why did they both have to go "flaunting my circumcision? I am not a poet because I'm a Jew ... It's an adolescent trick — this whimsical opening of another man's fly." Even Smith could not escape Klein's mild rebuke for the selection he had made in his *Book of Canadian Poetry* that year: "Your choice of my poems somewhat overemphasizes the Judaica."

It is ironic, and perhaps a mirror of his own ambivalence, that Klein at this very time was most strident in his attacks against American Jewish writers who seemed to be either ignorant or ashamed of their Jewishness. The older generation of American Jewish writers were, he believed, "irrevocably committed to the thesis that the less Jewish they appear, the more American they will be. They are, to vary a notorious formula of the last century, Americans by Jewish dissuasion." Klein was convinced that it was this very betrayal of their heritage that doomed them to secondary roles in American literature, as anthologists, reviewers, editors, and teachers. Having "nothing original to contribute" they merely write but "they do not create. One cannot create with another's genitals."

Klein hoped for a while that the younger generation of American Jewish writers might be different. He was slightly encouraged by the example of Delmore Schwartz, in his opinion a subtle and talented poet, who though limited in his knowledge of Judaism was at least prepared to state publicly that he considered his Jewishness to be a "fruitful and inexhaustible inheritance." But Schwartz was a solitary case. Klein would have liked to discover a similar measure of Jewish pride in Karl Shapiro, another young American poet whose work he greatly admired in the early forties. Instead he could detect only the familiar signs of ignorance and negativism.

There is not any indication anywhere that the poet is aware of the rich cultural heritage which should have been his ... nothing worthy of reference in a culture which has spanned the centuries and covered the continents.... Let us not be misunderstood; it is not the function of the creative artist to be a public relations counsel for his people, though it is no disgrace if he is. But surely Shapiro's poetry is in no way enhanced, his Americanism in no way made more authentic, by this studied — and unalleviated — denigration of his own.

The question of the relationship between the creative artist and his people was always of the utmost concern to Klein. As a writer he displayed a great sense of Jewish honor and pride, based on a genuine love of Jews, individually and as a nation. Even in his Zionism, what mattered most was not land, nor even language, but peoplehood. "It is the folk — and all of it, everywhere — which is of the essence. Domicile, status, speech, etc., these

KLEIN AND BESSIE IN THE EARLY FORTIES.

are but adjectival; the substance is *amcho* — thy people." Such sentiments most likely had their origins in his childhood. Klein, it will be recalled, was the youngest in a fairly large, close-knit family. The household he grew up in had been the constant gathering-place of older siblings, cousins, aunts and uncles, nephews and nieces. It was in this setting that he formed his strong sense of tribal loyalty and affection, beginning with kith and kin, and gradually extending outward to wider and wider circles. Ultimately his humanism and his sympathetic openness to people of all backgrounds were but the final extension of this love of family.

Yet there was also a countervailing force in Klein's character, an impulse towards privacy and individualism, and a chafing at the burden of having to be the hero and spokesman of the folk. Joyce's hero Stephen Dedalus epitomized the modern artist's refusal to "merge his life in the common tide of other lives." Home, fatherland, and church were the treacherous nets that Dedalus thought he had to fly past in order to attain the higher realms of freedom and art. Klein struggled all his life to assimilate and conquer this basic dogma of modernism.

The truly Jewish artist, in Klein's view, had necessarily to sacrifice a portion of his individualism. To be a poet of the people was to suffer a kind of anonymity and a frequent suppression of the private lyrical accent in favor of the public rhetorical voice. The Jewish writer is the Everyman of his people, a spokesman of the entire folk. Hence the aptness, Klein thought, of the *nom de plume* of the great Yiddish storyteller Sholom Aleichem — "the Jew's hello; the individual writer in his very signature announces the approach of the total heritage: Sholom Aleichem — here come all of us!" It was in this spirit that Klein sometimes described the folk song as the quintessentially Jewish genre. A folk singer is "no poet seeking esoteric themes and an abstruse vocabulary to express the uniqueness of his personality.... a folk singer does not choose his subjects; his subjects are chosen for him by the folk."

Klein too had his subjects chosen for him. In devoting so much of his talent to the public causes of the day, and especially as a ghostwriter for Bronfman, he invariably had to assume an anonymity that went against the natural wish in a talented artist for personal recognition and fame. Frequently there recurs in Klein's writings the image of the *lamed vavnik*, the legendary hidden saint whose righteousness quietly and imperceptibly sustains the very existence of the world. Like the *lamed vavnik*, Klein's unrecognized "Poet as Nobody" is "a number, an x ... incognito, lost, lacunal ... in a shouting mob, somebody's sigh."

In his worst moments Klein felt positively humiliated at the thought of allowing his eloquence and imagination to be used for mundane purposes. Writing once of Bialik he was surely thinking as well of his own case when he observed that there was often in the great Hebrew poet "a certain impatience with his people who demanded of him, at the slightest provocation, 'a poem for the occasion,' as if he was a fashioner of birthday greeting-cards, or a writer of rhymed obituaries.... One can well imagine the feelings evoked in the man whose forte was eternity, not time, and certainly not the incidental."

from STRANGER AND AFRAID

Why, then, do I not seek the road to escape? Why don't I change it, my name that seems a pornography? Why do I persist in my identity, flaunt it, boast about it? From what actual depths of humiliation does it spring, this weak faltering I'm-proud-to-be-a-Jew bravado, as if the thing was the result of an exercise of choice, and not a mere reconciliation with one's fate?

Is it the religion of my fathers that so ravishes me that I will suffer all these revilements? For the true faith? But that is absurd. To me the thirteen credos of Maimonides are mere literature, and the six hundred and thirteen injunctions of Holy Writ historic curiosities. I have lost my father's faith. I am not of the stuff with which one kindles auto-da-fés. Nor are my fellow "co-religionists." They, in fact, are not even curious about the six hundred and thirteen, and to them Maimonides is not even literature. That can't be the bond.

Then, perhaps, it is race, the cohesion of the chromosomes? Perhaps; the universal envies and the ubiquitous hatreds certainly do bestow upon us a distinctive identity. But that is a distinction which comes from without; it is not inherent. Moreover, I cannot entertain a loyalty based upon the assumption of race; it would belie all my human convictions. Besides, I cannot but ask: Am I really of the race? Would it not be a grand joke, an irony of the subtlest refinement if, searching my genealogy, I discovered that somewhere in the dark backward of time, my ancestors, through war or through passion, mingled their bloods with strangers? Would not there ensue the classic pay-off — the man persecuted, convicted, condemned — and it's all a case of mistaken identity!

Perhaps, then, it is mere indoctrination, the comfort of habit, which holds me to those I am accustomed to call my own, and to their traditions. That this is much due to it, I have no doubt. They are forever part of me, the ceremonials of my childhood. The seasons do not roll around but each one brings me symbols of the customs of my father's house; I cannot smell the winds of April but that I sense also the gust of air that flew into our banqueting house when the door was opened for Elijah to drink from his cup, nor can I hear sad music — music of the minor keys — without remembering the intonations of the synagogue. Good Canadian October, florid with leaves, still brings me the rites of the Feast of Tabernacles, and the memory of the branch-covered Succah my father built on the back-gallery, and the delicious fragrance of citron, redolent from the benedictive hand. And Purim, and the penny for the mask; and the Fifteenth of Shvat, New Year of the Trees. The calendar conspires for my soul....

Yet surely that which is indoctrinated can be exdoctrinated? Is it because — because I read a book— that I am forever bound not only to all its readers, but also to the non-readers who only heard of the reviews? ...

Shall I then be eclectic, and say that it is a combination of all of these factors — race, education, religion — that keeps me self-willed among the chosen? But the whole cannot be made up of deficient parts. What, then, is it, this secret force of the magnet?

I am beginning to think that it cannot be anything but honor. A sense of honor.

105

Ignoble and base is he who forsakes the weak in whose midst he finds himself to go over, and for that reason alone, to the camp of the strong. It is treachery. It is a coward's choice. It is a despicable desertion. Its perpetrator ceases to be not only Jew, but also man. It is the endorsation of iniquity — a kissing, a sneaking up to the other end of the whip. Who does this abjures his integrity. He is the man in the country of hunchbacks who wills to walk with a stoop — mean, wretched, and with no honor.

(mid-1940s)

from Journal, 1942

The voice of Rabinovitch, editorial, cantorial, touching the burden of Klein: I'd like you to do me a favor.

He wants a translation — only you can English my Yiddish — an appeal to the maestro for a worthy cause — only you can make it clear to him — or legal advice. No, not that; — you're too honest.

The library is having a campaign dinner. Need a guest-speaker. You? Speech! Speech! The bastard art — modulated wind, seduction lingual.

We are the people of the Book. When the Germans were still barbarians — as they have remained — shaking their spears in forests black, our ancestors etcetera. Spiritual resources. Am Ha-Sepher. We gave the world a ten-inch descalogue. Conjure with big names. The Bible! Talmud! Maimonides! Halevi! Bialik! Argumentum ad vulgum: The great literature in Yiddish. Not a jargon, forsooth! Peretz and Mendele — fathers of Yiddish literature. (They died childless, strangers say their Kaddish.) Contemporaneity: Of what avail our material struggles, if we win the world and lose our own souls? Erudition: As Emerson said, as Milton's lifeblood spoke, quoth Rabbi Yochanan ben Zakkai. Irony: The people of the bankbook, the moneytheists. (Laughter.) Not us, — disturbance in hall — not any here, the assimilators, the sellers of their birthright for an officer's mess. Peroration: Our strength in our ideals. Where is the wolf Assyria? Where is Rome? Where is Carthage? (Is there a Carthaginian in the house?) They may destroy our homes, uproot our people, slaughter our children, but the truths which Israel launched upon the world, they cannot destroy. (Applause.)

No; don't accept. Give him the negative, cordial.

Much as I am tempted to avail myself of your kind invitation — nothing would please me more than to be able to address the pillars of this cultural institution, so dear to my heart — my own membership dates back to 1922 — I am regretfully compelled to forego the proffered pleasure. There are a number of reasons, but I believe that three will suffice: Imprimis: medical instruction not to tax myself with oratorical effort — save forensic, to pay the doctor's bill. Secundo: I have made a resolve not to deliver any public addresses during war-time; and tertio: there are so many more who could do the job better than I.

Unuttered the fourth reason. I will not play second fiddle! Who was he, first invited, who shall not come, that I am now called to save the day?

Rabinovitch, inquisitive: I did not know you were so sick.

He wants a medical diagnosis. Ill himself, he seeks company. Spontaneous pneumothorax — the perforated bellows. But I won't tell him.

Rabinovitch, flattering: We were thinking of getting a New York speaker, but decided we could use home talent.

Aha, a prophet with honor in his country. Honor, for a piece of himself.

Rabinovitch, personalizing: I thought you would accept for sure. After all, it's your library.

Draftdodger, why don't you enlist? Don't you know we are fighting for civilization?

I am the civilization for which you are fighting!

*   *   *

The poetess to see me: crazy Slappho. Imagines herself in love with me, the grand passion, Eloise and Abie.

"I know that you talk so cruelly to me because you want to discourage me. But why be so conventional? What if I am married?"

(And at her back I always hear
The drenched diapers slapping near.)

"After all, it is the breast which speaks. We were made for each other! How we could take the world by storm. I with my poetry, you with yours!"

(Aroint thee, rump-fed runion
I wouldn't touch thee with a double pentametre!)

She takes out of her purse her be-prepared notebook, her book of verses, crusted with bread-crumb, kitchen-greased. She reads some lines about her baby, and about "beautiful Palestine." Her voice throbs. Tears come to her eyes: she moved herself. Her bosom heaves. "Don't you think I have something there? Don't you think it has feeling? Ever since I read those books you told me to read, I know that I'm improving."

(Quousque tandem ...)

"I was at the Canadian Author's Association Convention. I saw Mr. Spondee the well-known poet. He wanted me to leave him twenty poems. Twenty! Don't you think that's wonderful?"

(The Lay of the Fast Minstrel.)

"But all of this is so unimportant, compared to *us*! I know you are in a hurry, but just let me look at you a few minutes more."

She looks a few minutes more.

"O, if my children were only grownup, and my husband not so jealous."

(Blessed art Thou, O Lord, who hast invented jealous husbands!)

(September-October 1942)

from Design for Mediaeval Tapestry

The burgher sleeps beside his wife, and dreams
Of human venery, and Hebrew quarry.
His sleep contrives him many little schemes.

There will be Jews, dead, moribund, and gory;
There will be booty; there will be dark maids,
And there will be a right good spicy story ...

* * *

The moon has left her vigil. Lucifer fades.
Whither shall we betake ourselves, O Father?
Whither to flee? And where to find our aids?

The wrath of people is like foam and lather,
Risen against us. Wherefore, Lord, and why?
The winds assemble; the cold and hot winds gather

To scatter us. They do not heed our cry.
The sun rises and leaps the red horizon,
And like a bloodhound swoops across the sky.

(1931)

7

Tumultuous Night

THE FIRST DOCUMENTED REPORTS of the organized mass murder of the Jews of Europe reached the West in the spring of 1942. The world's silence, Klein told his readers in the *Chronicle* in July, was "eloquent of nothing so much as a sense of its own guilt."

Today the cables bring reports of the pogrom which lasted for two days in the city of Lemberg. Yesterday Slovakia — Nazi-dominated — boasted across the airwaves that it would soon be *Judenrein*. A week ago came the belated news of the continued and daily massacre of Jews in the Baltic countries. A month ago, the world heard of the holocaust in Kiev where forty thousand Jews were destroyed. A year ago, one read the report of the *shechitos* in Rumania.

We recount these atrocities, as if they were the items in a Cook's Tour Catalogue, the peregrinations of murder. It is in this same matter-of-fact fashion that the general press reports these matters. They are relegated to a footnote, a small item in the back page, these which should furnish the headlines of the day.

Where, he asked, is "the thunderbolt of invective which these events should call forth? Where are the keepers of the world's conscience, its intellectual leaders, guardians of the progress of the ages, and where the as-yet-unuttered *J'accuse* of our generation?" The complacent indifference of millions of decent people, churchgoers, leaders of society, enunciators of noble ideals, astounded him. "They regretted, perhaps, that these things should be; they no doubt found them distasteful, unpleasant to read about, embarrassing. But they did nothing. They did not interfere. They turned their heads away and talked about Western civilization."

As a potential victim of Hitler, Klein was not simply outraged but terrified. He was to recall the effect this welter of emotions had on him, in an unfinished novel written just after the war.

There wasn't a night — my mind had dwelled so long upon the theme — inhuman cruelty visited upon those whom I could not but regard as my substitutes — there wasn't a night of calm untroubled sleep. Once it was a man who looked like my father, beard, humility, and all, — I did somehow realize that my father was dead, and this unrealized subconscious of the subconscious did console me a little — who was being slapped and spat upon, and then from a rail hung by his feet, and his head dipped and raised, dipped and raised, a little lower each time, into a barrel of human dung. I was standing by, and my turn was next.... it was only upon waking, when the full realization of what I had seen came upon me, that I was seized with a sweating and heaviness that made it impossible for me to fall asleep again. I was frightened at the passive role I seemed to have played in the dream. To horror, there was added a sense of guilt.

His fears were intensified by local outbursts of anti-Semitic demagogy, coming mainly from extremist elements in Quebec. French Canadians were less isolationist now than they had been during the First World War, but they still opposed a policy of compulsory military service. Indeed, the ruling Liberal party had won the support of French Canada in the wartime election of 1940 by promising not to introduce conscription. Early in 1942 a plebiscite was called to release the government from that pledge. In March a French anti-conscription rally in Montreal ended with a rowdy parade through the main streets of the Jewish district. From *À bas la conscription* the shouts soon changed to *À bas les juifs*, and the marchers set to smashing windows, stopping streetcars, and assaulting pedestrians. The French Canadian Nazi leader, Adrian Arcand, was at the time in prison under the War Measures Act, but his small band of vocal supporters was still active in the anti-conscription movement. Klein warned that it was their unseen hand that had directed the rioters — "the same hand which, when less cowardly, lifted itself in Fascist salute to Arcand ... For this is Fascism, simple and unadulterated — native-born, home-made Fascism." The plebiscite on April 27 resulted, as expected, in a majority "Yes" vote in favor of conscription, but the country's sharp racial split was evident in the overwhelming "No" vote by French Canadians.

Klein personally was ineligible for military service because of his age and marital status, and perhaps also on medical grounds; "deficiency of gall" was the condition he reported, half-facetiously, in the only written mention anywhere of his exemption. There are indications in his semi-autobiographical manuscripts of the early forties that he was slightly self-conscious about being thus excluded from danger.

I feel like one who lives somewhere on an African veldt at the edge of a jungle. Now and again, a panther stalks forth from the leafy design of the horizon to maim or kill a disobedient child playing on the outskirts of our village. Then, my brothers, the hunters, take down their rifles and make ready for the hunt.... All about me the world is full of a terrible activity....

I cannot say that I remain, even from afar, untouched by these tremendous expeditions. I, too, would like to be of the Nimrods. Their curdling hunting-cries stir

me; their many lethal inventions arouse my curiosity. I watch with envy the raising of their gay banners and would like to form part of this pageant about which others, less sensitive than I, are already making songs....

Unfortunately — and perhaps fortunately — I must stay behind. The medicine-men have added an insulting initial to my name; and I am not fit for hunting.

So here I am, with the womenfolk. I am like one who in meditation watches a thunderstorm, and pares his nails.

As if to compensate, he became increasingly caught up in the notion that the poet had a special mission to fulfill as "part of the fighting forces ... the trumpeter marching into the fray." From the psalms of 1940 he turned to a series of haunting war ballads in 1941, inspired by the contemporary Yiddish balladist Itzik Manger. The crazed, danse macabre rhythms of these poems underscored Klein's unbridled anguish, but it was some other, more bellicose voice that he was still seeking: the voice of satire and invective that he finally settled on in his mock-heroic *Hitleriad*.

THE HITLERIAD BEGAN as a hundred-line poem in 1942 and reached its final length of nearly eight hundred lines by the spring of 1943. It was, in effect, Klein's major contribution in verse to the war effort, an elaborate poetic indictment of Hitler and his chief henchmen. At the time of its completion he was remarkably pleased with the poem; he spoke of it proudly as one of the very best things he had ever written, and for himself personally "a satisfying exercise in righteous hate."

In *The Hitleriad*, as in his editorials for the *Chronicle*, Klein sought to expose Hitler as a charlatan, a man of devilish rhetorical cunning whose essential wisdom was that "the lie, if oft repeated, is the truth!" In contrast there stood the messianic figure of Churchill, "the man who hated sham and cant." Klein marveled at the eloquence of the British prime minister's war-time speeches and commented on them regularly in his editorials. "No leader of Britain, within the memory of living man, has been such a master of the inspiring utterance ... here is language that is as if taken out of Holy Writ, the homely parable, the apt quotation, the ironical aside — all the verbal characteristics bespeaking the man endowed with a purpose and brimming with confidence." Part of Klein's intention in *The Hitleriad* was to achieve in verse what Churchill had already accomplished in his oratorical prose.

He had consciously chosen to write the poem from what he considered to be a universal rather than Jewish perspective. "The only thing Hebraic about it," he believed, was "perhaps its indignation and compassion." It was intended "as a prosecutor's indictment against 'that wicked man'." In style it was "neither lyrical, nor cerebral, nor pure poetry," but a revival of Augustan verse, "the poetry of wit and wrath." Klein's idea was to apply this eighteenth-century form not to literary squabbles, for which it was best suited, but to "mightier themes — systems and ideologies."

While he took personal pleasure in the technical virtuosity of the poem, he was convinced that its contents would appeal to a much wider audience than might normally be expected for poetry. He was eager, in fact, to see it published as quickly as possible, recognizing that it was essentially a propaganda piece and that its topicality would not outlive Hitler himself. "My dilemma," he told one publisher, "is this: I must have *The Hitleriad* published before the dog dies; yet I wish his death daily."

In June 1943 he sent a copy of the poem to E. J. Pratt in Toronto. Klein had written a glowing review of Pratt's *Dunkirk* a year and a half earlier, calling it the "first memorable poetic utterance" on the war. Now given the opportunity to return the compliment, Pratt wrote to Klein: "Your poem is grand." He strongly urged Macmillan to publish it, but to no avail.

Later that month Klein sent a copy to his editors at the Jewish Publication Society, half-heartedly suggesting that they append it to his manuscript of *Poems*, which at the time was still in limbo. Knowing their fastidiousness, he cautioned them: "It is, definitely, not characterized by feebleness or delicacy of expression." The Jewish Publication Society, however, was not interested in *The Hitleriad*.

As a last resort, Klein turned to the *First Statement* group, who without hesitation decided to print an edition of four or five hundred copies. In advance, selections of the poem were published in the August and October issues of *First Statement* magazine. Just then, Klein unexpectedly received word from James Laughlin of New Directions in Connecticut that a series of poems he had submitted a year earlier were to be published in the next *New Directions* annual. Encouraged by this acceptance, he sent Laughlin a manuscript copy of *The Hitleriad*. In January 1944 Laughlin made up his mind to publish it as a volume in his "Poets of the Year" series.

Klein was overjoyed. It was still not too late to have the Canadian edition halted; only a few pages had been run off, and he undertook to pay for the losses himself. He then quickly sent off a slightly revised version of the poem to the printer for New Directions, corrected proofs in April, and saw the first copies of the book in August 1944.

In the excitement of the moment, Klein unrealistically anticipated a very wide readership for *The Hitleriad* and offered to collaborate closely with Laughlin in promoting its sale. "What is essentially required are a couple of proper *blurby* reviews in the right places. The 'little magazine' reviews are good for one's immortal soul, but for one's mortal needs, give me a good spread in *Time* magazine, or a proper accolade in the *New York Times*. They set the tone, and all the bookstore registers echo their melody."

Laughlin was equally optimistic about the book's popular potential and tried very hard to get the influential Book-of-the-Month Club to comment on it in its monthly newsletter. Klein went a step further and attempted to persuade *Reader's Digest* and *Life* to publish part or all of the poem. He also reported to Laughlin that he had sent copies of the book to Churchill and Roosevelt. "These gentlemen, I gather by the papers, are soon to meet in Quebec. Ah, if we could only elicit from either of them — I rub my hands — even a snort of approval!"

None of these publicity efforts succeeded. Laughlin wrote to Klein of his disappointment that *The Hitleriad* had been ignored by a number of prominent American critics and reviewers who happened to be Jewish and who therefore might have been expected to take special note of the book. At this prompting, Klein's own vehemence was instantly unleashed:

You are right, right, full-face, dead-center, bull's-eye right! Myself I never would have volunteered that analysis of the Fadiman, Untermeyer, Cerf, Kreymborg attitude — you may think of this junta as the composite of their initials — myself, I had deluded myself into believing that this phenomenon was a racial, a family secret — but if you, a non-Jew, have observed it, have noted it, have written about it, — well, then the shame is out! Let it be discussed.

At first I had thought: Perhaps they haven't got around to it, perhaps they haven't had time to write about it, perhaps they haven't seen it, perhaps, perhaps, the poem is not quite the opus I had thought it was. This last was a doubt entertained only in my moments most unnerved; for after all, I was not deaf, I was not blind: others had found laudable things in it, and had so deposed, others had heard it read and were visibly and audibly affected. A crowd's laughter is not a studied thing.... Yet these four good men and true said nothing....

These arbiters of public taste — together with the lesser marranos — maintained their silence about *The Hitleriad* not because it was written by a Jew, but by a Jew not of their ilk. A Jew who admits it! A Jew who is in no way embarrassed by his nativity, who in fact is defiantly grateful that his lot is with the persecuted, and his heritage of the Talmudic, the prophetic, the biblic....

Let me make myself clear. I am myself not one of those I-am-proud-to-be-a-Jew

Jews. A Jew I am; the world knows it, and I accept that fact like the fact that I have two arms.... It is to be noted, in this connection, that in *The Hitleriad* I did not make any special point touching the suffering of Jews. That suffering was merely one aspect of a many-sided phenomenon. No, I wasn't displaying my Jewishness in the show-case; but neither was I hiding it under the counter, like contraceptives.

But this crew, dousing their Ellis Island smell with true New England spice, are not content unless they don starspangled thimbles upon their circumcised penises. Your desire to descrotize them, therefore, will never be fulfilled. They have themselves anticipated you. For they are also castrati....

At the same time I think these crypto-Jews deserve a good swift kick in the ass for their feigned unconcern. (Note: The Yiddish press, wherever it got a copy of *The Hitleriad*, responded warmly, gratefully, proudly. It may not have caught the allusions to Blake and Marlowe, but it knew damn well when I alluded to its own flesh.)... So let them go to hell. I have more important work to do....

It is surely a comment on the mood of the time that *The Hitleriad* received whatever praise it did. Among readers and reviewers who took note of it, the poem seemed to touch a sensitive nerve. Many, though, did not know what to make of it as literature. Irving Layton justly praised the poem's technical excellence but doubted whether the satiric mode was applicable to Nazi bestiality. "Mr. Klein must insist that Goebbels is halitotic, which is illuminating but is not exactly the circumstance that makes him so unpopular.... The section on Streicher, trenchant as it is, yet reminds me of a telegraph boy arriving with a singing telegram to a house where someone has just died."

Layton perhaps could not appreciate the unusual degree to which Klein was steeped in a tradition that did, in fact, allow him to make even Hitler the butt of satire. To the truly religious Jew, Klein once noted, "Hitler is not so much knave as fool." On the eve of the war he had applauded Chaplin's intention to treat the Fuehrer mockingly in *The Great Dictator*; like Chaplin, he wished to see in Hitler a clownish, ridiculous figure. The contemporary situation called to his mind the biblical Purim story told in the Book of Esther, in which the mortal enemies of Israel are seen in the end to be mere laughingstocks in a Divine comedy. For centuries the Jewish shield against suffering had always been humor: to combat evil one had only to expose its ultimate ridiculousness. Strange as the results of this aesthetic may now seem in certain parts of *The Hitleriad*, it must be said that Klein's weakness for black humor and melodrama, the mingling of laughter and tears, was profoundly Jewish and a hallmark of his Yiddish mentality.

WHEN THE FULL EXTENT of the Holocaust was revealed in 1945, Klein was stunned at the devastation. "For the past six years," he recalled,

while the Nazis themselves openly flaunted the murder-blueprints they had prepared, and while reporters standing upon the abandoned scenes of Gestapo atrocity sent accounts of the number of containers of human ashes they had discovered in the macabre buildings, the quantity of gold torn from the teeth of Jews about to be cremated, while all this was being attested, both as to place and as to time, as to method and as to result, Jews, and all civilized beings, secretly entertained a hope, a wish, a concealed but cherished incredulity. It can't be as bad as it's described! Inhuman monstrosity could not possibly go to such lengths! True, the villages and cities redeemed from the hands of the fleeing Germans were invariably empty of Jews. Perhaps, ran the secret hope, they have fled into the woods, they have changed their names, they are being concealed by friendly peasants... Come the end of the war in Europe, and they will reveal themselves.

The hope was doomed to frustration. The Nazi program for Jewish annihilation was by no means overestimated.... A generation, and more, has been wiped out.

Klein's initial response was one of grief and vengeful anger. In his 1945 poem "Elegy" he lamented the loss of one-third of the Jewish nation and hurled the curses of Deuteronomy upon the Germans. At the same time, he prayed for the speedy rescue of the survivors and for their reestablishment in a Jewish homeland. The shattered remnant of European Jewry, he felt, "ought to be regarded as the means for the maintenance and continuation of our people. Succor brought to these, therefore, is not an act of charity; it is an act of national reconstruction."

In the years that followed, Klein became increasingly outraged at the leniency with which many Nazi war criminals were treated by international tribunals. The cynical motives behind this policy deeply offended his sense of justice and gradually contributed to his darkening view of Western civilization. Only the complete rooting-out of Nazism, he believed, could prevent its resurgence.

Klein had been among the few writers in English to react to the Holocaust in the forties. His response was remarkably natural in its emotions, and gave powerful expression to the anguish of the moment. By the fifties, however, he could no longer summon words equal to the subject, and refrained from even attempting to deal with it any further, except to ask rhetorically:

Is there anywhere a Jeremiah with tongue so bitter and heart so clenched that his words would not issue feeble, inadequate, mocking, in the face of an annihilation so widespread and so wanton? Who is there who can descry, amidst the impalpables of the human spirit, the true measure of this vast anonymous loss? ... Here, certainly, memorials and threnodies would be but empty ceremony, not only futile to assuage the heart, but, in their very insufficiency, compressing and agonizing the heart still more. The thunderblast is not to be answered with a sigh. There is, indeed, no voice to utter such catastrophe; wailing is vain, and clamor almost obscene.

from THE HITLERIAD

See him, at last, the culprit twelve men damn.
Is this the face that launched the master-race
And burned the topless towers of Rotterdam?
Why, it's a face like any other face
Among a sea of faces in a mob —
A peasant's face, an agent's face, no face
At all, no face but vegetarian blob!
The skin's a skin on eggs and turnips fed,
The forehead villainous low, the eyes deepset —
The pervert big eyes of the thwarted bed —
And that mustache, the symbol of the clown
Made emperor, and playing imperial pranks —
Is this the mustache that brought Europe down,
And rolled it flat beneath a thousand tanks?

*   *   *

Judge not the man for his face
Out of Neanderthal!
'Tis true 'tis commonplace,
Mediocral,
But the evil of the race
Informs that skull!

116

You ask, is paragon'd
The Nordic in this thrall?
Why, chivalry's not found
In him at all!
And he's the beast not blond,
Nor is he tall.

His strength is as the strength
Of ten, and ten times ten;
For through him, magnified
Smallness comes to our ken —
The total bigness of
All little men.

          *   *   *

The dossier, then; the facts, the untampered text:
Let *this* world know him, ere he goes to the next!
Where was he born? (Born is the word that I
Use, seeing *littered* is not poesy.)
Where was he born? In Braunau at the Inn —
And Austria paid for that original sin! —
Born to a father, old and over-wined
Who had he slept one night, had saved mankind!
At first hight Shicklgruber — 'what a name
To herald through the mighty trump of fame' —
Heil Shicklgruber! Shicklgruber, heil!
Methinks this lacks the true imperial style,
And certainly no poet's nor mob's tongue
Could shake from shekel-shackle-gruber — song!
The gods are kind. His father changed his name,
And saved, at least the Shicklgrubers' shame....

          *   *   *

So, you may say, he was a miracle
Of bold persuasion and of iron will —
And sure he needs no courage who has skill!
What skill? And what persuasion? Skill to use
Hatred as bomb, and rhetoric as fuse?
Persuasion to persuade the Swabian mind
It was the unwhipped cream of humankind?
A bag of tricks, a mountebank's recipes,
Fit only for the half-mentalities
By birth and training sedulously bred
To swap, for circuses, their daily bread....

CROWDS THRONG PHILLIPS SQUARE AND ST. CATHERINE STREET IN DOWNTOWN MONTREAL ON MAY 8, 1945.

Reflections on V-E Day

Not with surprising suddenness did it come; it did not come — as in the dark days we had hoped it would — as a miraculous flash on a radio, a startling announcement lifting us from the depths of despair. By installments, with forewarnings, parceled in rumors, it finally arrived, and even then was only quasi-official: *the Nazis had surrendered, unconditionally.*

How difficult it was to articulate the proper response! So much hope, so much day-in-day-out longing was wrapped up in the coming of this announcement, — this, the day for which we had hoped! — that thoughts stumbled over one another; and the mind was confusion, and the heart a bursting inexpression. Us the moment found on St. James Street: inglorious place. In an instant the street was a bedlam of joy, the tall buildings smiled with hundreds of faces, the paper that streamed from the windows was itself an extended and ubiquitous smile. Everybody said unrememberable things; it wasn't really speech; it was ejaculation, brimful and jubilant. Girls danced, soldiers were borne up on shoulders. People danced in the streets; even those who walked alone glowed with an inner illumination.

118

And we could not help reflecting upon the great kindness which had been vouchsafed to all of us to be permitted to behold this day. Five years ago — let it be frankly admitted — we saw about us only darkness palpable. The great trek which we had made through history seemed about to come to an end. The enemy appeared invincible, and to us Jews, implacable. A Haman had arisen who meant to obliterate our people, to destroy us, beyond remnant, and beyond memory. For the time being, his ravages were confined to Europe, but his intentions were never concealed — he meant to make the whole world the scene of his totalitarian iniquity. Every Jew felt the Nazi tentacle stretch out to reach him, personally. Until the last Jew was cremated, Hitler, we knew, would feel that his task had not been done. Surely, in all our troubled history no such threat had ever been lifted against us.

Now, in the hour of triumph, we could take the Nazi propaganda against us, and make it into a crown, even as we had made the Yellow Badge the shield and ensign of nobility. The arch-enemy of our people had fallen into the dust, miserable and ignominious; the murder he had planned was only partially accomplished; his grand scale of slaughter had been frustrated. Whence could one summon the voice, and whence the hallelujah, that could utter adequate thanksgiving for that this thing did come to pass?

How often, in the past, have we as a people boasted of the ordeals and martyrdoms which we have survived! Antiochus, Pharaoh, Haman, Torquemada, Chmelnitzki — these were names which marked the danger-points of our survival. We had outlived them, and their wicked intention; and ever thereafter, their appellations were like a pendant of grim bloodstones which we wore upon the throat of our history. Sometimes, indeed, we made out of these names a playground for humor, a field for our wit. Pharaoh outlived was a comic character; Ahasuerus outlived was a drunkard and fool.

I wondered what place Hitler and his doings would now occupy in our folklore. I thought about the past years, and the words *blitzkrieg, lebensraum, festung Europa* — portentous terms! — and how henceforth they would sound in the vocabulary of civilized man. But of one thing I was certain — these words and their kindred would never form part of our humor.

For while the bombs were silent, and while the bombast sounded, we could not help but think upon our missing. Conservative estimates place the number of our martyred at five million; only the months to come will reveal the actual figure. Yes, we have survived; but as we take count of our numbers and take stock of our condition, we discover that we have survived, bleeding and maimed. We are less by one quarter of our population.

The poison that has been brewed in Nuremberg still spreads its fetid odor across the face of Europe; much still remains to be done before victory is translated from its military language into a living and meaningful reality. In the meantime, for the great blessing, the supreme boon, gratitude and thanksgiving. For the day, *dayenu*; for the rest, He who has led us thus far, will lead us still.

condensed from the **Canadian Jewish Chronicle** *(May 11, 1945)*

NAZI SOLDIERS WATCH THE BURNING OF THE WARSAW GHETTO.

from Elegy

A world is emptied. Marked is that world's map
The forest color. There where Thy people praised
In angular ecstasy Thy name, Thy Torah
Is less than a whisper of its thunderclap.
Thy synagogues, rubble. Thy academies,
Bright once with Talmud brow and musical
With song alternative in exegesis,
Are silent, dark. They are laid waste, Thy cities,
Once festive with Thy fruit-full calendar,
And where Thy curled and caftan'd congregations
Danced to the first days and the second star,
Or made the marketplaces loud and green
To welcome in the Sabbath Queen;
Or through the nights sat sweet polemical
With Rav and Shmuail (also of the slain) —
O, there where dwelt the thirty-six — world's pillars!—
And tenfold Egypt's generation, there
Is nothing, nothing ... only the million echoes
Calling Thy name still trembling on the air....

Vengeance is thine, O Lord, and unto us
In a world wandering, amidst raised spears
Between wild waters, and against barred doors,

There are no weapons left. Where now but force
Prevails, and over the once blest lagoons
Mushroom new Sinais, sole defensive is
The face turned east, and the uncompassed prayer.
Not prayer for the murdered myriads who
Themselves white liturgy before Thy throne
Are of my prayer; but for the scattered bone
Stirring in Europe's camps, next kin of death,
My supplication climbs the carboniferous air.
Grant them Ezekiel's prophesying breath!
Isaiah's cry of solacing allow!
O Thou who from Mizraim once didst draw
Us free, and from the Babylonian lair;
From bondages, plots, ruins imminent
Preserving, didst keep Covenant and Law,
Creator, King whose banishments are not
Forever — for Thy Law and Covenant,
O, for Thy promise and Thy pity, now
At last, this people to its lowest brought
Preserve! Only in Thee our faith. The word
Of eagle-quartering kings ever intends
Their own bright eyrie; rote of parakeet
The laboring noise among the fabians heard;
Thou only art responseful.

                        Hear me, who stand
Circled and winged in vortex of my kin:
Forego the complete doom! The winnowed, spare!
Annul the scattering, and end! And end
Our habitats on water and on air!
Gather the flames up to light orient
Over the land; and that funest eclipse,
Diaspora-dark, revolve from off our ways!
Towered Jerusalem and Jacob's tent
Set up again; again renew our days
As when near Carmel's mount we harbored ships,
And went and came, and knew our home; and song
From all the vineyards raised its sweet degrees,
And Thou didst visit us, didst shield from wrong,
And all our sorrows salve with prophecies;
    Again renew them as they were of old,
    And for all time cancel that ashen orbit
    In which our days, and hopes, and kin, are rolled.

(1947)

from Barricade Smith: His Speeches

Where will you be
When the password is said and the news is extra'd abroad,
And the placard is raised, and the billboard lifted on high,
And the radio network announces its improvised decree:
You are free?
Where will it find you, that great genesis?
Preparing your lips for a kiss?
Waiting the call of next in a barber-shop?
Rapt with the ticker's euphony?
Or practising some negroid hop?
Where will you be?
When the news is bruited by the auto horn?
Holding a pair of aces back to back?
Paring a toe-nail, cutting out a corn?
Or reading, with de-trousered back,
Hearst's tabloid, previously torn?
Or will you be — O would that you should be! —
Among those valiant ones returning to their homes
                              To tell
Their daughters and their sons to tell posterity
How they did on that day,
If not create new heaven, at least abolish hell.

(1938)

122

8
The Multiplying Word

Klein's mounting sense of accomplishment in the early forties made him more eager than ever to free himself from the reins of his law practice and to devote as much time as possible to literature. In 1942 Smith had encouraged him to apply for a Guggenheim fellowship to spend a year on the translation of Bialik's poetry. Klein hesitated, fearing that such a project, important as it may have been in his own estimation, would not meet with the approval of the Guggenheim committee. Finally, he submitted an application in October 1943, listing Smith, Pratt, and Brown among his references. He was deeply disappointed, though not surprised, to be told early in 1944 that his request had been turned down. Brown's suggestion afterwards that the Guggenheim committee was "not very favorable to creative projects" did little to console him.

Sam Bronfman had come to know Klein well by this time and recognized his desire to pursue a literary career. Klein's pride, however, would have precluded any mention between them of outright patronage. It was only by indirect means that Bronfman would ever be able to extend financial help. As a prominent donor to McGill University, Bronfman was in a position to influence Klein's chances of obtaining a lectureship in the English department, and he let him know of the fact. Klein was prepared to accept this much assistance from Bronfman and decided to wait for the right moment to avail himself of it.

In the spring of 1944, he was suddenly confronted with an altogether different avenue of escape from his law practice. Canada's socialist party, the Cooperative Commonwealth Federation, or CCF, needed a candidate to represent it in the federal riding of Cartier, where Klein lived.

The CCF had already been in existence for over a decade. Two of Klein's closest friends, David Lewis and Frank Scott, were among the original builders of the party, and their steady enthusiasm undoubtedly made an impression on him. The CCF had scored its biggest electoral gains so far at the level of provincial politics, especially in the Prairies. With its sights set on the coming federal election, it now hoped to achieve enough momentum to launch itself into a position of national significance.

Cartier riding had been allotted as a "Jewish seat" early in the century by the Liberal leader of Canada, Wilfrid Laurier. S.W. Jacobs was the first Jew to win Cartier for the Liberals in 1917, and Peter Bercovitch followed in his steps in 1938. Bercovitch died in office in 1942, and a by-election to fill his seat was held in August 1943. Lewis entered the race as the CCF candidate and anticipated his stiffest competition, as usual, from the Liberal. Unexpectedly the victory went to the communist Labor-Progressive Party candidate, Fred Rose. The communists were subsequently accused of having won through unscrupulous tactics, such as registering "boarders" from outside the riding to swell the vote for Rose. Their success, however, was mainly a result of public enthusiasm for Soviet Russia, seen then as a heroic embattled ally against Germany.

Klein was shocked and distressed at Rose's victory. During the campaign he had warned Lewis against alienating the Zionist element in Cartier. Lewis's Jewish-socialist Bundist background cost him the support of the influential Labor Zionist groups, who might have come out more strongly for him had he taken a clear pro-Zionist stance in his campaign.

In preparation for the next general election, the CCF now had to choose a new candidate to represent it in Cartier. Lewis, embittered by his loss, decided to stay out of the riding and instead persuaded Klein to seek the nomination.

Until this time Klein had shown little inclination to enter politics or to devote himself to the goals of a party. If he could be labeled a socialist, it was not because of any economic doctrine to which he subscribed but simply out of a heartfelt concern for the downtrodden and a biblical sense of outrage at injustice. Nonetheless he was tantalized by the prospect of a seat in Parliament; any change in his life, he seemed to feel, was bound to be an improvement. He recognized that the fight for Cartier was liable to be vicious, but tried to look past it to the reward of victory. In March 1944, warming up for the anticipated campaign, he began delivering his first political speeches to Jewish labor audiences.

His formal nomination at a local CCF meeting on April 2 went unopposed. In his acceptance speech he made it clear that his strategy would be to unite the divergent ideological camps within the Jewish community under the CCF banner. Certainly this was a sensible approach for him to take; socialism always had a strong appeal in working-class Cartier, and Klein was already well known and respected as a spokesman for all of Montreal Jewry. He concluded his remarks in a light vein, speaking of his intention to play down his poetic career. At the same time, he added, it was fitting that a poet should "go forth to pluck a Rose."

:אראקטמעריסטיש פאר דער שטימונג פון די בירגער אין קארטיע
יונען די ווערטער פון מר. בערנסטיין, וואס האט זיין סטאר אויף
זיין פטריום: "מיר האבן געזען וי פרעד ראזע האט זים ווירדע
אין שטאליע געערדם און געארבעט פאר קארטיע ; נט אונגסם 1943.
ער לאזונג דערציילט דעם אמת. ער האט געוואונען; רעספעקט
פאר קארטיע און ער האט געוואונען אונזער רעספעקט".

דעם ווֹ־טן יוני ווידערוויילט
פרעד ראֹז

FROM A BROCHURE ISSUED BY THE
FRED ROSE CAMPAIGN, 1945.

The day following his nomination found him both elated and apprehensive. He sensed envy in the stares and congratulations of his lawyer friends. On reflection, it occurred to him that his connection with Bronfman might be used against him in the campaign. When they met a few days later, he playfully feigned concern lest *he* mar Bronfman's Liberal associations and confided frankly that he would have preferred a teaching post at McGill to a seat in the House of Commons.

After only a week he began to have serious misgivings about his decision to run. He wondered why he, a poet, should allow himself to be contaminated by political struggles. "Here are so many mean motives, so many ignoble drives; in poetry, only cleanliness, starched words, and the smell of air." Why then, he asked himself, was he running? "I am not driven by ambitions in that direction; and I surely have too much humor to have a mission. It must be — for the exercise."

In late April he explained his hesitation to Brown:

The last thing I ever expected to do was to run for office. My political commitment — tell it not in Gath — was partly a rebound from the Guggenheim rebuff. For poli-

125

tics, or rather for political campaigning in the particular division in which I am to run, I have certain talents; these talents, as all political talents, I never esteemed highly.... Even now I would much rather hold a minor lectureship in a university which would provide me with a minimum of congenial work and a maximum of leisure to work upon the hundred "projects" which agitate me, than be an M.P., let alone a would-be M.P....However, since things are not as I would have wished them to be, I intend to fight the good fight on the field that has been chosen for me. My sole regret is that every one of my political speeches — and in Cartier you have to make plenty, and in three languages — will cost me at least three poems...

All through the spring and summer, long before any serious electioneering would normally have begun, Klein kept up a busy schedule of political speech-making before various groups in Cartier. Towards the end of the year, however, he withdrew from the race almost as suddenly as he had entered it. Early in 1945 he admitted openly that he had learned his lesson: "Politics is not my meat; it gives me indigestion." His withdrawal may have been urged upon him out of tactical considerations as well, for splitting the Jewish vote between the Liberals and the CCF only threatened to hand another victory to Fred Rose. Thus it was that the CCF did not field a candidate in Cartier in the election of 1945. As it turned out, Rose retained his seat anyway, winning over sixty percent of the vote that June.

In January 1945 Klein briefly considered moving to New York. The American Jewish Committee was about to launch *Commentary* magazine and was searching for an editor. Klein discreetly let it be known through intermediaries that he was available, but he evidently never filed a formal application for the job. He probably knew very well that his recent foray into socialist politics and his ardent, outspoken Zionism would have been sufficient to disqualify him in the eyes of the Committee.

At the same time, a tempting offer was extended to him by Meyer Weisgal, then secretary-general of the American section of the Jewish Agency for Palestine, who invited Klein to come to New York to take on a variety of tasks as a writer and publicist for the Zionist cause. The work promised to be rewarding and stimulating, but Klein backed away from the opportunity. His many ties to Montreal had given him a sense of security that he was not ready to forego. Bronfman, in particular, was reluctant to see him leave and assured him again that a lectureship at McGill could easily be arranged on very short notice. In February Klein apologized to Weisgal for having to say no, and explained: "The objective that I primarily seek is the life academic, and not the life political; and despite the usefulness and the rewards of the work which you discussed, and despite the fact that I have talents which could advance that work, I must stick to my original decision — to devote myself to those creative undertakings which are to me the *summum bonum*."

BRONFMAN'S CONTACT AT MCGILL was F. Cyril James, the principal and vice-chancellor. James evidently acceded to Bronfman's wish that a part of his annual contribution to the university be earmarked for Klein's salary as a lecturer in the English department. The details were worked out in the spring of 1945, and James met with Klein at the Faculty Club in May to explain the arrangement. Klein was to get a visiting lectureship in poetry for three years. He would receive the salary of a full-time assistant professor and teach nine to twelve hours per week. It was an "experimental thing," James cautioned, and added frankly that Cyrus MacMillan, the chairman of the English department, was dubious about it — Klein hadn't a Ph.D., he had been away from the university a long time, and, besides, "Mac" didn't much fancy his poetry.

Klein assured James that he was delighted about the job. Inwardly, however, he was full of apprehension, not only about MacMillan but about whether he would be successful as a teacher.

I am worried about the students: A Jew teaching English poetry! About students who will have come back from the wars: And where were you all this time? About the subjects I will teach. About what will constitute the measure of success. About the "experimental" nature of the thing; and then, what? Return to the Law? I'll never do that. O, that my father had left me an inheritance.

Klein turned for advice to Harold Files, a veteran member of the department. Files had been a supporter and mentor of the *Fortnightly* group back in the twenties, and as a teacher of modern literature and creative writing was far more enthusiastic about Klein's arrival than MacMillan was. He later recalled how the suddenness and manner of the appointment caught everyone by surprise.

In certain ways it was an odd transaction, out of line with the usual mode of appointing to the Faculty. Apparently it came about through an agreement between Principal James and a member of the Bronfman family who had undertaken to pay Klein's salary, and so make a gift of his services. It was without question a desirable windfall ... but at that particular moment, Dr. MacMillan had left Montreal and had not been consulted or asked for an opinion. Nor was I, who was as Dr. MacMillan sometimes put it "second in command." I first learned of the appointment from Klein himself who appealed for advice on taking the next step. Our talk was very cordial, and my advice was that he get in touch with Dr. MacMillan *by any possible means,* and work out with him whatever plan of work, conferences, lectures, would be acceptable to them both.

I learned later that summer that his efforts to make contact had failed. When the registration of students was actually and dizzily under way, I was startled by Abe's sudden appearance at my office door, to say that he had been completely, at all points, baffled, and had no sense of belonging in the McGill scheme of things. It was quite clear that Dr. MacMillan was not pleased by the manner of the appointment. Something had to be done fast, and I dropped all other business while Klein and I sat down to work it out together.

from Journal, 1945

May 4, 1945: Had lunch with Dr. James at the University Club. A club right out of a cartoon in *Punch*, deep leather seats, trophies on the wall, lackey at the desk, heads in newspapers, and frigidity pervasive everywhere....Waited for the Dr. who arrived — a punctual man — at the first tick of one. So good to see you, he said, have you washed up? I had, so he went himself to the rear of the club to doff his clothes; I could hear the mumblings of the old dodderers in the lavatory.

We went upstairs, up a carpeted staircase that seemed to say — Come, curl yourself upstairs in me. He ordered two martinis. I had accepted just to be sociable; the damn stuff is too heady for me; I find it a handicap in conversation. (I shall never suffer from gout.)

Discussed the war, Germany was capitulating by installments....What will the Jews do, he asked. I said Jews were in a dilemma. Five million had been murdered, and those who survived would very likely not want to return to the scene of their martyrdom. Palestine, I told him, was the principal subject of discussion in regard to the Jews of Europe.

A difficult problem. I agreed. I showed him that I knew the English viewpoint, nonetheless, all we wanted was 8800 square miles. Ibn Saud could hide that in his flowing robes.

A great man, Ibn Saud. I met him when I went to see my brother who was a councillor at his court. Very primitive. Justice Solomonic....

I could gather from the Dr. that he was in love with primitive things. The bloody picturesqueness of the Arabs is our most difficult obstacle in appealing to the English. They prefer natives. They are colorful, and easier to deal with. But the goddam Jews, they are always quoting from the same books as you read, unpleasant occidentals. The doctor did not say that, but that was the wind that blew from his remarks.

We proceeded to lunch. He looked for subject of conversation. Do you do any gardening, he asked. No, I said, I don't, neither I, nor my ancestors for two thousand years. Just haven't had the chance.

How do they manage in Palestine?

That precisely is the miracle of our generation: Lawyers, doctors, university graduates, all took to the farm. Blackest of labor, and made a success of it....

Still on the primitive, I thought the manner of Mussolini's death was abominable. I was revolted by the desecration of his body.... I admitted, however, that I might not have felt the same way if it was Hitler who was hanging in that fashion — side of beef, strung upside-down from a hook.

He didn't. He would feel the same way, if it was Hitler. I thought, Naturally. To you he was only a belligerent. To me, he was a blood-enemy....

Our coffee we had downstairs. The Dr. probably remembered that I liked to have my cigarette with my coffee, and in the dining room smoking was prohibited. Last time, the dessert was an ordeal to me, without nicotine.

Finally he got down to the subject. I was to get a Visiting Lectureship in Poetry ...

He and I drew up a rubric for the kind of course he would like to give (a tempting enough dish), and we rushed it down to the Dean's office for approval. Dr. MacMillan, taken even more by surprise than I, thought best to consent (though he confided to me later in the day that such a course would not get off the ground). Klein and I had good hopes, posted advertisements, word got round, and on this short notice there were soon more than a score of registrations.

There were no further hindrances and in a short while all of Klein's classes were filled. Still, he kept apart from MacMillan and most of the other faculty members. He hardly ever socialized with them and spent as little time as possible on campus. By contrast, he enjoyed very friendly relations with several of his students. He had a devoted following among a small group of them and would occasionally wander over to a nearby student tavern with them after classes. A few of his students began writing poetry and later were to embark on literary careers, remembering him and very much inspired by his example.

Klein was naturally a stimulating and entertaining teacher. His courses were the first in modern poetry ever to be given at McGill, filling what must have been a considerable hunger. In the classroom he liked to encourage spontaneous discussion, but nevertheless always came prepared with copiously detailed lecture notes. As might be expected, he stressed close reading of individual poems and a sensitivity to the nuances of language. Two textbooks he relied on heavily for his courses were Louis Untermeyer's anthology of modern American and British poetry and the newly popular and influential textbook of the New Criticism, Brooks and Warren's *Understanding Poetry.* Though modern poetry was his main subject he was also called upon to teach some courses in seventeenth-century prose and poetry as well as nineteenth-century romantic and Victorian poetry. When Files became chairman of the department in 1947, he invited Klein to give a course in Canadian literature. Klein turned down the suggestion, explaining that he was already "saying what he felt the impulse to say" and that the subject of Canadian literature did not stir his enthusiasm.

While teaching at McGill, Klein still used his law office as his principal place of work. Students who were unable to meet with him during his hours on campus might sometimes come down to his office on St. James Street. It was thus that he was able to maintain contact with his more important legal clients, while actually spending most of his time in the office reading, preparing notes, and writing. All along he continued working for Bronfman and kept up his weekly columns and articles for the *Canadian Jewish Chronicle.* The routine afforded him sufficient opportunity to pursue some long-delayed projects and to branch out into new areas of literary creativity.

from COMES THE REVOLUTION

In an unpublished novel written in 1946 Klein drew on his knowledge of politics in Cartier riding and of David Lewis's 1943 loss to Fred Rose. As this excerpt begins, the narrator, Mort Snyder, has been trying to win the confidence of the Communist Party leaders in Cartier.

Then I got my lucky break. In one of the slum constituencies the sitting member had popped off, a by-election had been called, and the Party had decided to contest the seat. Krantz had been defeated there before, a couple of times, but that didn't matter, the fight would be worth it, at least in propaganda, and anyway, an election was as good, if not a better way to carry on the Party work, than trying to invent slogans for the week. Also the time being what it was — Russian victories coming in on the airwaves, morning, noon, and night, — and the place what it was — a constituency largely inhabited by citizens of foreign extraction — this would be a great opportunity, it was felt, to concentrate the Party guns on international affairs, to go again, but this time with meaning, into the song and dance about Yalta, Yalta.

So a democratic convention was called, and the name of Theodore Krantz was spontaneously proposed, and adopted, unanimously.

By the time the campaign came into the hot weeks, there were four candidates in the field: Krantz; and a rich Liberal lawyer who had the backing of the government, stuffed shirt by the name of Lazarus, Edgar M. Lazarus; and Milton Charles, a popular local boy who ran C.C.F.; and fourth some illiterate shirt vendor who had made a lot of money during the war and now wanted his relatives to appreciate that he was really somebody. At first, it looked as if the fight would be exclusive between the Liberal and the C.C. heifer, with Ted coming in a poor third, — the fourth guy, of course, didn't stand a chance at all, he'd probably be betrayed even by his kith and kin — but as the campaign progressed and the canvassers came back from the stoops with their report cards, it became clear that Krantz was very much in the running after all. This made everybody sorry they didn't have a better candidate than Ted, but there was nothing to be done about it, he was there, he had a right to be there, and you didn't go changing horses in the middle of the race.

The board of strategy then made some rapid calculations from the report cards, and figured it out that the big danger was the socialist Charles, who though he couldn't win himself might pull away enough votes to kill Ted's chances. So he was *it*.

They ran him ragged. Every day there was a new pamphlet, in two colors, showing what a dirty doublecrossing betrayer this Charles was, betraying both the constituency and the Soviet Union, how he was really in the employ of the big corporations, and how he was making himself a willing tool of the capitalist candidate to split the labor vote. Magil came down specially from Toronto and devoted an evening, at an open air meeting on Fletcher's Field, to Lazarus's lackey. He laughed at Charles's academic distinctions, he mimicked his Oxford accent — for him that wasn't hard — he contrasted Charles's career with Krantz's — Krantz sitting in jail because he dared to speak out for his class, and Charles sacrificing himself for the workers by making two-hour speeches. Magil made quite a comedy out of the fact that Charles was a little fellow, pint-size, although Krantz wasn't bigger, only stouter. By the time Magil was through, Charles was a fascist, done up brown. A good time was had by all.

Then the guys got really cocky. They challenged Charles to a public debate, what the French here call a contradictory assembly. Each speaker is given some time to talk up his ideas, to show his stuff, and the audience decides who made the nicer promises. Of course no vote is taken then and there, nor is the applause clocked, but an impression is left, and the Party thought the impression would be all in its favor. It was to be a show, and if everything went right, it was to be our show.

True, the braintrusters didn't think very much of Krantz as the great spellbinder, but they weren't very worried about it either. In the first place, the fact that the other guy was so smooth, and he, Krantz, seemed so simple, would work out they figured in Krantz's favor; the citizenry, particularly of this slum district, didn't like smooth guys who spoke with an Oxford accent and manicured their nails. They wanted one like themselves, and that was Krantz. Moreover, the organizers, just so as not to leave everything to psychology, would see to it that the Victory clubs would swarm out to the meeting, the cliques and claques would be strategically placed, and everything would run according to Hoyle.

The Oxford man accepted the challenge. Whatever he may have lacked, confidence he had plenty and to spare. Krantz was just his meat. To put on a show with the stuttering inarticulate deep-thinker who opposed him — that suited him fine.

Me, I thought so too. It's all very well to have your cliques and all that, but at a public meeting, strangers, not to speak of the supporters of the other guy, are bound to slip in, and while the crowd might cover up for the showing of their native son, the seams were bound to show and there's a limit to the extent to which people can be kidded.

So this was my chance.

The hall was packed, and the overflow stood out in the street looking up at the loud-speakers. Ted spoke first. When he rose there was a thunder of applause, the gang was all there, he grinned in that sheepish way of his, then he began slinging the Party line. There was nothing new and nothing smart in what he said, just the old rehash, but every time he said certain words, like *Yalta, Teheran, Soviet Union, Unity*, the mob just went crazy with hand clapping.

Then the chairman called on Milton Charles. I had heard him before, at those Labor Forums where I used to speak myself, and he was no slouch. His voice was like a bell, and he could handle those long sentences like nobody's business. Now he was soft and reasonable, now he lifted his two puny fists, and you would have said the law was being handed down from Sinai. In fact, it was this that made me dislike the guy so much. I don't mind a guy who is on the make, but a guy who is on the make and tries to let on that he's doing all this for your good, he, he wants nothing out of it for himself, that sticks in my gorge. And that was the act he was always putting on.

Anyway, this night he was as good as ever. He had it all over Krantz like a tent, and although the stooges did their best to sit there unmoved and poker-faced, you had to hand it to him — he was making himself felt. It wasn't what he said, but how he said it; you couldn't help but admit that the guy would make a Member of Parliament, and that Krantz beside him was nowhere. The whole thing began to look like a bad idea. If there were any impartial voters in the crowd, there was no question who had won them, and when he sat down, and the applause broke out, it showed.

The meeting was then thrown open for questions. There were a couple of questions and they were duly answered.

This was my chance. I had no intention of asking a question, and didn't; I made a speech. I had thought about this speech ever since the meeting had first been announced, I knew my man Charles, and I had all the arguments and the wisecracks prepared. I didn't know whether I was as good as I had hoped to be, these things you know never turn out exactly the way you plan them. Every speaker, they say, makes three speeches every time he speaks, the speech he prepares, the speech he actually shoots off, the post-mortem he goes over on the way home; but I knew that if I was halfway decent, I would have that mob with me. And they were. I remarked that I would try to be sincere, although I didn't think that I could be as sincere as Mr. Charles, because Mr. Charles, everybody no doubt had noticed, used the words *sincerely* and *honestly* and *truly* instead of commas. I had myself counted forty *sincerelys* in that number of minutes. I was suspicious of a guy who every time he caught his breath told you that he was telling the truth. So I couldn't be as sincere as he, but as an ordinary citizen I could have an opinion, and it seemed to me for a number of reasons that it was Ted Krantz, perhaps with not as many gestures, and certainly without Charles's great dramatic talents, who had most appealed to my commonsense. First of all it was a question of fairness. Krantz had fought the fight in that constituency for years, he had been in there pitching while Charles was away in England, taking tea with the kindly Sir what's-his-name, and it was nothing but right, particularly according to the Oxford rules of cricket, that now Krantz should consolidate labor support about him. Second, it was a question of tactics; anybody could see, and certainly a great scholar like Mr. Charles, that what Mr. Lazarus was hoping for was that the worker's vote would be split, and he could walk in between the crack. And thirdly —

"Question! Question! Come to the question!"

This, from Charles's several supporters. Annoyed, they were looking for the muzzle.

"No speeches! Question!"

The chairman, who at least wanted to look fair, interrupted.

"Mister — er, will you put the question?"

"Snyder, Snyder is my name, formerly Captain Snyder, of the Second Armored Corps, four years overseas. I think that after having stayed out of this constituency for four years, and having kept my mouth shut all that time, that now I should be entitled to say a word. Do you agree?"

The Commies took the cue.

"Let him speak! Let the captain speak. Go on! Go on with your speech!"

"Yes, Mr. Chairman, I'm coming to the question, but first I must make clear why I put this particular question that I am going to put. Thirdly ..."

And I went on with my thirdly, and my fourthly, and seeing that I had been compelled to speak of my military record, I wondered about Mr. Charles who I had understood had declared that the fight against the Hitler tyranny was of no particular interest to the Canadian working class, and then, changing my tone, and putting on the wrath and indignation number, I got really mad about all those who made a career of running down the Soviet Union, which, in the final analysis, was the only power that had really stood up to Hitler, and which, whether in peace or war, allowed no race discrimination in its territory. I had gotten the loud cheer, but at this the acoustics were really strained, and no maybe. The place was full of hunkies and such, and I was getting the bravos in all languages.

"Come to the question! The question!"

"All right, I'll come to the question." Everybody waited. The C.C.F.'er strained forward on the platform.

My question is: "*What in hell is Mr. Charles doing in this constituency?*"

And, of course, I sat down. The place was in an uproar, what with cheers, and belly-laughs, and pounding of chairs. Charles got up, and was motioning for attention. He wanted to answer. But, as Gerard would have said, the instinctive good sense of the masses always comes to the fore at a moment of crisis. As if it was all previously arranged, and believe me it wasn't, the masses began getting up from their seats and were leaving the hall. They trekked out in whole groups and rows. They made all the noise they could too, and loudspeaker or no, Charles couldn't get a word in edgewise. He was talking to retreating backs. The meeting dissolved. Mr. Charles gave up.

I was in. There was no question about that.

Lullaby for a Hawker's Child

Sleep, hungry child, within your crib.
Father will bring you a silken bib
And he will set upon your cradle
A golden plate and a silver ladle
And darling waking in his bed
Will find sweet cakes and raisined bread.

And son will traffic in the town
Wearing his father's cap as crown
His father's purse upon his throat
And ride on our caparisoned goat
Crying, Cold Ale! and loaves red hot!
Sleep, hungry child, sleep, weary tot!

(1934)

9

Kith and Kin

THE BUSY, OFTEN FRENETIC pace of Klein's work life during the forties was offset to some degree by the comfortable stability of his home and family. For almost the entire decade the Kleins lived at 4857 Hutchison, the middle floor of a handsome triplex near the corner of St. Joseph Boulevard. The neighborhood, with its quiet, tree-lined avenues, was at the respectable edge of the old Jewish immigrant district, bordering on well-to-do Outremont.

The Klein household was pleasantly crowded and lively, with three young children growing up. Colman's brother Sandor was born in 1941, and their sister Sharon in 1945. Klein's aging mother, Yetta, lived with the family until her death in 1946.

It was in this somewhat cramped setting that Klein spent probably the happiest and most fruitful decade of his life. Since there were no rooms at all to spare, he did not have the luxury of a private study or even a desk. In the middle of the large square kitchen was a dining table at which he would frequently sit and write. What would normally have been the dining-room area, next to the kitchen, was made into the family living-room and became the center of the home. Here Klein had his favorite reading place, a stuffed wing-back chair alongside a wall of books.

Klein's son Colman retained warm memories of life during this period.

My parents' relationship was very openly affectionate and loving, with lots of hugging and kissing and consideration for one another. My mother idolized my father. Though she had a remarkably strong character in her own right, she always showed her concern for him in the most self-effacing way, by attending to all his creature comforts and making sure his house was an island of peace and calm. There was never any sign of discord or difficulty between them, at least none that we as children could ever detect.

My mother served as my father's sounding board, his first editor. In the evenings she would hear or read whatever he was writing, and then give her approval or tell him if something didn't sound right. There would be a lot of talk and discussion, whether about his work, or books they were both reading, or the day's news. Later at night, from my bed, I could hear the tap-tap of the typewriter in the living room or the kitchen — my mother would be typing from one of his manuscripts or from his dictation.

Friday nights they would usually go out with a few close friends to a movie. They were both great movie fans. Saturday was spent quietly — my father might do some writing in the morning, maybe catch up with a little work at the office, and then just relax in the afternoon.

Saturday nights there would always be a big family get-together at our house. Partly because my grandmother lived with us, but also, I suspect, because of everyone's fondness for my parents, our home was the headquarters of a veritable clan of aunts and uncles, cousins, and second-cousins. Most of the women would sit and talk in the living room, and some of them would regularly join the men at poker around the kitchen table. Every now and then my father would sit out a game and duck into a corner somewhere to read while munching on a crusty piece of rye bread.

My mother was in a way the matriarch of the whole extended family. Everybody would come to her for practical advice, sympathy, warmth. Even my friends regarded her as someone they could talk to with complete ease about any subject. I couldn't really say that she shared my father's intense concern for the Jewish community and the larger world beyond. Her center was her house, her family, her husband.

My father was quite helpless himself when it came to even the simplest domestic chores, and left nearly all the household and childrearing duties to my mother. He obviously had a very traditional notion of his parental role: a father's function, aside from being the breadwinner, was to derive *naches* (pride and pleasure) from his children. He would always come to watch whenever one of us performed in the school play, and would dutifully attend all the "meet-the-teacher" affairs.

Klein sent his children to Hebrew day school through the elementary grades, and then encouraged them to continue their education at public high schools, in the belief that they should broaden their horizons. At home he tended to restrain his own didactic impulses. He rarely read aloud the poems for children that he had written in the thirties, though he did make up delightful bedtime stories. Rather than push any of his children in a preconceived direction, he let each of them develop independently. Whenever he noticed one of them becoming interested in a new subject or hobby, he would buy some appropriate books and secretly plant them on a lower shelf in the library where he knew they would be discovered.

Klein's customary way of spending time with his children was to take them, most often individually, on certain regular walks and outings. The annual trip to Mount Royal every spring after the thaw was one of Colman's favorite adventures.

My father knew certain special places where trilliums grew, adder's tongue, bloodroot. He was fascinated, would show us every year how the bloodroot yielded its bit of dye. We would collect a great big bunch of these lovely flowers and run back home

DESPITE HIS OWN CHILDHOOD FEAR OF DOGS, KLEIN GAVE IN TO COLMAN'S WISHES AND BOUGHT HIM A COLLIE FOR HIS ELEVENTH BIRTHDAY. COLMAN RECALLED: "IT WAS A MARVELOUS, SWEET-TEMPERED COLLIE, AND MY FATHER LEARNED TO LOVE IT VERY MUCH. IT WAS A TIMID DOG, PERFECTLY SUITED TO MY FATHER — SO TIMID THAT IT WOULDN'T WALK DOWN THE STAIRS FROM OUR SECOND-FLOOR LANDING TO THE STREET BELOW. MY FATHER WOULD CARRY THE DOG DOWN THE STAIRS AND UP AGAIN!"

before they wilted to give them to my mother, who would always feign surprise: "What a nice thing to do — for me!" That was beautiful.

I remember also accompanying him at times to the Eagle printing room when he would go to deliver his weekly editorials. He knew I was fascinated by machinery and would take me through the entire printing apparatus, introduce me to the typesetters, and always make sure to have my name set for me in lead.

On Saturdays he would occasionally take me along with him to his law office, which was then in a dark old building on St. James Street. This was his work world to me — the gray and dark-brown paneled walls, the desk, the bookcases, the heavy cigarette smoke. Before leaving he would open his office cabinet and stuff my pockets with elastics, pencils, and writing pads.

Sunday mornings we would often go for a walk down Park Avenue, ending up at the YMHA on Mt. Royal Avenue. The "Y" had a marvelous gymnasium and swimming pool. My father, unfortunately, was no athlete. We'd go down to the pool and stand on the viewing platform for a few minutes to watch the swimmers, but he never once actually took me swimming. We'd go to the upstairs lounge, the library, the soda fountain. All along the way he would be greeted warmly and respectfully by people he knew from the Zionist Organization or the *Chronicle,* and he would stop to chat with many of them, wisecrack, share stories. That, after all, was the main purpose of taking a walk in those days.

BESSIE KLEIN WITH HER SONS, COLMAN AND SANDOR.

IN THE SAME WAY THAT HE THRIVED on the closeness of his immediate and extended family, Klein took for granted the compact community life that still existed in the streets of Montreal's Jewish district. The prosperity of the post-war years, however, would bring unexpected changes to this milieu. The world of Jewish Montreal in which he had been raised, and in whose image he had formed his social ideals, was now about to vanish into bourgeois suburbia. The late forties saw the beginning of the move outwards to more open spaces, new houses, and posh synagogues and Jewish centers that gave renewed currency to old jokes about the "edifice complex." There was no visible trauma in this exodus from the ghetto — on the contrary, there was great relief in leaving behind the harsh memories of the Depression era. Returning from military service, many children of poor tradesmen and shopkeepers were enabled by government grants to attend university, shed their working-class backgrounds, and enter into professions. Acceptance among their non-Jewish colleagues and neighbors came with surprising ease.

The gradual break-up of the immigrant community, occurring at the same time in many other North American cities as well, had cultural implications for Klein of which he was painfully aware. The imminent demise of the Yiddish language, and the dying-off of the generation that could still recall its East European roots, meant that fewer and fewer readers would ever be able to understand, let alone appreciate, his unique experiments in the Judaeo-English idiom. Soon, it appeared, he would need to annotate his writings even for Jews.

Through the forties and early fifties, Klein was in fact haunted by the melancholy realization that the entire culture of East European Judaism was gone forever. Reviewing a new book in 1945 by his good friend, the Montreal Yiddish poet J. I. Segal, he spoke knowingly of the pathos of nostalgia.

It is that beautiful way of life represented by the Chassidic milieu — a beauty intrinsically involved with the beautiful associations of childhood — which, seeing that it is gone, and its values discarded, gives his heart its pain. When it is realized, as his poems amply realize, that that way of life is vanished, not only by the ravages of time, but by the horrific destruction of the evil which usurped the world for a decade, that pain reaches the degrees of agony.

In the aftermath of the Holocaust, Klein saw himself as being among the lonely survivors, the last of a disappearing breed.

> Myself to recognize: a curio;
> the atavism of some old coin's face;
> one who, though watched and isolate, does go —
> the last point of a diminished race —
> the way of the fletched buffalo.
> Gerundive of extinct. An original.
> What else, therefore, to do
> but leave these bones that are not ash to fill —
> O not my father's vault — but the glass-case
> some proud museum catalogues *Last Jew*.

Klein's faith in the future of the Jewish people would, of course, be strengthened by the establishment of the State of Israel in 1948. But even there, he feared, the heritage of Jewish Diaspora culture would be in danger of extinction. "In recent years," he was to note with dismay in the early fifties, "there has arisen, particularly in Israel, a sect of philosophers, narrow, intransigent, insular, who would treat all of Jewish exilic history as one vast cultural blank; only that will they recognize as authentically Jewish which has issued out of Israel, all else being but expense of spirit and sheer loss." It was this fierce Diaspora-negating chauvinism that he disliked in the younger generation of Hebrew poets in Israel, though he excused it as "only a reaction from the experiences of exile. It would vanish. It did not belong to the essential thoughtways of our people."

While the decline of the Jewish culture in which he was rooted was disheartening to Klein, it did seem to validate his own efforts as a bearer of the tradition in a new language. So much of his artistic enterprise, after all, was basically that of the translator, rendering the spirit of one culture in the language of another. In one of his fictional self-portraits of the late forties, Klein went so far as to represent himself not as an author of original poems but as an English translator of the classic Hebrew poets.

Not an easy task had it been, but a ceaseless unrelenting struggle: again and again they stood in opposed deadlock, the intransigent Hebrew meaning, the Saxon syllables aloof and unaccommodating. But the struggle had not been without its own reward, for it had been a wrestling with an angel. And though foredoomed to defeat, who would not wrestle with an angel? . . .

So as to communicate the archaic flavor of the original Hebrew, Halevi he had translated into Chaucerian English; Alharizi's poem — the one in which every line begins with the letter Resh — he had Englished into a rumble of recurrent r's; he had imitated the couplet of the rhyming homonyms; he had reproduced acrostics, horizontal, vertical, and transversal; and for the purpose of communicating to the gentiles some feeling for the language which had no vowel letters, but only vowel pointillation, he had boldly made use (but only in one rendering) of a disemvowelled prose — he could not but smile now at the splutter with which the Psalmist, quoted in one of the pieces, had issued from his pen: Fr thr is no fthflnss in thr mth; thr inwrd prt is vry wickdnss; thr thrt is an opn splchr.

Klein apparently regarded Yiddish as an even more difficult language to translate, in part because of its multilingual fabric and its intimate nuances.

Take — may it not harm you ! — the exclamation, *Oy veh!* Bold, indeed, would he be who sought to transliterate this *cri de coeur* with a lorryman's *O, woe!* The personal and historic associations which vibrate from the phrase cannot be Englished. The epic memory which is evoked by the two monosyllables is not conjured by an English equivalent. One does not translate a groan.

Besides actually translating many important Yiddish and Hebrew authors, Klein consciously worked at synthesizing a style — almost a separate dialect — that would express as faithfully as possible the content of Jewish civilization in a rich, authentic English. It was this goal, probably more than anything else, that animated his endless obsession with language and linguistic experimentation, and that sent him in search of models among the great English Hebraists such as Milton and the authors of the King James Bible.

Whether English could ever, in any significant way, compete with Hebrew or Yiddish as a vehicle for expressing Jewish culture was a question that Klein seemed reluctant to explore deeply. His touchiness on this subject was noticed by the poet and critic Melech Ravitch, whose friendly efforts at drawing him closer into the Yiddish literary community in Montreal met with little success. Klein was an acute reader and student of Yiddish literature, but never ventured to write in any language other than English.

When Ravitch once asked him flatly how he could presume to be a Jewish writer and not write in a Jewish language, Klein seemed to take offense and petulantly walked away from the conversation — stung as much perhaps by the rightness as the wrongness of the question.

IT WAS NOT ONLY THE LINGUISTIC gap that was widening. The very type of Jewishness that Klein represented was itself proving too tenuous to survive much longer. In his own life he had been able to straddle the traditional religious world of his parents and the secular world of modern North America. The mixture was remarkable but unstable; given the stresses of increasing assimilation, it could not easily be built upon or passed on.

Klein's secular form of Jewish traditionalism was not unusual for his generation, especially in Montreal. Though he observed hardly any of Judaism's ritual practices and prohibitions, he was very sympathetic to religious ideals. In a letter to a friend, he referred to himself once, albeit in a light vein, as "deeply religious... in an unorganized way." Theology was one subject he generally avoided, both in his personal writings and in his conversation. "Gentlemen do not argue about religious convictions," he told his readers in the *Chronicle,* and on several occasions coyly remarked that his relationship with Divinity was "a purely personal affair, modeled upon the dictum of Heine: *Dieu me pardonnera, c'est son métier....* Profounder subjects we have left to the specialists in the field."

At home and with his family, religion for Klein was a matter of a few vestigial traditions. Bessie for most of her life kept a kosher kitchen and lit Sabbath candles every Friday evening. Klein rarely attended synagogue, except occasionally on the High Holydays. The more popular and colorful festivals of the calendar were usually observed at home, though as a rule only in a perfunctory way.

To Klein there was no great contradiction in the fact that he veered from religious tradition in his private life while at the same time insisting on the integrity of the tradition in public. He mocked the iconoclastic, antinationalist excesses of Reform theologians, whom he perceived as

methodically eliminating the entire body of Jewish rite, custom, and ceremonial, burning Maimonides in effigy, flinging through the windows of their temple *mitzvah* after horrible *mitzvah,* until of Judaism, as of the vanishing Cheshire cat, there remains only an empty Freudian grin, a grotesque surrealist "moral law," a dangling unrooted kindliness towards "our co-religionists."

He had a much higher regard for the Reconstructionist movement and for its founder Mordecai Kaplan, whose concerns for the survival of the Jewish people and the renewal of its ancient civilization he naturally shared. Yet when the Reconstructionist Prayer Book was published in 1945 he deplored its prosaic language and arid rationalism. "Such language cannot exalt, and there is no worship without exaltation... A prayerbook without a mystique is a contradiction in terms... litanies are made by poets, not logicians." Klein condemned the fanatical attacks leveled against the editors of the Prayer Book by the Union of Orthodox Rabbis, but wholeheartedly agreed that it was wrong of the editors to have excised so many references to traditional doctrines. It surprised him, in fact, that the Reconstructionists, who for two decades had valiantly defended all that was "good, true, and beautiful" in Jewish tradition, now discarded much of it.

We believe this to be an error, for traditions, we think, though scientifically untenable can still be retained as evidences of that continuity of which the editors speak in their introduction. Indeed, though they may lose, with the passage of time, a great deal of their validity, with the passage of time they indubitably take on new meanings and a richer color. Such, indeed, is the Protean potency of tradition...

A modernized and Americanized Passover *Haggadah* issued by the Reconstructionists evoked a similar reaction from him: "It is the very quaintness, it is precisely the old-fashioned and quasi-medieval flavor of the *Haggadah* which endows it with all its charm and beauty." Klein's feeling for tradition was based largely on a nostalgia for childhood and on an aesthetic preference for the archaic and the sublime. The notion that the recovery of the authentic scriptural and literary sources of Judaism would be sufficient to sustain a living Jewish culture was something that he and many of his generation of Zionists had absorbed from the teachings of writers like Bialik and Achad Ha'am. If Klein was more sensitively religious than others of that school, it was in his conviction that the simple faith of pious Jews like his parents was precious and irreplaceable, particularly in times of adversity.

How happy, indeed, is that orthodox Jew, who considers the world, its savages rampaging upon the stage, the righteous suffering, and the wicked prospering, and who loses not his optimism, who abandons not his faith, knowing that the ways of God are mysterious to man, and that it does not behoove the simple soul to seek to analyze the inscrutable methods of Providence.

Confessing to his own unfitness for the "'sweet simplicities of the unquestioning faith" he envied in others, he nevertheless felt that even just to envy was "in itself an act of faith."

YETTA KLEIN, SKETCHED BY ERNST NEUMANN.

from STRANGER AND AFRAID

Lately, when I would sit in my red rep chair, engrossed in a book, valet to some statesman, or poet, or buccaneer, I would suddenly raise my head, and surprise her, presumably in the act of knitting, watching me. The doleful expression on her never particularly joyful face — tears upon parchment — at once saddened and enraged me. I knew what that expression meant — it was criticism: once he was so full of promise and of hope, and now, look at him, blighted, ambitionless, a reader of books. Like the rest of them he might have been, only more successful, a buyer of fur-coats for his mother, a car-owner, a proprietor — instead, distorted values had steered him away from what was rightfully his. She was, of course, occasionally proud of my unpragmatic achievements, achievements she did not understand but read only in reflection in other people's compliments — she wasn't unpleased; my son, she would say, *has a name*; but it wasn't a real pride, only a consoling substitute, a sort of defensive honor.

Everything about me seemed to call forth her pity, — my frustrations, my not being wealthy, even the complexion I had inherited from her. No doubt if I was rosy with health, fleshful and colorbright, she would still have worn that melancholy pall upon her. For she has a talent for sadness, my mother, a gift for misery, both native and indoctrinated. For her the happiest days in the calendar are the fast-days, the non-eating Mondays and Thursdays, and the anniversary penances in gratitude for some long-forgotten and since-nullified salvation of Jewry. And as for the Sabbath before the Blessing of the New Moon when, alone by the window in her room, her *siddur* and her handkerchief on her knees, she sits weeping the old-fashioned Yiddish of seventeeth-century prayerbooks, addressing herself to God for that he should preserve her children and her children's children that they come not unto the sons of men for favors, that they be not shamed of men, but that they live, decent and honorable, because of thy lovingkindness, O *Rebono shel Olam* — I remembered them from my earliest childhood as events which at first made me sorry for her, and then angered me with their servility. God, I felt sure even then, did not ask for such weeping and ululation.

Later I realized that these prayers were their own reward. They answered my mother's needs, first for drama, because they placed her on the center of the stage, then for snobbery, because they established relations of intimacy with God Himself, and finally for self-pity, because that was the major theme of this liturgy. The same attitude showed itself in the other activities of my mother's pious routines. Some people go to the country for picnics, but my mother visits the Jewish cemetery where lie buried our discarded family bones, including those of my dear father. There she takes her position at his tombstone, and weeping, tears up clumps of grass and places them — an old rite — upon the granite; and she talks to the granite, as if through a side-entrance she would seek to storm the Heavenly Court. These activities, of course, wring her heart; she returns home, pale and tired, to rest in her low chair, pensive for hours. Secretly she is filled, I know, with a sense of great worth, the elation of piety. Not she like the other Sabbath-breaking and perruqueless apostates who emigrated to Canada, but beloved of her God, the God of her hometown Ratno, than which no other place, except Jerusalem the Holy, is saintlier.

Nor are these self-abnegations confined to doings sacred and ritual; even from a family party she will return, full of pride at what she didn't eat there. "It was a wonderful spread," she would say, "as from the generous hand of the Czar. Whatever in the world is good to eat, that was on plate and dish. Others there were who grabbed, devoured, guzzled, as if they had just come off the boat from hungry Europe. Mrs. Cohen — the one who is president of the Ladies Auxiliary, kept eating on both jaws, and you should have seen Mrs. Grossman, she crammed her fat little *kaddish* I thought he would burst. Me? I put nothing to my lips, I did not touch as much as the size of an olive. A cup of tea, that I had. Do I, then, lack for food at home? (This, for pride.) Am I sure that the dishes are kosher? (This for piety.) I don't need their food, thank God. And as for the tea, well, I drank it, of course, you can't, after all, spit in a person's face."

(mid-1940s)

144

from THE INVERTED TREE

Klein's family members appear frequently in his semi-fictional journals and unfinished novels of the forties. Elizabeth, in this excerpt, is his wife Bessie, and Samuel is their younger son, Sandor.

The first installment of spring is about to be made. Already as I pass Fletcher's Field and sloping Mount Royal — my own parcel of imported Nature — I can smell the earth giving off the odor of rebirth, the cleansed musk of last year's autumn, whose snow-soaked leafage now feeds the delicate white teeth of April. The snow has melted quite away, look to the clouds if you would see it! Even the dust and dirt and soot of the chimney-puffing and sand-strewing months which until yesterday smudged the cool linens of the year — the stableboy's bootprints on the princess's bed — have disappeared, gone down, to nourish roots and to support grasses. As yet the fields look brown and squishy with last year's sloshed stubble; one singing night of rain, one day of pin-prick showers, and the chlorophyll will rush to its face again the green and comely blush; people will come out of their houses housing winter into a new, a just-delivered season. April with her long hair freshly washed, and her clothes smelling of Sabbath.

It is Sunday, there is no school, and Colman is bored.

You promised to show me the flowers on the mountains, daddy, he says. Let's go today.

But I don't think the flowers are out yet. Next week perhaps. If it will be nice outside.

It's nice outside today and maybe there are flowers. I saw a kid carrying flowers on Park Avenue. A whole bunch of them.

They must have been bought in a flower-shop. The flowers on the mountains are of a different kind.

Free?

Free, when they are there.

Colman, disappointed, looks to his mother.

Why don't you take him out sometimes, she says, like other fathers do? She says this privately, with gestures, whispers, so that Colman should not hear his father invidiously compared. Aloud, and freely, it's such a nice day, dear, and you promised him a long time ago — the time you were supposed to take him to see the skiers — that you would show him how flowers grow. It's only a couple of blocks away.

Yes, daddy, you promised; and we'll bring the flowers home for Mummy.

I was getting the business all right. Touched, Life upon his little head, said Elizabeth, lapsing into benedictive Yiddish. The little gentleman, the sweet lover. Come, let him go out with his daddy for a change.

For a change? Didn't I take him to the Y.M.H.A. last Sunday for a coke?

Yes, last Sunday you took him to the Y.M.H.A. for a coke. Big doings.

And didn't you enjoy it, Colman, watching the swimming pool, the gym, the basket-ball game, the library, the goldfish?

But I would like the flowers better. I want to get some of those flowers that the Indians used to use to paint themselves, like you told me.

Colman was beginning to get that sunrise glow around his eyes, his lips pouted at the world's injustice and plighted troth not kept.

There, said Elizabeth.

All right, all right, I said, I'll make like a father.

*   *   *

We entered the woods through the Mount Royal Avenue gate, always open, sunk in the soil, which leads to the cemetery. It is hot, the trees are bare, and the sun, unhindered, comes pouring down upon the grassless earth, in many places still wet with soggy leaves and little mirrors of water in the hollows. Colman is wearing his rubber boots, and enjoying the mud into which he can now slip with impunity, so receptive it feels, so intimate it sounds. He has picked up a fallen branch and is using it, with exhilarated bravado, as a weapon against unseen foes, Indians and such-like, and against shrubs, bushes, vines, exposed roots. Victorious, his mind moves on to new fields of conquest. Where are the flowers? he asks.

146

These are wild-flowers we are looking for, special flowers that grow only in the woods. You have to know the snooks, we will soon come on one.

True enough, I soon descried a piece of white peering above a brown burden of dead leaves. Blood-root! "Come, Colman." We climbed the knoll, he going first so that the released twigs should not lash him in the face, and at last he saw the blossom too. He plucked it. The plant gave way before his careful ritual grasp, coming up with its bleeding roots, its clinging soil, its delicate thin rootlets. "Is this really blood?" He looked at me as if he had perhaps done something wrong, guilt and elation in his face, thrilled and shuddered. Reassured, he was like a bird, an excited bony bird, hopping from hill to hill, pecking at white here, jumping at yellow there, sometimes duped by brown, gulled by green, disappointment flooded by quest, his constant talk a bird's bubbling.

A lovely morning we had, full of discovery, discovering the three-leaved and three-petalled trillium, the robin, its red bib, its tuxedo stance, and the mound, hit by sunlight, quivering with the yellow adder's tongues, vibrating in the small breeze on their fragile stems, between their long-leaved brown-speckled sheathes. And the crackle of dry branches under our feet, and the smack of the juicy soil. Poking at leaves, surmising the rot of maple, the punk of tree-trunk, skeleton elmleaf, the thick preserved mummy-leaf of oak. In the air, spangles of sun, dart of sparrows, and bird-whistles vaguely identified. And whenever we wanted him, our third companion, Echo.

Homeward bound, Colman proudly entered our street, flanked by his envious friends, his fingers stained, his rubbers muddied, his little trousers linted by contact with sharp shrubbery, his legs scratched, but bearing bouquets for his mummy who stood on the balcony, smiling us all the way up to our doorsteps.

Hurriedly he mounted the stairs — the anemic petals of the blood-root were already limp, and the cluster was falling away in his hands — From daddy and me to Mummy and Baba and Samuel, he said. Baba glowed; Mummy melted, and Shmulikl wanted to touch, to hold, to smell, to appropriate. Some flowers — and over Elizabeth's protests — some blood-roots for Samuel, the rest placed in two vases and one glass of water.

These flowers have no odor, but my house was full of fragrance.

Not to mention, of course, muddy footprints, dried burrs, and crumbs of root-earth.

(early 1940s)

147

from Parade of St. Jean Baptiste

Quebec, Quebec, which for the long blanched age —
infidelium partes — multiplied
pagan its beasts and painted savages —
(while Rome was rounded with St. Peter's dome
and Europe vertical with tower and cross
supported constellations) — is still rich
of realms spiritual the Jesuits founded,
and Sabbaths of the monks of Yamachiche.
Crosses of clergy, luxe armorial,
still vivify with their insignia
the evangelical air, and benedictions
douce-digital from priest and eminence
still quadrilate the inhospitable tense.

(1947)

10

Fame, the Adrenalin

IT WAS DURING HIS FIRST YEAR of university teaching that Klein was inspired to write a series of poems that were to form the core of his last and finest collection of verse. He began working on his "Quebec poems," as he originally called them, in the spring of 1945. Three of these poems, including one entitled "The Rocking Chair," were published in magazines later that year. He went on enlarging the series and in July 1946 sent eleven of his favorite pieces to *Poetry* magazine in Chicago. In his covering letter he introduced the poems as his "Suite Canadienne," and commented:

For an interval I have abdicated from the Hebrew theme which is my prime mover to look upon the French Canadian in this province: we have many things in common: a minority position; ancient memories; and a desire for group survival. Moreover the French Canadian enjoys much — a continuing and distinctive culture, solidarity, *land* — which I would wish for my own people. So maybe I've not abdicated, but am only traveling incognito, disguised as a Frenchman.

Klein clearly felt that as a member of one minority he was well equipped to understand, with an insider's empathy, the virtues and foibles of another. Many of his portraits of Jews and French Canadians contain the same distinctive mixture of satire and sentimentality. His basically conservative nature was attuned to the traditionalism of French Canada as he knew it in the thirties and forties, wherein he saw upheld life's simple, eternal verities: faith and family, order and common humanity.

The editors of *Poetry* magazine accepted seven of the eleven poems for publication in their July 1947 issue. Klein placed several others in various Canadian periodicals around the same time, and by the fall of 1947 had assembled enough additional material to form a manuscript, *The Rocking Chair and Other Poems*, which he submitted at the end of October to Lorne Pierce of the Ryerson Press in Toronto. "I have wanted for a long time to be published in Canada," he told Pierce, "but hitherto the subject matter of my verse has been such that American publication recommended itself; the present volume, however, is concerned almost entirely with the Quebec scene and the Canadian outlook."

Two weeks later Klein was informed by the editors of *Poetry* magazine that he had been awarded their annual Edward Bland Prize for his "Seven Poems." One of the first people with whom he shared this gratifying news was David Rome, then the press officer of the Canadian Jewish Congress. Rome recalled how pleased and excited Klein was that afternoon. "He came into my office with the idea that these poems, so sympathetic to French Canada, written by a Jewish poet, ought to be placed before the French Canadian cultural public as an instance of Jewish goodwill and of the possible harmony that could exist between these two communities in Canada." To Rome it was an unforgettable example of Klein's inordinately objective awareness of the social and political implications of even his most purely literary work. Having long admired Klein's poetry, he readily agreed with the suggestion.

The Congress, as it happened, was particularly concerned at the time with the need to counter anti-Semitic influences that had flourished in French Canada during the war years. Rome's proposal to distribute a reprint of the "Seven Poems" to selected members of the French community in Quebec, mostly clergy, was implemented immediately, and a modestly produced booklet entitled *Poems of French Canada* was issued by the Congress in late November. In the following months two more editions were printed, *Seven Poems* and *Huit poèmes canadiens*, the last containing a new "bilingual" poem that Rome favored, "Parade of St. Jean Baptiste."

Pierce all this while had been putting off a final decision on Klein's manuscript. In January 1948 he at last wrote to say that Ryerson would indeed publish *The Rocking Chair* early that summer. The book came out just a month behind schedule at the end of July.

The Rocking Chair represented the culmination of Klein's fruitful association with the Montreal poets of the forties. But there were other important influences as well, foremost among them the work of the rediscovered Victorian poet Gerard Manley Hopkins. Klein had begun reading Hopkins closely around 1940 and was to maintain an almost obsessive interest in his poetry well into the late fifties. He was undoubtedly attracted by Hopkins's intense religious vision of nature, his Shakespearian language and craftsmanlike experiments in rhythm, and the strangely neurotic tension between Hopkins's ascetic life and sensuous verse. And what could have been more fitting than to invoke a Jesuit poet while writing about Catholic Quebec?

The other great influence on Klein's style in *The Rocking Chair* was the poetry of the highly-regarded young American Karl Shapiro, whose Audenesque poems he had first noticed in the pages of *Poetry* magazine at the start of the decade. He found Shapiro's voice unique in American literature — "a perfect, an impeccable re-creation in words of the very sound and texture of the American scene, together with a rich sensuality, reminiscent only of Keats — if Keats had lived in an age of department stores." The title of Shapiro's first book, *Person, Place and Thing*, would indeed have been an apt subtitle for *The Rocking Chair*. Echoes of Shapiro's rhythm and syntax can be heard in many of Klein's poems from the mid-forties.

Klein in 1944 had publicly lamented the fact that Shapiro's writings revealed a certain "Jewish self-hatred," or at the very least an unfortunate disregard of his heritage. Nonetheless, perhaps out of a sense of homage, he instructed Ryerson to send Shapiro a copy of *The Rocking Chair*. The personal acknowledgement he received from the American poet could not have been more flattering:

I don't know quite how to praise your work. It wants praise, it is the only poetry by a Canadian that can take its place with the best in English of our time. Doesn't it take a Jew to deny the torpor of Canada? I don't mean this in any chauvinistic way but only that you are lucky in your consciousness. In another sense it is too bad to visit our consciousness on the nations. Still, we can't help it.

Shapiro, it turned out, had also seen Klein's earlier remarks about him, and in a postscript asked:

Were you the one who once wrote about me that I was a lost Jew? It is true but I am not a Christian. I am less Christian than anything but quite a long chalk from Jew. Must one be one or the other?

Klein began drafting a long reply to Shapiro, but then apparently changed his mind and never mailed it.

Canadian reviewers and critics who had been following Klein's progress over the years immediately recognized *The Rocking Chair* as his most accomplished work. The most lavish praise of all came from Rolfe Humphries, the distinguished American translator and poet, who reviewed the book for the *Nation*, and who thought that its best poems were "as good as things of Baudelaire, Rilke, Auden."

It would have seemed natural for Klein to continue working this popular vein and to produce more poems on the Canadian scene. This did not happen, in part because he rarely liked to repeat himself, and also because the particular social mood that had given rise to these poems was already on the wane. *The Rocking Chair* was, to a considerable degree, the product of a rare, invigorating burst of patriotism that affected many Canadians in the immediate aftermath of the Second World War. Klein too experienced this sense of national pride and optimism that was suddenly in the air, the feeling that Canada's time had, in some sense, finally arrived. He believed that such a moment in a country's history was an auspicious one for the future of its literature. "Canadians today are more inclined to receive serious writing than they ever were before," he wrote in February 1946, replying to a questionnaire from the Toronto poet Raymond Souster.

Two causes have militated toward this end. First, the experience of the last war, which brought everyone closer — excuse the expression — to the eternal verities; ... and, second, the position which Canada now occupies in world affairs, a position which brings with it a sense of importance, strength, confidence ... geopolitics has converted our country from a flanking colony to a central state ... our diplomats speak modestly of a Middle-Power. We are even worth spying upon. All has changed; our sinews, our muscles, our thinking; only the voice, as yet, is not commensurate with the body.

In the same breath, Klein cautioned against the dangers of parochialism among Canadian writers. Asked by Souster whether he tended to be influenced more by English or American writers, and which he considered the healthier influence for Canadians, he quickly adopted a cosmopolitan stance.

I have never really made a distinction ... I have considered all English writing as a single entity.... As for myself, I am influenced — forward or backward — by everything I read or see. Moreover, since what I seek is the human, I do not confine myself to writing English or American.... In the final analysis, a writer gets influenced by those things which do best harmonize with his own temperament. For Milton even Hebrew influence was healthy.

The same cosmopolitanism expressed itself in his derision of the notion that Canadian writers ought to stress Canadian backgrounds and locales in order to give their work a truly national flavor. "The proper study of mankind is Man — not paysage." He granted only that a writer's Canadianism might be one particular source of his universal themes, and though he made no mention of the fact to Souster, he was himself working at that very moment on his "Suite Canadienne."

OF ALL THAT HE WROTE, Klein considered only his poetry to be "serious writing" — defined by him simply as "writing that may enter the corpus of lasting literature." Still he did not belittle what he called "hammock literature," such as mystery novels, which served, he believed, a legitimate purpose. No strictly serious writer, he felt, could expect to be rewarded in any way by contemporary society. "The writers of detective yarns command more attention, more respect, and of course, more gratitude palpable."

Evidently feeling entitled to some share in these rewards, he repeatedly tried his hand at commercial fiction. In the early forties he made several starts at a popular sort of novel centering on the life of a Jewish Montrealer not unlike himself. None of his first efforts in this direction were satisfying, and he simply left them as fragments in his files, perhaps for later use. It was around this period that he would sometimes speak to his poet friends of how he in fact "hated writing prose."

In 1946, however, he finally managed to complete his first novel — a spy thriller, originally titled *Comes the Revolution*, based on the Igor Gouzenko affair. Gouzenko was the cipher clerk in the Soviet embassy in Ottawa who had defected in September 1945 to disclose the existence of an elaborate Soviet-Canadian spy ring. Several of the Canadians involved were well-known Jewish communists, including Fred Rose, the newly re-elected member of Parliament for Cartier riding.

Klein seized on the Gouzenko story as perfect material for a spy novel. He was personally acquainted with many of the peripheral figures in the scandal and knew their political milieu intimately. He cast as his hero and narrator a cynical, unsuccessful Montreal lawyer, Mort Snyder, who is paid by the RCMP to infiltrate the suspected spy ring. While supposedly keeping an eye on Gouzenko for the communists, Snyder actually helps Gouzenko defect. Unlike his counterpart in real life, Klein's fictional Gouzenko, named Krilenko, is killed in the end.

As a thriller, *Comes the Revolution* is written to formula. It is well paced and does have a few moments of genuine suspense. Ultimately, though, it is an exercise in ventriloquism, for there is little in it of Klein's own rich language. He admitted to publishers that he had set out deliberately to imitate the hard-boiled American style of a writer like James M. Cain. Klein had a poet's ear for street slang and one can sense the pleasure he must have had in working up the lingo for this novel.

He submitted the manuscript under the pseudonym of Dan Mosher. First he tried to sell it to *Collier's* magazine for serialization. Then from the spring of 1947 to the fall of 1948 he sent the manuscript to nearly every major American publisher of popular fiction, with no success. At one point he decided he needed a more distinctive title and changed it to *That Walks Like a Man*. In April 1948 Gouzenko himself published a personal memoir called *This Was My Choice*, and in July the *Saturday Evening Post* printed a serialization of Evan John's novel *The Network*, based on the same story material. Klein felt he had missed his chance at a literary scoop and finally gave up looking for a publisher.

Among the last pieces of fiction that he wrote in the forties were two short stories, "And the Mome Raths Outgrabe" and "Letter from Afar." The former, a surrealistic satire on the various competing schools of modern literary criticism, was published in the Canadian literary magazine *Here and Now* in 1949. "Letter from Afar," written probably in the same year, is a clever fantasy concerning what Klein speculated to be the "true" fate of the victims of Stalin's show trials. It is a story that reflects his continuing interest in the subject of communism and in particular the Marxist idea of the dialectic. On submitting it to an American literary agent he was advised that it was too intellectual in style for the American magazine market.

Klein's unfinished and unpublished stories from the forties were to serve as preparatory exercises for his one and only published novel, written in 1950, *The Second Scroll*. What he learned, above all, was that his own best efforts tended to be autobiographical and journalistic. When it came to writing realistic fiction, he lacked the sheer inventiveness of a natural-born storyteller, preferring instead to rely on given facts and personal experience. Perhaps his greatest difficulty as a fiction writer was that he was never as interested in imagining characters as in dramatizing ideas. Thus in *The Second Scroll* he would confine himself to writing about figures who either were based on real people he knew, or were essentially character types representing abstract historical movements and ideas. Writing a spy thriller gave him, if nothing else, the practice he needed in shaping the plot of a novel, in particular a novel built on the devices of suspense. This exercise would have a clear effect on *The Second Scroll*, a story modeled outwardly on the pattern of a detective's pursuit.

TOWARDS THE END of his three-year lectureship at McGill, Klein was offered a promotion as an incentive to stay on, but by this time all the excitement and novelty of teaching had faded. Giving the same courses year after year was boring, he complained, and the alternative of constantly preparing new courses entailed more work than he had bargained for. So, without any apparent misgivings, he chose to leave McGill at the end of the spring term of 1948 to return full time to the practice of law, where, he rationalized, "the duties are less onerous and the rewards — when they come — more generous." Klein assured his closest colleague in the English department, Harold Files, that it had been a most pleasant and useful experience and that he had learned much from it. At Frank Scott's urging he advised Files to recommend Patrick Anderson as his successor to teach modern poetry at McGill.

In retrospect, it is tempting to wonder what might have happened had Klein remained in academe, which seemed to be as congenial and desirable a setting as he was likely to find. Part of the almost sad irony in his leaving McGill when he did was that he wanted more time for himself — not really to practice law, nor even to write poetry, but to pursue a project in literary scholarship of the most academic nature imaginable: a comprehensive and detailed commentary on James Joyce's *Ulysses*.

His interest in *Ulysses* had been building for over two decades. From his first reading of it in 1927, he felt certain that it was destined to be recognized as the literary masterpiece of the century. Its brilliant language and its web of obscure allusions formed a vast riddle that he was determined to solve. Through the thirties and early forties he re-read it about every second year and made new annotations in his copy each time.

Klein was considerably less interested in Joyce's later novel, *Finnegans Wake*. Following its publication in 1939 he wrote to Leon Edel, his fellow Joyce-enthusiast, to say that after several weeks of evenings on the book he could "only descry here and there a bright constellation, the rest being fog and nebula.... it does seem a great waste of seventeen years of genius." On further consideration he judged that Joyce had failed in *Finnegans Wake* by carrying his multilingual experimentation to "ridiculous extremes." The book's technique, he believed, was better suited to poetry than to prose. Klein himself composed a number of poems in "Finneganese" in the early forties.

Joyce's death in 1941, and the closing of his canon, probably marked a turning point in Klein's obsession with the man and his work, just as Bialik's death in 1934 had prompted him to begin his translations of the Hebrew poet. But it was only while lecturing at McGill in the late forties that he found the opportunity to get down to serious work on Joyce. As a teacher he was ideally suited to give an entire course on *Ulysses*, but that would have put the university in too awkward a position, since the book was not at the time legally obtainable in Canada.

In his conversations with Files, Klein occasionally revealed the extent to which Joyce fascinated him, as artist and as person. Among other things, Klein shared with Joyce an inordinate sensitivity to language, an intellectual compulsion towards order, and a pedantic yet earthy sense of humor. Joyce's training at the hands of the Jesuits reminded Klein of his own early schooling under rabbinical orthodoxy. "Both," as Files noted, "had been schooled in the tradition of a dogmatic culture, based on centuries of historic process and growth, with prolonged insistence on a system of logical and orthodox thinking about necessary moral, theological, and social commitments; and both had broken through those nets, and taken a self-reliant stance, even while saturated with the thoughts that had dominated their forebears and their race."

What Klein finally set out to do in his study of Joyce was to produce a thorough page-by-page commentary on *Ulysses*, "tracking down," as he explained to Edel, "all the allusions, indicating in the abstruser stream-of-consciousness paragraphs the mental associations and sequence, explicating text, and relating the parts to the whole." By the middle of his last year of teaching at McGill he considered that the "general spade work" was completed and that he could begin writing.

No task that Klein undertook ever gave him as much pleasure as his work

The Oxen of the Sun: The Labyrinth Charted

Month	Pagination	Embryological Indicia	Recapitulation	Evolutionary Stage	Parody Style
Prelude	377 to 378			Creation of World/Azoic	Sallustian-Tacitean
The First	378 Some man ... to 381: Almighty God	Fertilization and Mitotic development	Calypso	Proterozoic: Archæozoic	Old English Wayfarer and Traveller poems. Mandeville
The Second	381: This meanwhile to 384: About that present time	External genitalia appear	Telemachus	Mesozoic	Malory's Morte d'Arthur
The Third	384 to 386: To be short, this passage	Centres of ossification	Nestor	Tertiary	Elizabethan Chronicles
The Fourth	386 to 388: There-to Punch Costello ... pea	Sex differentiated	Scylla-Charybdis	Quarternary	Milton/Taylor Browne/Hooker
The Fifth	388 to 390: brenningly biddeth	Heart sounds heard	Cyclops	Early Paleolithic	Bunyan
The Sixth	390 to 392	Foetus, if born, dies	Wandering Rocks	Late Paleolithic/Neanderthal Man/The Flood	Pepys Evelyn
The Seventh	392 to 409	Child may be born and live	Proteus	The Age of Cultivation	Defoe-Swift
THE SEVENTH — 7:1:a First	392 to 395: for a' that	Ravishing, Rapeseed	Nestor	Azoic/Archæozoic	Defoe-Swift
7:1:b Second	395 to 397: larum in the antechamber	Pod or Two Testibus ponderosis	Telemachus	Mesozoic	Steele-Addison
7:1:c Third	397 to 399: store of knowledge	Spontaneous movements Amniotic Fluid	Calypso	Tertiary	Sterne
7:1:d Fourth	399 to 400: with ... a heart	Recognition of sex	Scylla-Charybdis	Quarternary	Goldsmith
7:1:e Fifth	400 to 401: Supreme Being	Lanugo	Cyclops	Early Paleolithic	Burke
7:1:f Sixth	401 to 402: ... laugh together	"In readiness to burst anon"	Wandering Rocks	Late Paleolithic	Sheridan

Month	Pagination	Embryological Indicia	Recapitulation	Evolutionary Stage	Parody Style
THE SEVENTH — 7:2:a First	402	"Oblivious of ties of nature"	Cyclops	"Lowest strata ... to seedfield and ploughshare"	Junius
7:2:b Second			Scylla-Charybdis		
7:2:c Third	to		Calypso		
7:2:d Fourth			Telemachus		
7:2:e Fifth			Nestor		
7:2:f Sixth	402: acid and inoperative		Wandering Rocks		
7:3:b	403 to 405: whom God has joined	Triplets	W. R./Telemachus/Calypso	Mesozoic	Gibbon
7:3:c	405	Triplets	Telemachus Nestor/S-C	Tertiary	Walpole
7:3:d	406	Twins	W. R./Calypso	Quarternary	Lamb
7:3:e	407 to Taurus	Quadruplets	S-C/Calypso Nestor/Telem.	Early Paleolithic	de Quincy
7:3:f	407 to 409: ... constellation	Triplets	W. R./Telemachus/Cyclops	Late Paleolithic	Landor
The Eighth	410 to 411: Lafayette	"Little Old Man"	Aeolus (7 recapitulations)	The Age of The Old Man	Macaulay
The Ninth	411 to 421	Parturition	Hades	Civilization/The Incarnation	Huxley to Carlyle
THE NINTH	411 to 413: to save her own	PARTURITION	45 recapitulations — HADES — Proteus	CIVILIZATION/THE INCARNATION	Huxley
	413 to 414: good and faithful servant		27 recapitulations		Dickens
	414: "There are sins" to "silent, remote, re-proachful		4 plus 5 recaps		Newman Pater
	415: He frowns a little to utterance of The Word		18 recaps		Ruskin
	415: Burke's! to 416: A truce to		Par. I:48 rec's Par. II:81 rec's		Carlyle

KLEIN'S DIAGRAMMATIC SUMMARY OF HIS ANALYSIS OF THE "OXEN OF THE SUN" CHAPTER OF JOYCE'S *ULYSSES*.

on *Ulysses*. Each discovery that he stumbled upon whetted his appetite for more. In a physician's office he found an old textbook on obstetrics that helped him decipher a crucial chapter of the novel. At the McGill Library he spent many hours hunting down mysterious names and expressions, and immersing himself in the writings that Joyce had drawn upon. Once, after coming across a rare dictionary that Joyce was said to have used, he triumphantly told Frank Scott that he was at last able to explain the precise reason for every single word in *Ulysses*, "even the and's and the but's."

In the spring of 1948 Klein began corresponding with a young American Joyce scholar, Ellsworth Mason, who had learned of his project from Edel at a Joyce Society meeting in New York. Mason encouraged Klein and furnished him with clues and ideas that proved fruitful. In late June Klein sent him the preliminary draft of his first article on *Ulysses*, a microscopic examination of the "Oxen of the Sun" chapter. Mason found Klein's analysis ingenious — too ingenious, he feared, for while it revealed patterns buried deep in Joyce's text, it ignored contradictory patterns on the surface. Klein remained undaunted and proceeded to publish his article in *Here and Now*.

In July, following Scott's suggestion, he wrote to Henry Allen Moe, the director of the Guggenheim Foundation in New York, explaining in rather elaborate detail the nature of his work on Joyce and seeking advice on how to obtain a grant. He calculated that if he could devote to the work half his days for the following two years he would "be able to give to the publisher a completed manuscript of about five hundred pages of condensed and hitherto unsuspected explication." This labor of love, he said, would involve a personal loss of at least $4,000 each year.

His plea evidently made no great impression on Moe. In February 1949 Klein turned to Edel for sympathy. "Earning my daily bread greatly interferes with my work on *Ulysses*. I haven't touched it now for two months. Already I have stolen from my family for this purpose enough; it should have been a labor for an Academy, not for one man doubly beset — beset by the non-paying clients he has, beset by the clients he has not."

Several weeks later he wrote to James Laughlin of New Directions, asking almost desperately for help in securing a patron. Laughlin had already expressed interest in seeing the final manuscript of his commentary, and Klein was counting on New Directions to publish it if nobody else would. Finding a patron, however, was more than Laughlin could do for him.

Klein never asked Bronfman to support his Joyce work, probably out of pride and a feeling that such esoteric research would make no sense to him. Saul Hayes, the executive director of the Canadian Jewish Congress, tried to encourage Klein to seek Bronfman's help, assuring him that it would be granted. Klein was taken aback at the mere suggestion. Such an idea, he insisted, was out of the question: he would not dream of letting Bronfman risk embarrassment in Catholic Quebec by being connected in even the remotest way with the writings of the anti-Catholic Joyce!

Encouraged all the while by Mason's stimulating correspondence, Klein kept up the work in his spare moments and completed a second article in April. His hopes for financial support, however, seemed dimmer than ever, and he frequently wondered whether to continue. As it happened, unexpected events interposed at this time, forcing him to put *Ulysses* aside for a while.

IN THE SPRING OF 1949 Klein was suddenly back in politics. Fred Rose, the communist member of Parliament for Cartier, had been arrested and convicted of espionage and was now in prison. In a 1947 by-election, his seat had been won by a Jewish Liberal and former member of the Quebec Legislature, Maurice Hartt. Late in May 1949 a general election was called for June 27. Once again Klein was approached by his friends in the CCF, and once again he agreed to accept their nomination.

Faced with what he regarded as an excellent chance of winning, he chose to put out of mind his earlier distaste for political campaigns. Hartt, he thought, had proven himself utterly incompetent in Parliament and needed only to be held up to ridicule to be defeated. The communist candidate of the Labor-Progressive Party, Harry Binder, was certain to lose, since Rose had thoroughly discredited the party in the eyes of his embarrassed constituents. Binder himself had been found guilty in 1940 of sabotaging the war effort by

A MUD HOLE IS NO SUBSTITUTE FOR A PLATFORM *!!*

A MAN TO BE PROUD OF ?

KLEIN

DIRT IN CARTIER...

The candidate of the C.C.F. splinter party has no platform and is ashamed of the anti-Zionist policy of MacInnis, who said in Parliament, "The treatment of the State of Israel by the Labour Government in England is proof that we are not pro-Zionist". This C.C.F. puppet is trying to cover up the statement by wallowing in filth, vituperation and dirt. — Is this a man to be proud of?

We do not hear the C.C.F. puppet speak of Cartier's problems or high policy or discuss a platform. All he does is indulge in personalities, and sling mud.

IS THIS A MAN TO BE PROUD OF?

Maurice Hartt has already proven his worth. His opponents cannot discuss it, and it is only by subterfuge that they try to avoid the solid accomplishments of Maurice Hartt as a public representative at Quebec and Ottawa. During a decade of service he has protected the dignity and the rights of and obtained privileges for the electors of Cartier.

The man to be proud of is MAURICE HARTT

DO YOUR PART — RE-ELECT HARTT

---

calling on Canadians to give up their struggle against Hitler and had been sentenced to three years in Kingston Penitentiary. A fourth candidate, Maurice Hébert, represented the Progressive Conservatives, a party which could expect only marginal support in Cartier.

Klein's initial campaign strategy was to portray himself as a true son of working-class Cartier, a devoted Zionist, a man of culture, a leader in the Jewish community. To the many French Canadian voters in Cartier he appealed for support as "un vieil ami," one who had taken his law degree at the Université de Montréal and had served many French Canadian clients, especially during his sojourn in Rouyn. As evidence of his sympathetic understanding of their culture, he pointed with pride to *The Rocking Chair* and quoted from the glowing reviews it had received in the Quebec press. On June 11 his campaign received an unexpected boost from the announcement that *The Rocking Chair* had just been awarded the annual Governor General's award for poetry.

Klein persisted in conducting a very personal sort of campaign, making as few references as possible to the CCF and its national platform. Max

לעצטער וואל מיטינג

פאר דער דערװײלונג פֿון

א. מ. קליין

סי. סי. עף. קאנדידאט אין קארטיער

זונטיק, 8 אוונט, דעם 26-טן יוני

אין ארבעטער רינג זאל

4848 סט. לארענס בולוואַרד

הערט א. מ. קליין, פראפ. פ. ר. סקאט, נאַציאנאַלער פֿאריצער פֿון
דער סי. סי. עף. און פֿאַרשטײער פֿון אַלע אָרגאַניזאַציעם
וועלכע שטיצן א. מ. קליין.

FINAL MASS RALLY

For the Election of

A. M. KLEIN

C.C.F. CANDIDATE IN CARTIER

Sunday, June 26th at 8 p.m.

WORKMEN'S CIRCLE CENTRE

4848 St. Lawrence Blvd.

Hear A. M. KLEIN, Prof. F. R. SCOTT and representatives of organizations supporting A. M. Klein

Win back Cartier's good name!

Elect A.-M. KLEIN, *A Man to be Proud of*

C.C.F. ELECTION COMMITTEE

LEFT, A FLYER PUT OUT BY THE MAURICE HARTT CAMPAIGN. RIGHT, A POSTER ANNOUNCING KLEIN'S FINAL RALLY ON THE EVE OF THE ELECTION.

Garmaise, his former law partner, normally a Liberal supporter, kept an old promise and came to Montreal from Rouyn to lend a hand in managing the campaign. Klein confidently wrote and designed all his own posters and flyers. The slogan he adopted was one which accurately summed up the appeal he hoped to make to the voters of Cartier: *A. M. Klein — a man to be proud of*.

Hartt's campaign relied on the traditional loyalty of Canadian Jews to the Liberal party. In 1949 the pro-Liberal sentiments in the Jewish community were especially strong because of the government's recent recognition of the State of Israel. Hartt seized on this point and tried to associate the CCF with the Labor government in Britain, whose foreign secretary, Ernest Bevin, had become in Jewish eyes the personification of anti-Zionism. In response, Klein immediately cited his own editorials against Bevin as well as numerous pro-Zionist statements by CCF leaders throughout the forties. He was deeply hurt by the grotesque unfairness of Hartt's slander and as the campaign progressed his counterattacks grew increasingly personal. Quoting Hansard, he ridiculed Hartt's tactless pronouncements in

from CCF Campaign Speech

Ladies and gentlemen, electors of Cartier:

During the past two weeks, as my opponent Mr. Maurice Hartt, the member sitting on Cartier, found his position growing worse from day to day, he has looked wildly about him for desperate remedies for his desperate plight.... Hartt grasped at whatever came into his head, and sought — against all rhyme and reason — to denigrate me a Bevin's agent. Mr. Israel Rabinovitch, editor of the Canadian Jewish Eagle, has characterized this slander for what it is. Said Mr. Rabinovitch: Electors of Cartier are as likely to believe that Klein is an agent of Bevin's as they are to believe that the cow jumped over the moon and laid an egg....

And so the uncomfortably sitting member for Cartier has taken to a new strategy. A. M. Klein, he and all his speakers repeat, is a fine man, truly a man to be proud of. It is an endorsation which, after the endorsation of the many groups in Cartier, I did not require, nor did expect; circumstances, however, seem to have extorted the fact from the opposition. A fine man, a scholar and a gentleman is Klein, — admitted, but, adds Hartt, he is misguided, misguided by the C.C.F. whose banner he bears.

Mr. Hartt's strictures against the C.C.F. are singularly at variance with the statements not only of C.C.F. leaders, but of leaders of the Liberal Party. For Mr. St. Laurent it was who said that C.C.F.'ers were only "Liberals in a hurry." Mr. Hartt apparently prefers to remain a slow, a very slow Liberal; such indeed he has been, slow to defend the rights of his electors, slow to maintain the honor of his community; in a hurry only to uphold the principle of Hartt for Hartt's sake....

Mr. Maurice Hartt, I offer you one last opportunity to return to the slogan with which you began your campaign: "Let my record speak!" I do now challenge you to mount the same platform with me, in the good old tradition of Quebec, to debate your record, any time, any place.

Whether you accept this challenge or not, in the hearts of the people of Cartier the verdict is already prepared. They know what are the real issues — to them, your cartoons are just so much ostentation. Cartier wants cheaper bread — not lavish circuses. Cartier wants legislation — not vituperation.

Cartier cannot vote for Hébert. The candidate of the party of reaction has no appeal to a constituency made up of wage-earners and working people.

Cartier finds it unthinkable to vote for Binder. It particularly resents the fact that the Labor Progressive Party could find no better candidate to offer them than a man who had spent two years in Kingston Penitentiary. Cartier wants to forget the affair of Fred Rose, not to repeat it.

Electors of Cartier, there is only one candidate in Cartier for whom you may vote in all conscience, without anxiety, and to your own best interest. That is the C.C.F. candidate A. M. Klein. I must warn you, electors of Cartier, that plans are on foot to thwart your will, to frustrate your intention. Vote early, electors of Cartier, and frustrate the frustraters.

condensed from Klein's script of a radio address (June 21, 1949) the House of Commons and finally rested his entire case to the voters of Cartier on the argument that such an uneducated and uncultured man as Maurice Hartt would only continue to embarrass them in the eyes of the rest of Canada.

Klein was the sole author of all his speeches and radio addresses. As a speaker he was in top form, and his rallies drew such large, enthusiastic crowds that he became increasingly certain of victory. His campaign staff knew, however, that most of his audiences came simply to enjoy his rousing speeches, and not to send him to Parliament. Throughout the campaign Garmaise frequently heard people saying that they would have certainly backed Klein had he been running for the Liberals, but that they had no interest in voting for the CCF.

As election day approached, Klein was supremely optimistic, while most of his staff was resigned to defeat. The results of the voting on June 27 were even more disappointing than any of them had expected. The Liberals, under their new national leader, Louis St. Laurent, won a landslide victory across the country. Hartt was swept along with fifty-three percent of the vote in Cartier. The great shock was that even Binder did better than Klein, winning twenty-one percent against Klein's fourteen percent. The Progressive Conservative candidate fared only slightly worse.

Klein perhaps should have been consoled by the fact that it was the party, and not its candidate, that had been spurned by the voters. Across Canada, the election was one that appeared to spell the end of the CCF's hopes of ever becoming the official opposition party in Ottawa. Klein tried to put on a brave face and shrug off the defeat as mere "politics," but privately he expressed a bitter sense of rejection: the community whose great champion he had been all his life had now rudely turned him down. His appeal to the voters had indeed been so unabashedly personal that he could hardly have interpreted the results in any other way. When the CCF asked him again the following year to accept the party's nomination as its standard bearer, he absolutely refused. One such humiliating defeat had been enough, and he said his final farewell to politics.

A VIEW OF MONTREAL'S HARBOR, AS SEEN FROM THE TOWER OF THE CHURCH OF NOTRE DAME DE BONSECOURS.

Grain Elevator

Up from the low-roofed dockyard warehouses
it rises blind and babylonian
like something out of legend. Something seen
in a children's colored book. Leviathan
swamped on our shore? The cliffs of some other river?
The blind ark lost and petrified? A cave
built to look innocent, by pirates? Or
some eastern tomb a traveled patron here makes local?

But even when known, it's more than what it is:
for here, as in a Josephdream, bow down
the sheaves, the grains, the scruples of the sun
garnered for darkness; and Saskatchewan
is rolled like a rug of a thick and golden thread.
O prison of prairies, ship in whose galleys roll
sunshines like so many shaven heads,
waiting the bushel-burst out of the beached bastille!

Sometimes, it makes me think Arabian,
the grain picked up, like tic-tacs out of time:
first one; an other; singly; one by one; —

to save life. Sometimes, some other races claim
the twinship of my thought, — as the river stirs
restless in a white Caucasian sleep,
or, as in the steerage of the elevators,
the grains, Mongolian and crowded, dream.

A box: cement, hugeness, and rightangles —
merely the sight of it leaning in my eyes
mixes up continents and makes a montage
of inconsequent time and uncontiguous space.
It's because it's bread. It's because
bread is its theme, an absolute. Because
always this great box flowers over us
with all the colored faces of mankind...

(1947)

Letter to Karl Shapiro

Dec. 27, 1948

Dear Mr. Shapiro
It was very kind and most generous of you to take the trouble to drop me your note of congratulation. In the light of the question put in your postscript, the body of your letter was indeed generous to a degree, for verily I am the one who once mourned you as a lost Jew. I say "mourned" because it was a sadness and not an anger which moved me, a mood of regret and not of anathema. Please believe me — this is not cant. I recognized the uniqueness of your talent — its vigor and its sensitivity, its being within the tradition and its newness — and I was mortified to think that you were lost to those who needed you most.

Had my feelings then been other than as I have described them, your letter would have covered me with embarrassment and confusion. As it is, it is the most welcome letter I have received this year. I see in black and white that you do not belong to *them*. I know now that you never did, I knew always that we never could — even when accepted, embraced, baptised, they hang the hyphen upon our necks, like the leper's clapper — and I see that you now know that you don't. Your poem on the recent Maccabaean events in our history elated me; the letter before me — its very existence, compliments aside — won back your name for me — Shapir, the pleasing, the acceptable.

But, you say, I am quite a long chalk from Jew. Brother, you perpetrate a naiveté: you assume it is a matter of choice. It is in this sense, and not in any arrogant sense,

163

that we are a chosen, and not a choosing, people. Choice, if any, does not lie between Christian and Jew, but between the manners in which one accepts or rejects the *fait accompli*. One can either — here I go, professorial and avuncular — associate one's Jewishness with all the negativism history, like a mad Rashi, has appended to it; or one can feel oneself, and develop oneself as part of a great tradition, a tradition whose fruitfulness is by no means exhausted. I recall a symposium published in 1940 on the question "what my Judaism means to me." Delmore Schwartz participated and said that he cherished his Jewishness because it provided him — with an additional source of anguish! This is like the circumcised one who insisted on showing everyone his operation. David Daiches said that the fact that he knew he was a Jew (his father is or was Rabbi in Edinburgh) resulted in his acquiring, when he was at college, an excelling knowledge in — Scots dialect poetry! This is — like nothing I know. Both gentlemen see in their heritage — only succession duties. Of its inventory they have no idea.

That inventory is both valuable and extensive, and its items are not confined to the Hebrew tongue. The Talmud, and your own name, which issues therefrom, are both Aramaic; Maimonides did not spurn the Arabic, Mendelssohn judaized even the German, and as for English, it is already a vessel prepared. Milton prepared it.

Now the continuation of our own culture stands before the Jewish writer as *the* challenge. The hiatus of the Diaspora has been closed — closed even for those who still remain therein. We do not write any longer *in vacuo*; we write in the aftermath of a great death, European Jewry's, and in the presence of a great resurrection. Our miracle, moreover, owns to a miracle's greatest virtue — contemporaneity.

You speak of the Jewish consciousness. You recognize it, then, and I need not argue it. Remains only to *visit* (italics yours) that consciousness upon our own chain of being, and not elsewhere. Saying which I hear your *tu quoque*: And what have *you* to do with French Canada? It's a long story. Two books I wrote, both stemming out of my ancestral traditions; both praised ancient virtue; when I looked about for those virtues in the here and now, I found them in Quebec. Now I have no illusions about my province, its clericalism, its frequent reaction, etc. — but here was a minority, like my own, which led a compact life; continued, unlike my own, an ancient tradition, preserved inherited values, felt that it "belonged."

Now, of course, I do not require my Gallic prototype's beatific vision; the original is re-building.

And how it is to be rebuilded is a matter of concern to me, though I may never dwell therein.

unfinished draft, from Klein's private papers

The Rocking Chair

It seconds the crickets of the province. Heard
in the clean lamplit farmhouses of Quebec, —
wooden, — it is no less a national bird;
and rivals, in its cage, the mere stuttering clock.
To its time, the evenings are rolled away;
and in its peace the pensive mother knits
contentment to be worn by her family,
grown-up, but still cradled by the chair in which she sits.

It is also the old man's pet, pair to his pipe,
the two aids of his arithmetic and plans,
plans rocking and puffing into market-shape;
and it is the toddler's game and dangerous dance.
Moved to the verandah, on summer Sundays, it is,
among the hanging plants, the girls, the boy-friends,
sabbatical and clumsy, like the white haloes
dangling above the blue serge suits of the young men.

It has a personality of its own;
is a character (like that old drunk Lacoste,
exhaling amber, and toppling on his pins);
it is alive; individual; and no less
an identity than those about it. And
it is tradition. Centuries have been flicked
from its arcs, alternately flicked and pinned.
It rolls with the gait of St. Malo. It is act

and symbol, symbol of this static folk
which moves in segments, and returns to base, —
a sunken pendulum: *invoke, revoke;*
loosed yon, leashed hither, motion on no space.
O, like some Anjou ballad, all refrain,
which turns about its longing, and seems to move
to make a pleasure out of repeated pain,
its music moves, as if always back to a first love.

(1945)

JEWISH REFUGEES FROM EASTERN EUROPE ARRIVING IN ISRAEL, LATE FORTIES.

from THE GOLEM

For its sins that were many (so is it received of our ancestors), for its sins that were many the stock of Israel, banished its land, goes vagrant over the world. Flung and dispersed, as from the hand of the sower, our scattering lies in the farthest corners of the continents. We are chaff driven before the wind which even when fallen to the ground, no growing grows from it. Therefore, in the mid watches of the night and at high noon's blaze, we dream Jerusalem. We would return. We would fare back. We would return, but we know not the highways, we are lost among the paths, we seek to come there by the straight road or by the roundabout, but always are we turned off wandering, or herded back, or, caught between gates, held.

Yet do I hold firm to the belief that our journeyings, which are under Providence, even when they run circuitous and in directions away from our purpose and hope, are journeyings which tend ever and always toward Zion.

Such passage, to what may it be likened? It may be likened to the flight of the pigeon which, though buffeted by storms and far from its dove-cote, by an inner sense, in an inscrutable course over the trackless skies, wings it, homing. To the contentions of that fish called salmon which, struggling against currents and leaping over weirs, through devious channels makes ever toward its hatching place. To the bee, buzzing zigzag among flowers, that after many honeyless sallies at last sips sweetness.

(early 1950s)

11

O Zion,
Altogether Beautiful

Within a few weeks of his dejecting loss at the polls Klein was preparing to undergo the most elating experience of his life. For many years he had yearned to visit Palestine, now the State of Israel, but, could not imagine how the opportunity would ever be granted to him. Quite unexpectedly in the spring of 1949 the Canadian Jewish Congress proposed to send him for the month of August on a fact-finding mission to Israel, Europe, and North Africa. Klein's task was to survey Jewish refugee problems and, on returning, to deliver a series of speeches about his trip at fund-raising rallies across Canada. The offer came from Saul Hayes, the executive director of the Congress, and Klein gladly accepted.

Israel was barely a year old that summer. The birth of the Jewish State had been announced from Tel Aviv on May 14, 1948. No day in Klein's life could possibly have aroused deeper emotions in him.

My life was, and is, bound to the country of my father's choice, to Canada; but this intelligence, issuing, as it did, from that quarter of the globe which had ever been to me the holiest of the map's bleeding stigmata, the Palestine whose geography was as intimately known as the lines of the palm of my hand, filled me with pride, with exaltation, with an afflatus odorous of the royal breath of Solomon. I was like one that dreamed. I, surely, had not been of the captivity; but when the Lord turned again the captivity of Zion, I was like one that dreamed.

As the date of his departure approached, Klein grew dizzy with excitement. In mid-July he made his tour of the various consulates to obtain the necessary visas. Arriving at the Israeli consulate, he relished the thought that by legal fiction it was really a parcel of Holy Land in Montreal. "One was almost tempted to plant an orange tree in the consulate — if it observed international law, it should grow." Klein was only the ninth person to be issued an Israeli visa at Montreal — a good omen, he noted: "Klein — nine — sign. Fine."

His journey was to begin in New York on Sunday evening, July 31. Earlier in the day he met with Leon Edel for lunch in a Manhattan restaurant. They talked of old friends, of Montreal, of the bondage of Klein's law practice, and of his wish for a patron to allow him to complete his study of Joyce's *Ulysses*. Noticing the brightness in Klein's eyes as they spoke about Joyce, Edel asked smilingly, "I suppose you planned this so that you might stop in Dublin on the way?" Klein laughed: "You are right — I go to Jerusalem to visit Dublin!"

His plane left New York that night and, after four airport stops in Europe, arrived in Israel on Tuesday morning. From the airport at Lydda he took a taxi direct to his hotel, the Eden, in Jerusalem. It was about noon when he arrived; exhausted after two nights and a day without sleep, he immediately dozed off in his hotel room. The irony of it struck him afterwards — succumbing to the weakness of the flesh while his spirit hungered for visions of the land he had waited so long and journeyed so far to see — "to slumber in Eden!"

In the evening he was awakened by A. H. Friedgut, a former acquaintance from Canada whom he had arranged to meet. They drove through the city to the outskirts of Jerusalem and up to the top of Mount Herzl. There they lingered for an hour under the moon and stars, overlooking the panorama beneath them. Klein was spellbound, rapt in a meditative trance. They hardly spoke at all, either then or on the way back to the hotel. Friedgut heard him say quietly "Oh, God" — and that was all.

The next day Klein contacted the Jewish Agency to confirm arrangements for a quick tour of the country. Using Tel Aviv as his base, he went on a series of excursions to the major cities and towns, including Haifa, Beersheba, Safed, Nazareth, Jaffa, and probably Jerusalem again. Among the agricultural settlements he stopped at was Ein Harod, where he spent a night. Like many visitors, he was struck by the actual modernity of a land that in his imagination was still ancient. The rejuvenation of the language of the Bible, its transformation into a tool of everyday commerce, startled and delighted him. Every scene was a feast for his senses and a stimulus to fanciful poeticizing.

The sole and solitary rose growing in the only garden of Beth Eshel in the desert. Red in the face with defiance against the surrounding wilderness ... At Haifa, the little cups of Turkish ... The Yemenite newsboy shouting, Idiot! Idiot! Peddling the daily *Yediot* ... The waterworks in the Negev with all the machine-parts identified in Hebrew. *Lachatz*, said the device on a circular face. The word had always meant to me *oppression*, as in the Haggadah: *lachatz asher haim loichatzim oisom*. Now it owned to a new and happier meaning: water pressure ... The wild whirling pressure of life at Tel Aviv's most congested intersection at the Mograbi. A constantly improvised hora ...

"At Beersheba, in company of Beduin, sat on a camel to be photographed ... The camel is the most ill-mannered of all beasts. As I sat, warrior-like, at his hump, he turned his muzzle: Who's this? Most disconcerting. Camel peculiar also in motion, going step by step, nodding acquiescence. The yesman of the desert ..."

Jerusalem, the lovely stone of its mansions. A debt to Sir Ronald Storrs, who had insisted under British regime that all Jerusalmite houses be built out of the stone of the country. Excellent Judaean quarrying. Result — Arab snipers frustrated by solidity of Jewish residences. House after house — pockmarked. The New City has had its infantile disease ...

Mea Shearim — the hundred gates. An understatement. The most tortuous labrinthine winding area of all my peregrinations. The Underground's underground. But really not a part of Israel — a part of Eastern Europe. Hebrew is tabu, too holy for weekday use. The little yeshiva boys with great big calves' eyes, and long black garments, and serpentine side-curls. Faces like a page of Gemara: centre, text; on the left a *payah* of Rashi, on the right a *payah* of Tosfoth ... And the odor — not of sanctity ...

He kept an intermittent record of his sojourn in what he called his "Notebook of a Journey," published in the *Canadian Jewish Chronicle* in seventeen installments from August to December. The early segments were mailed to the *Chronicle* and began appearing before his return; it was a pleasant experience, after so many years as editor, to be playing the role of a

169

real newspaperman, filing reports from the scene of his investigations. The "Notebook" became in the end the raw material for his speeches as well as for the novel he was to write that winter.

Beyond his fresh, childlike excitement at everything he saw, Klein experienced in Israel an almost religious sense of the miraculous. There was above all the miracle of "the brands plucked from the burning" — the salvation of the last remnants of European Jewry and the arrival of immigrants from all the lands of their dispersion. Further, there was the "miracle of David slaying Goliath" — the victory of the Israelis over the Arabs. Wherever he went he found that even the most skeptical believed "something messianic, millenial had occurred."

Klein happened to be in Israel when the remains of Theodor Herzl, the father of modern political Zionism, were being transported from Vienna to Jerusalem. The reburial was originally scheduled to take place on August 4, the ninth of Ab, the day of memorial for the destruction of the Temples. Klein had timed his stay in Jerusalem so as to be present at the ceremony. "It would have been indeed an apt conjuncture," he wrote, "a coincidence such as had found favor in the eyes of the Talmudists who in their vision of the fitness of things had seen the Messiah as being born on this ninth day of Ab."

To his great dismay, the event was repeatedly postponed, and in the end he missed it. When Herzl's coffin was finally flown to Israel on August 16 Klein was in Tel Aviv, nearing the end of his two-week visit to the country. He was presumably among the thousands of Tel Avivians who filed past Herzl's remains lying in state in the Knesseth Circle that day. To this extent, at least, he could claim to have witnessed the return to holy soil of the "prince and seer of my vision and my life." The next morning he was on his way to Paris and so could not follow the cortège to Jerusalem and see the coffin reach its destined terminus atop Mount Herzl.

Klein stayed in Paris for five days and then proceeded to Casablanca via Marseilles. Three days in Casablanca were followed by three days in Rome. While in Italy he made an excursion to Bari, on the Adriatic, one of the main camps of Jewish refugees embarking for Israel. Klein then returned to Paris for three more days. He left France on September 1, stopped in Ireland, and arrived back in New York on September 5.

From his speeches and "Notebook of a Journey" it is clear that the most affecting part of his trip outside of Israel was his visit to the infernal mellah, or Jewish ghetto, of Casablanca. In a very different way, as a former classics student, he was deeply moved by the art and architecture of Rome. Altogether, Klein spent a considerable part of his time in Paris, and yet there is hardly any record of what he did or saw there. His "Notebook" is similarly evasive about Ireland — there is not even a mention of Dublin, which he surely must have visited, but only a brief reference to his having been delayed

at Shannon airport. These gaps may perhaps be explained by the fact that as an emissary of the Canadian Jewish Congress Klein had little business in Paris and none in Dublin.

On his return to Canada Klein began fulfilling his speaking obligations to the Congress. The speeches he gave that fall and winter were among the most electrifying of his entire career. He played mercilessly on the heartstrings of his listeners. His poetic phrases, his vivid images, his humor, the dramatic range of his voice, his sheer vitality, all produced an overwhelming emotional effect. He was "burning," a friend recalled, "aflame, out of control in a way."

The first of these speeches was delivered at a Congress convention in Toronto in late October 1949 and has survived as one of the rare recordings of Klein's voice. It was a "mingled picture" that he set out to paint for his audience, containing "bright areas of effulgence" and "dark patches of unreality." He began by depicting the sad condition of the last of the war refugees, whom he saw at Marseilles, Rome, and Bari. He spoke of the squalor and degradation of Jewish life in the mellah of Casablanca, which was typical, he noted, of all Jewish ghettos in the Arab world. Next to these scenes evoking pity and fear he juxtaposed pictures of contemporary Israel in all its glory — the coming of immigrants on Jewish boats under Jewish flags,

171

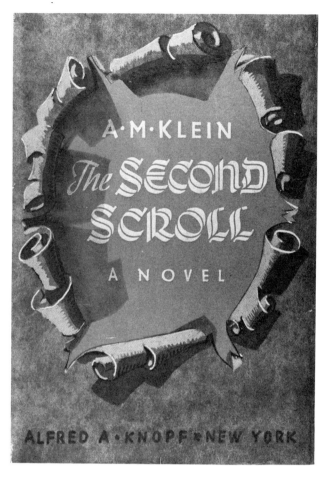

the transporting of Yemenite Jewry "on eagles' wings." He saved for last what to him was most moving of all, his witnessing the arrival in Tel Aviv of Herzl's coffin, and finally punctuated his address with an appeal for contributions to Israel.

Such, in broad outline, were the speeches he delivered to dozens of Jewish audiences in Canada, and then all across the United States as well, on behalf of the United Jewish Appeal. At first he enjoyed the speaking tours and was stimulated by new contacts and appreciative audiences. Over the next few years, however, the routine became both strenuous and monotonous, driving him perilously close to the brink of exhaustion.

OUT OF HIS EARLIER SPEECHES and the "Notebook of a Journey" Klein drew together the elements of his novel, *The Second Scroll*. In April 1950 he mailed the manuscript to the New York publishing firm of Alfred A. Knopf. Several weeks later he received a brief letter of rejection from one of Knopf's editors, Herbert Weinstock, saying: "While we all admire your writing,

MONROE ABBEY, ON BEHALF OF THE EXECUTIVE OF THE CANADIAN JEWISH CONGRESS, RECEIVING A COPY OF *THE SECOND SCROLL* FROM KLEIN.

we feel that this book fails of its intended effect, largely because it sprawls in a structural sense."

Klein revised the manuscript sometime during the summer of 1950. It is impossible to say just how much of it he rewrote, since no copy of the original version, rejected by Knopf, has survived. That he found time at all to devote to the work that summer is itself surprising. His speaking engagements for the United Jewish Appeal entailed two lengthy trips to California in May and June. In August he attended a five-day poetry conference at Harvard University's summer school. That same month the Kleins were getting ready to move into the new home they had just bought at 236 Querbes in Outremont. In addition, of course, there was the usual routine at the law office and the *Chronicle*, and probably even some sporadic work on *Ulysses*.

Klein resubmitted his novel to Knopf at the end of the summer. In September Weinstock forwarded it to one of the firm's outside readers, Maurice Samuel, confessing that parts of the manuscript fascinated him but that most of it simply went over his head. Weinstock was evidently unaware that Samuel had been an admirer of Klein's work for nearly twenty years. As it happened, Samuel was genuinely moved by the novel; in his excitement he telephoned both Klein and Weinstock as soon as he had finished reading it.

The gist of his initial reaction was later printed on the Knopf dust jacket: "Among the books that have been written since the creation of the State of Israel, this is the first that rises to the height of the occasion."

In October Weinstock sent Klein an official offer to publish *The Second Scroll*. The copy-editing was completed in January 1951, and Klein took this last opportunity to make some minor changes. The manuscript then went to the book's designer, Lucian Bernhard. Klein saw the first proofs of Bernhard's work in April and was generally pleased. His only complaint was about the use of the Star of David at the head of each chapter — "a much too obvious symbol," he feared, "usually associated with religious tracts or the writings of professional Jews." Even more upsetting to him was the fact that his essay on the Sistine Chapel could not be set on the printed page exactly as he had intended, in imitation of the layout of Michelangelo's ceiling. The essay follows closely the progression of large biblical scenes visible overhead in the chapel, from Noah's drunkenness, near the entranceway, to the rear panels depicting Creation. Klein wanted his Latin quotations from the Prophets to appear in pairs on either side of the text, corresponding to Michelangelo's portraits of prophets and sybils along the edges of the chapel ceiling. Unfortunately the page was not wide enough to allow this, and the quotations had to be placed one under the other. Klein received the first copies of his book about the middle of August 1951. In the end he was delighted with its physical appearance and sent his compliments to the designer.

The explicator of Joycean arcana soon began applying his analytic methods to his own writing. Within a month of the novel's publication, Klein elaborated on its structure and symbolism in detailed letters to both Leon Edel and A. J. M. Smith. He explained how on a first level he regarded *The Second Scroll* as a record, a memento of his pilgrimage, "a scripture to witness to the fact that I had beheld the glory of the Jewish State's beginning, the consolation of our people's rescue." Complete sections of his "Notebook of a Journey" were therefore incorporated into the novel, mixing fact and fiction. The original journey began in Israel and ended in Europe, but Klein felt that the novel demanded the reverse, a "rising progression." Klein was sent on his trip by the Canadian Jewish Congress, but the novel's narrator is sent on a mission that would have been even dearer to Klein's own heart — to search out the new poets of Israel and produce a volume of translations. Many of the novel's incidental details are actually based on fact, especially the descriptions of locations and the delineation of minor characters. Klein relied on personal memories in portraying his narrator's childhood. In the opening chapter, in fact, there is only one invented character, and that is the mysterious, unseen hero, Uncle Melech. The rest — family, teachers, neighbors — all are accurately named and sketched from life.

And where *does* Uncle Melech derive from? Clearly he is larger than life, a universalized figure. But the seed of such a character may have been planted in Klein's subconscious mind when his wish to attend Theodor Herzl's reburial was, because of repeated delays and postponements, frustrated. Here, perhaps, was the source of his plot — the quest for a heroic Jewish personality, an idealized father-figure, genius, savior, and alter ego, who constantly eludes the worshipful seeker.

Klein's hero is named Melech Davidson, that is, King, son of David: the Messiah. The narrator is engaged, then, in a messianic pursuit. What he discovers in the end is that the Messiah is in fact the entire Jewish people. He is "the ubiquitous anonymity of universal Jewry's all-inclusive generation, he is the resurgent creativity of the incognitos of the folk."

Hints of Melech's symbolic role as Messiah are scattered throughout the novel, with frequent allusions to Christ, whom Klein invokes as an exemplar of martyred Jewry. Like Jesus chasing the moneylenders from the Temple, Melech puts a halt to the proceedings at the Warsaw Bourse. During the war, he is buried beneath corpses and rises from the dead. Melech is flogged. He is tempted by Settano, a figure of Satan. In Casablanca he leads the blind and the maimed. When he meets his death he is "annointed" with gasoline.

The novel also contains numerous hints equating the Messiah with the "incognitos of the folk." Many of the characters share the same regal name in different languages: Melech, Krul, Dauphin, Ketter, Krongold. The search for Uncle Melech leads to a curious "catalogue of incognitos," thirty-six names representing the thirty-six anonymous saints of Jewish legend.

The double theme of the last chapter — the search for Uncle Melech and the search for the poetic, the creative — this too is intended to reinforce the idea that the Messiah is embodied in the mass, the folk. The narrator has been searching everywhere for the most promising new poets of Israel, but he is disappointed, until he discovers the "poetry" of Israel in the miraculous rebirth of the Hebrew language itself, in the streets and shops, all about him. "It was there all the time — the fashioning folk, anonymous and unobserved, creating word by word, phrase by phrase, the total work that when completed would stand as epic revealed!"

Melech's life story is recognizable as the career of the archetypal modern Jew. The movements are classic: the abandonment of religion, the flirtation with Marxism and Christianity, the passionate humanitarianism, the trauma of the Holocaust, the return to Zion. Melech's life is at once a recapitulation of modern Jewish history and a summation of the lives of many individual Jews, such as Klein himself.

Yet, if Melech's story typifies modern Jewish history, it is also a timeless story. For Klein, Jewish experience in the twentieth century had assumed mythic proportions and was linked with the mystique of Jewish peoplehood

PART OF THE TEAM INVOLVED IN THE CBC RADIO PRODUCTION OF *THE SECOND SCROLL*, MAY 7, 1952. FROM LEFT TO RIGHT, NORMAN TAVISS, AN UNIDENTIFIED BOY, RUPERT CAPLAN, LORNE GREENE, BUD KNAPP, STANLEY MANN, AND ALBERT MILLER.

in its four-thousand-year history. He saw in modern events "a recurrence, in large outline, of the events recorded in the Pentateuch." Hence the *second* scroll — a new Pentateuch. Klein was instinctively drawn to cyclical views of history and believed in the need to recreate the classical forms of Jewish expression for each new generation.

THE SECOND SCROLL was the most widely read of Klein's books. Favorable reviews appeared in many American and Canadian periodicals, and it was publicized wherever he went on his speaking tours. On numerous occasions he was asked to give a reading and lead a discussion of the novel. A second printing was issued in February 1952. In May 1952 the CBC presented a ninety-minute radio dramatization of *The Second Scroll*, directed by Rupert Caplan and narrated by Lorne Greene. Klein thought it was "splendidly done." He began inquiring about the possibility of selling the movie rights, but nothing ever came of this.

The immediate popularity of the novel had a decisive effect on the course of Klein's activities in the fifties. First, it forced him to reassess his own standing as a writer. Having Knopf as a publisher meant that he had finally "made it" — there was no going back now to small presses. The success of the novel also helped restore Klein's image as a specifically Jewish writer, not only in the view of his audience but also in his own eyes. Thus in the early fifties he turned again to the translation of Yiddish and Hebrew literature and to the use of Jewish themes in his own fiction and drama. The Bible began to compete with *Ulysses* as his prime obsession. He became interested in contemporary Israeli culture, and he pondered long and hard over the future relationship between Israel and Diaspora Jewry.

For a brief while Klein seriously considered moving to Israel. It would have been quite difficult for him, practically and emotionally, to uproot himself from Montreal. As much as he longed for Zion, he also loved the land in which he had been raised. He feared and opposed the narrow, Diaspora-negating chauvinism that he already saw developing in Israel. He may even have felt that living in Israel might stifle his creativity, that he could thrive best in his more cosmopolitan exile. "To lie at ease in Zion," he wrote in 1953, "is, of course, a thing not to be despised. Yet is it a thing confined. After a little, ensues monotony, the deadly pall of iteration. ... Yes, Egypt was an ordeal, and one would gladly forget its fleshpots, but were not the Egyptians parted from more than their mere jewels? Was there not carried across the Red Sea a knowledge unknown to the Patriarchs? ... The mind, too, is a Nile, and has its alluvium; not negative entirely was the experience of Mizraim."

Klein chose to remain in his "Mizraim," his Canadian Diaspora. He planned a second visit to Israel in 1955, but the trip was canceled because of his precarious emotional state following the onset of mental illness. From then on he could only dream of Israel; he would never be well enough to make the journey again.

from Speech to the Canadian Jewish Congress

…There is also the tragedy which takes place unobserved and unnoticed, unpitied and unwept, in a corner. There is the tragedy of quiet desperation, of thousands perishing unknown against the wall, unnoted and unobserved. That tragedy I beheld in Casablanca.

You have heard a great deal of Casablanca. I went to visit Casablanca. I stood there on the spot and I saw these things with my own eyes, which were your eyes.

There is in Casablanca a mellah. A mellah is a ghetto in a Moslem country. It is not a ghetto through the accident of neighborhood; it is a ghetto dictated and a ghetto imposed. In this mellah in Casablanca there live huddled together in hovels of the most abominable character twenty-five thousand Jews. Their condition and their plight is typical of the plight of Jews in Moslem countries. Throughout the whole of Morocco there are two hundred thousand Jews. In all of the Moslem countries of the world today there are nine hundred thousand Jews. And the condition of the nine hundred thousand Jews is as the condition which I am about to describe prevailing in the mellah of Casablanca.

I left the hotel one morning — it was a sunny morning — to enter the mellah of Casablanca. It was but three hundred yards away. Casablanca is a beautiful city, a city of the twentieth century. It has wide boulevards, with plane trees and palm trees on either side. It has streets distinguished by the noblest names of French militarism. It is a city of this century. It has sumptuous hotels. We crossed from the hotel, three hundred paces, to enter the mellah, the area of tortuous streets and serpentine alleys dedicated to Jewry.

I slid into the mellah. I say *slid* with intention aforethought, for no sooner did I pass, but the area changed, and slime and ordure was before me. I *slid* because I slid also away from the twentieth, and nineteenth, the eighteenth, back into the twelfth century. And the first things that encountered me on my path — were hands. A multitude of hands! A forest of hands! The five-fingered plea, the petitioning palm, the civic gesture of the mellah of Casablanca; beggars everywhere. Indeed, beggars were scattered in various corners — they were Jews — these beggars were scattered in various corners, and they were pleading for the paltry pittance which they could get at the hands of a tourist. I made to throw them some pennies. My guide sought to stop me in the midst of my gesture. He said: "If you do so there is no end, there are twenty-five thousand of them." I persisted. And then there occurred to me that which was a searing of my heart. For this Jew who picked up the few pennies threw himself to the dirty cobblestones and smote his forehead thrice upon the floor in gratitude and oriental obeisance.

I could not imagine that this was real. Is this some oriental mirage? Is this some dream or some nightmare out of the Arabian Nights? Has Hollywood come here to stage a scene? But it was real! The stench and odor of eight centuries of unsanitation brought me back to reality.

There is no water in the mellah — twenty-five thousand people live there without water. Across the street there are these sumptuous hotels with hot and cold running water, all the time, plenty of it. And here there are people begging for a drink, begging for water. This is done with malice aforethought; this is the design.

I asked myself, is this Casablanca? Why, to me Casablanca was a beautiful word — the "white house." This is the place where there gathered the two mighty titans of contemporary politics to discuss the great new world, the brave new world, which was to be fashioned after this war. It was indeed Casablanca.

I asked myself, how do these people live? And the answer was, they do not. The mortality rate in the mellah of Casablanca is fifty percent. There are no statistics, but if you compare the records of those circumcised with the records of those who reach the age of bar-mitzvah, at the age of bar-mitzvah fifty percent of the young boys of the mellah are missing, they are dead. This is due to trachoma, which is ubiquitous; to ringworm of the scalp, which I saw treated in the various hospitals of the J.D.C. in Casablanca — hair by hair, a painful treatment; and to tuberculosis — I went to the *chadorim* of Casablanca, there was not a Hebrew teacher, there was not a teacher, in some schools, nothing more than little girls and little boys in shirts, no socks, no shoes, no nothing, just sitting in shirts, their mothers were maids in some Arabic or Moslem house, and they were being kept there by this Hebrew teacher, all suffering from tuberculosis.

The situation was appalling. And then there came to my mind a question for which I was ashamed no sooner did it prompt itself. I asked myself, are these people *Jews*?

Are they Jews? My friends, they are the descendants of the noblest sires in Jewish history. Their forefathers were the advisors and counsellors of kings and princes. They are the direct descendants of the Golden Age of Spain. Once, once, their ancestors counseled and advised prince and caliph. Once, their word was current in the courts of Spain. Today they are now paupers on a — on a heap of ordure, in the mellah of Casablanca.

This cannot be. This must not be. And the plight of the Jews in Casablanca — I have no complaint against the French Government; Casablanca is a protectorate of the Republic of France, the French Government has its own problems, and indeed would find it extremely difficult to introduce any reforms over the opposition of the Moslem population — for the plight of Jewry under *all* Moslem countries is the same. A Jew in Moslem countries, where Moslem law prevails, must not walk on the sidewalk in the presence of a Moslem. He must not ride a donkey, for that he would look down upon a Moslem. He must not mount a horse, for a horse is a noble animal. He must not wear white, the Jews of Casablanca wear black. And when a Moslem in his conversation happens to use the word *Jew*, he apologizes to his fellow as if he had uttered a term of pornography.

Nine hundred thousand of them live in this condition in the various countries of Moslem domination. They must be saved. They must be saved, my friends, for three reasons. First, because they are Jews, they are part of the body of our people. Second, because they are hostages in the hands of Moslem governments, who would wreak upon them and upon their persons whatever vengeance they wish to direct against the State of Israel. And third, because the State of Israel requires them, the State of Israel needs these nine hundred thousand or such of them as can be saved....

(October 24, 1949)

179

A psalm of Abraham of that which is visited upon him

A prowler in the mansion of my blood!
I have not seen him, but I know his signs.
Sometimes I hear him meddling with my food,
Or, in the cellar, poisoning my wines.

Yet face to face with him I never come;
But by a foot-print, by a book misplaced,
Or by the whorl'd impress of a thumb,
Or by the next day's meal, its metal taste,

I know that he has breached my household peace!
I know that somehow he has let him in!
Should I then run to a window, and shout *Police*!
I dare not. For I know him. My own kin.

(1941, revised)

12

A Prowler in the Mansion

I̲N THE EARLY FIFTIES, the last productive years of his life, Klein suffered a gradual mental breakdown from which he never fully recovered. By the end of the decade he had lapsed into an almost total silence, which remained unbroken until his death in 1972.

Many of Klein's later writings provide a special sort of record of the conflicts and pressures he was experiencing during the onset of his illness. Indeed, the closer one looks at these writings, the greater the psychological depths one discovers. Yet at the same time it is difficult to know whether Klein's words may be taken at face value, for at the end he was losing the ability to distinguish between the real and the imaginary. That is to say, the very pressures to which he was reacting were themselves likely to be grossly distorted in his mind, if not altogether delusional.

Premonitions of mental illness seem to occur in Klein's writings of the early forties — in his "prayer of Abraham, against madness," for example, or in the enigmatic "psalm of Abraham, of that which is visited upon him," where the sense of paranoia is heightened by a fear of some innate affliction. From the same period there is his "Portrait of the Poet as Landscape" — originally entitled "Portrait of the Poet as a Nobody" — with its ominous undercurrent of depression and inner loneliness. Here, however, Klein speaks in the third person, ostensibly not about himself but about poets in general. "Some go mystical and some go mad," but surely not he who in 1950, being interviewed for *Saturday Night* magazine, pointed to his conventional, unbohemian life as "proof of the error of the idea that to be a poet 'you must be somewhat cracked'."

It is hindsight that now accentuates these scattered clues. That Klein of all people would one day succumb to mental illness was certainly the last possibility that any of his friends or family could have imagined. His lively intelligence and robust sense of humor had always seemed the very essence of sanity.

The causes and precise nature of Klein's breakdown remain a mystery to this day. His sons, Colman and Sandor, the only surviving members of his immediate family, do retain vivid memories of their father's illness but still can only guess at its origins. Colman, who was in his middle teens at the time of the breakdown, has speculated that a variety of factors may have been involved. Apart from any unseen biological determinants that might have been operating, the most obvious antecedent, in his view, was his father's overwork and exhaustion during the early fifties. From late 1949 until the fall of 1952 Klein spent about half his time traveling and speaking all across the United States and Canada. He took very seriously the need to raise money for the fledgling State of Israel, and for a while was probably the single most popular speaker on the United Jewish Appeal circuit. In the spring of 1950, capitalizing on his success with American audiences, he joined the distinguished roster of lecturers and performing artists handled by the Jewish Center Lecture Bureau in New York. This brought him a steady stream of invitations from communities across the continent. There is every indication that he enjoyed speaking and made interesting new friends wherever he went. "It was the travel that he disliked," Colman recalled.

He missed the comforts of home, some of which he was quite fussy about. He also was leaving himself less and less time for his other work, especially his writing and above all his Joyce commentary. I think he finally just overworked himself, trying to do too many things at once. . . . After a few years of this routine he began to take sick — I think it was a self-protective mechanism, completely unconscious — he developed backaches which prevented him from going out on the road. That to me was the first sign — the beginning of a withdrawal from his self-imposed obligations.

Another factor possibly leading to the breakdown, according to Colman, was Klein's growing cynicism about the world in general. The euphoria of the early post-war years had given way rather quickly to the realization that international justice and morality were not necessarily destined to prevail after all. His election defeat in 1949 reinforced these feelings of pessimism with a sense of personal betrayal. In the end, he fell into the belief that there "must have been evil forces arrayed against him, people who wished him harm."

Colman tends to concur as well with those who speculate that Klein's wanderings into the labyrinth of *Ulysses* could have contributed to his breakdown. Here, as with every other possible explanation, it is difficult to separate the cause from the effect.

Klein had been temporarily distracted from his Joyce work by the election campaign in June 1949 and his subsequent trip to Israel. An article on the opening chapter of *Ulysses,* completed just before the campaign,

ISRAEL AND NORTH AFRICA: A report of a tour through Israel and the Jewish communities of North Africa — a dramatic record of The Thousand and One Nights of recent Jewish history.

A POETRY RECITAL: A reading from his own works, with commentary.

TEN DECISIVE EVENTS IN JEWISH HISTORY: Why we are what we are to-day.

THE POETRY OF CHAIM NACHMAN BIALIK: Illustrated with his own English translations.

THE PSALMS: A book review.

TEN GREATEST JEWS: The titans of Jewish thought and history.

JAMES JOYCE'S JEW: Why did this greatest writer of our century choose Leopold Bloom as principal protagonist in ULYSSES?

And assigned topics (Judaica, current events, or literature) by arrangement and on due notice.

A. M. KLEIN
POET—LAWYER—PUBLICIST—ORATOR

appeared in the American literary magazine *Accent* in the spring of 1950, and the notice it attracted prompted him to pick up where he had left off. By this time, however, his interest in Joyce was beginning to appear frighteningly obsessive. F. R. Scott, who accompanied him to a poetry conference at Harvard University in the summer of 1950, heard him deliver a strikingly impassioned speech at one session, in which he portrayed Joyce as a humiliated pauper and neglected genius. Sitting near Scott was the American poet and psychiatrist Merrill Moore, who remarked to him afterwards: "Your man Klein is ill, seriously ill. He wasn't talking about Joyce, he was talking about himself!"

Klein's numerous books and notes on Joyce took up a good deal of space in the private study he now had, upstairs in his home on Querbes Avenue. During one of his intense periods of research Sophie Lewis happened to visit for an afternoon.

Klein could hardly wait for our lunch to be through. He said, "You must come into my study, I want to show you something very important." Bessie and I followed him in, and there on the wall he had all sorts of maps such as are used, I suppose, in naval headquarters. Pointing very animatedly to the maps, he began explaining certain nautical allusions he had just discovered in *Ulysses*. He got so worked up after a while that I couldn't follow a single word he was saying. I just nodded and said "How marvelous!" Otherwise, the atmosphere was so tense, I think he would have actually pounced on me, whether verbally or physically.

An academic colleague, Wynne Francis, remembered going to see Klein around this period at his new law office, a strangely "gloomy and dingy" room in the generally bright and modern University Tower on St. Catherine Street.

When I entered he was sitting at his desk with an immense array of papers and books all around him. I thought to myself: I'm intruding, he's probably preparing a case. But it turned out the books were Browne's *Religio Medici* and Burton's *Anatomy of Melancholy*, and he was at work on his Joyce. Instead of attending to the business for which I had come to see him, he very enthusiastically began to show me all his discoveries for the day — he had them all underlined in red ink and was marking them down and relating them to his Joyce study. I had never realized until then the degree to which his interest in literature invaded his law office hours.

Late in 1950 Klein wrote his third and final Joyce article, an explication of the second chapter of *Ulysses,* and accepted an invitation to read it at a meeting of the James Joyce Society in New York in February 1951. The event proved to be the high point of his career as a Joycean. Leon Edel, who was in attendance, remembered it as one of the most brilliant lectures he had ever heard. Klein requested in advance that his listeners come with their copies of *Ulysses* in hand and, like a Talmud teacher, made them turn back and forth to specific pages and paragraphs, which he elucidated with beguiling cleverness and wit. The article was subsequently published in James Laughlin's *New Directions* annual for 1951.

Joyce studies, in the form of courses, dissertations, articles, and books, were just then coming into vogue on American campuses, and Klein was anxious to finish his great opus before anyone else might overtake him. In August 1951 he was immersed in the third chapter of *Ulysses* and happily reported to Laughlin that these thirteen pages in Joyce had already yielded him over a hundred pages of commentary. Just a few weeks later, however, he was distracted by the excitement of seeing his novel published, and once again left his work on *Ulysses*. From that point on he never managed to regain his momentum. Early in October 1952 he made a last fitful effort to pick up the threads of his complicated research, and even wrote to Ellsworth Mason to ask if they might resume their correspondence on Joyce, which had broken off three years earlier. But in mid-October, evidently fatigued by mounting pressures, Klein suffered a slipped disc and was immediately forced to curtail his work and cancel all travel engagements for the winter. Distressed and in low spirits, he wrote to Edel in a tone of mysterious finality: "I must tell you now that because of other plans I am putting my Joyce work aside."

In retrospect it seemed to Edel that Klein must have "tuned in to the mad side of Joyce," creating a kind of *folie à deux*. Mason, who had been his most helpful critic, finally concluded that Klein's exegetical approach had been completely misguided, depending as it did on "the ability to settle on evidence that proves one's point while ignoring evidence close by that disproves one's point."

If Klein had gone astray, it was in so idolizing Joyce that he began to treat his novel as holy writ. The interpretive method that he adopted was inspired by the classic Jewish commentaries on the Bible, where every single word must be explained and accounted for. Often the aim of such a commentary is not to provide the simple meaning of a word or phrase, but to uncover subtle and complex hidden meanings. Klein began by looking for the simple meanings but then quickly proceeded to subtler levels, forcing the elements of his text into large, predetermined schemes. Common sense and inductive reasoning count for very little in such an approach; what is needed rather is bold ingenuity and imagination.

During the fifties, more and more of Klein's thinking gradually came to display the same excesses that he had brought to his reading of Joyce. The symbolic import of even the simplest tale or event became grotesquely distorted in his mind, and like a cabalist he would ponder the secrets hidden in random signs and ordinary conversations. Finally, there remained but a short step from his over-reading of *Ulysses* to the delusions and illogical perceptions of paranoia.

KLEIN HAD ENCOUNTERED a series of difficulties and frustrations in 1952 and his forced rest probably came as a relief. One of the most disappointing episodes of his entire career was his involvement in the production of a play that had a very short, unsuccessful run on Broadway in the spring of that year. The play, performed under the title *Conscience,* was an adapted version of *The Hands of Eurydice,* the work of a Brazilian-Jewish physician and playwright, Pedro Bloch. The venerable Yiddish actor Maurice Schwartz had been on a South American tour in 1950 or 1951 when he discovered Bloch and decided to bring his play to New York. Schwartz first had the script translated from Portuguese into English by a Brazilian drama critic, and then asked Klein to revise it and make any modifications he thought appropriate for a North American audience. For his part in the venture Klein received a straight fee and was also assured a small share of the box-office take. He welcomed the opportunity to try his hand at serious script-writing and probably imagined that he was embarking on a path that would finally lead to popular recognition.

Schwartz had originally been attracted by certain theatrical aspects of Bloch's play: it employed only one character, to be acted by Schwartz himself, and it allowed for spontaneous audience participation at various points. Klein was equally fascinated by the play, but for reasons having to do more with the script itself. While working on the play he became so deeply involved in the mythological and psychological levels of the story that he failed to notice its glaring defects as a stage piece. Schwartz gradually became aware of the play's problems and expressed his concerns to Klein in February 1952, a month after receiving the revised version from him. Losing his temper, Klein accused Schwartz of failing to recognize Bloch's "insight and genius," and proceeded to defend the play in a series of revealing letters to his now reluctant collaborator.

The play is essentially a monologue in which Robert Burgess, a frustrated would-be writer, narrates and dramatizes his life story. As the scene opens, Burgess has just returned home to find his house abandoned and his family gone. It becomes apparent that Burgess had previously left home to run off with a young temptress, Eurydice, and that after becoming disenchanted he had murdered her and resolved to come back to his family. The entire play consists of Burgess's hysterical and pathetic plea in self-defense.

To Klein it was a "great Greek tragedy." He explained to Schwartz that the tragic element lay in the fact that Burgess himself was the cause of his own ruin. "He is a victim of himself.... the hell is of Burgess's own making." Though he tries to justify himself by "throwing the blame on his wife and his household menage," the audience is not fooled. Elaborating further, Klein described Burgess as a split personality, one side of him longing for the "safe domesticity of his wife," the other attracted by the "color and adventure of life with Eurydice. Between the two he becomes the broken, storm-tossed figure that we see." In particular, Klein noted, it is Burgess's manner of speaking that reveals his tragedy. For whole passages he talks "quietly, reasonably, almost ingratiatingly, and then — suddenly, because of a word, or a memory — off he goes into a tantrum of emotion."

Klein's extraordinary enthusiasm for this truly unremarkable play may have been due to a repressed sense of identification with the character of Robert Burgess. Before the final English title of the play had been settled on,

Klein approved of Schwartz's suggestion that it be named *You!* "I can see it on the billboards," he wrote enthusiastically to Schwartz, "a challenge — an invitation — an indictment — a moral lesson. For printed in that way, it tells the reader *You!*, I want to speak to you, you think this play is about me, it is also about *You*, and *You*, and *You*."

Schwartz's misgivings were ultimately confirmed. On May 15 Klein traveled to New York to attend the premiere performance at the Booth Theater. One of the many unflattering reviews of the play was delivered by Brooks Atkinson in the following morning's *New York Times*:

As the evening drags along [Mr. Schwartz] acts more and more for his private enjoyment — mumbling to himself, racing through the scenery, still talking, taking fine books off the library shelves, tearing pages out of them, pitching the books into the wings, crumpling up letters and tossing them on the stage, kneeling in the spotlight, addressing incoherent soliloquies to a bizarre bas-relief that is momentarily bathed in rosy light... by the time the play is half over, Mr. Schwartz has gone so deep into some private actor's reverie that he has closed the door on the rest of the world.

Most of the other New York critics were kinder to Schwartz and came down harder on the play itself — "a lugubrious rococo and desperately out of date charade ... hopelessly hackneyed and relentlessly purple ... accompanied by some remarkably primitive language," according to Walter Kerr in the *Herald-Tribune*.

The play closed after four performances, and the original plans to bring it to Philadelphia, Toronto, and Montreal were canceled. Back home Klein grumbled to friends about Schwartz's acting but assumed no responsibility for the graver faults of the script.

Putting this unfortunate experience behind him, he kept on pursuing a great variety of literary projects, all competing for the little time that he had left between his constant trips out of town. Among several plays that he had started writing, the only one that he managed to finish was *Worse Visitors We Shouldn't Have,* the script for a Jewish musical comedy based on the Hershel Ostropolier legend. Klein had worked his way through several drafts of this play, starting in the early forties, and was especially proud of some translations of Chassidic folk songs that he had written for it. Another play that he was working on in 1952, *The Icepick,* was to have depicted Leon Trotsky's last day, leading up to his assassination. Klein completed a rough outline and a first draft of the opening act. Yet another of his works-in-progress that spring was a musical comedy called *O Canada,* of which only a few pages of tentative ideas and lyrics have survived.

Klein's major effort in fiction during this same period was an unfinished — in fact, barely begun — historical novel, *The Golem.* Throughout the forties he had amassed a wealth of notes on the famous Jewish legend of the sixteenth-century Golem of Prague, a human creature said to have been fashioned out of the mud of the Moldau River and animated through mystic incantations by Rabbi Judah Loew. This colorful fable spoke to Klein of the awesomeness of human creativity and in particular of the power of language seemingly to bring forth life. The opening sections that he finally composed, probably around 1952, reveal glimpses of a masterful Hebraic-English prose style that he was laboring to perfect for this novel.

A major translation project that Klein had started working on in 1947 and 1948, and which he resumed with increased earnestness in 1952, was an English rendition of selected Talmudic legends and sayings, taken from the modern Hebrew compilation by Bialik and Ravnitzki, *The Book of Aggadah*. In late May 1952 he told his editor at Knopf, Herbert Weinstock, that he planned to complete the manuscript by the end of the year. "I have in mind the eventual publication of an attractive, largely-spaced book that may have a constant sale — the material is classic — as the perennial bar-mitzvah present." Weinstock responded with interest, but Klein abandoned the project in October, at about the time he suffered his slipped disc.

THE YEAR 1952 ALSO SAW a buildup of tension in another area of Klein's life — his continuing work as a hired writer and public relations consultant for Sam Bronfman. As always, this work was divided between Bronfman's two main areas of activity, Seagrams and the Canadian Jewish Congress. One of the last assignments that Klein undertook in the latter field was a full-scale history of the Canadian Jewish Congress. The idea of commissioning such a history had been bandied about the Congress in the late forties and became a serious project in 1949, in reaction mainly to Bronfman's fierce craving for glory and public acclaim on the occasion of his tenth year as president. Klein was assigned the job by Saul Hayes, the Congress's executive director. It was understood from the outset that the history was to be written on a rather grandiose scale, much in the manner that Klein was already accustomed to treating Bronfman. With occasional assistance from David Rome, the organization's press officer, Klein worked on the history in periodic spurts through 1951 and 1952. On the publication of *The Second Scroll* in the fall of 1951, expectations were raised that this next work of his would be just as moving and eloquent. Klein did in fact try his best to dramatize what was really no more than a humdrum institutional history, but the results were somehow doomed to be disappointing. Hayes and Rome read each of his successive drafts and plied him with instructions on how to correct and improve the work. Worn down by this process, Klein finally submitted his last draft late in 1952, around the time that he was convalescing at home. Hayes and Rome decided not to push the matter any further and subsequently reported to Bronfman that the manuscript was unacceptable for publication. Klein was paid for his services but his history of the Congress was shelved.

The entire affair sparked a sharp anger and resentment in Klein, as if a delicate nerve had been touched for the first time. The rejection of his manuscript at this point in his literary career must have struck him as a gross impertinence, coming from critics who ought not to have meddled and who, in his view, were unqualified to stand in judgement of his writing. In all his years of working for Sam Bronfman, he had stoically managed to tolerate the interference, as he saw it, of Bronfman's many advisors and underlings. Now such repeated assaults on his pride were at last becoming unbearable. "The

Inspection Mon 16 1952

KLEIN, SECOND FROM RIGHT, AT AN INSPECTION TOUR OF A NEW SITE FOR THE JEWISH PUBLIC LIBRARY.

lot of the artist in contemporary society is not a happy one," he remarked in an editorial in April 1953.

If he caters to what his audiences expect from him, he is thereby deemed to be no artist, but a mere graphologist in public relations; if he sticks to his bent and paints as his own mind conceives and his own eye sees, he is dubbed peculiar, erratic, even surrealist. When, moreover, the artist labors to please an audience that is itself divided in taste, he is well on the way to developing a case of multiple fragmented schizophrenia.

To what degree Klein's personal relationship with Bronfman may have contributed to the tension is difficult to determine. It seemed clear that their warm feelings of friendship for each other were as strong as ever. Yet to certain close acquaintances Klein spoke of his work for Bronfman with increasing bitterness. Despite his quite respectable earnings during the early fifties and the growing potential of his law practice, he still claimed that he needed the extra income.

The actual chores that he regularly performed for Bronfman were simple in themselves. The speeches to be delivered at Congress gatherings and Seagrams meetings were fairly standardized by this point. Somewhat more interesting were the feature essays that he wrote anonymously for several of the lavish annual reports issued by Seagrams in the fifties. Klein was also called upon to read and criticize the drafts of several books that had been commissioned by Seagrams during this period.

Whenever a private working session was called for, Bronfman would send his chauffeur to pick Klein up and bring him to the family mansion in Westmount. These occasional evening meetings were pleasant and relaxed. Klein normally did not care for liquor of any kind, but could not refuse the head of Seagrams. He was a much-liked guest in the household and came to know some of the family members quite well. It was probably no secret among them that Klein authored many of the rhymed birthday and anniversary greetings that they received from Sam Bronfman.

Beneath the superficial affability, however, Klein must have felt a certain uneasiness. For many years, especially through the forties, there had been the strange and sometimes embarrassing incongruity of a prominent poet and CCF socialist associating with a business mogul. To most onlookers, Klein never seemed able to reconcile these contradictory images.

In addition, the consulting work that he did for Seagrams brought him into contact with other advertising and public relations professionals, and there were times when he seemed to fear the prospect of finding himself reduced to their level. "Some of our most distinguished starving poets," he observed in 1941, "have at last found their daily bread in the large advertising agencies." In 1949 he tried to establish his own consulting firm, called "Your Copy," whose service would have been to analyze advertisements — "psychologize" them, as his brochure stated it — and thus warn clients of any undesirable "associative ambiguities" that might detract from the intended effect. The venture evidently foundered at the outset. In a sardonic essay in the *Chronicle* that year he described the advertising copywriter as a "usurper" of the poet's role in modern society.

The vanishing poet: where has he gone to? ... the most unlikely of places. Who would have thought to look for him on the exchange, in a mart, in a marketplace? ... For the vanished poet was now in an advertising agency, a copywriter!

It was, as we have said, to be expected. Hitherto he had dealt in words, but profitlessly, and without fame; what more natural than that he should forsake the milieu of his futility to move into a sphere where words, though issued anonymously, at least were rewarded with coin of the realm — and much of it ...

Thus did we find him, the mislaid poet.

In the final analysis, it was Klein's personal affinity towards Bronfman that must have outweighed the negative aspects of the job. David Rome, who

from Speech for Seagrams Meeting

Ladies and gentlemen:

I would like to speak to you this evening not about the isolated details of our own business, but about Industry as a whole, about Industry as one of the great civilizing factors of the world we live in.

I think it can safely be said that the progress to which we have attained in our way of life has been due in large measure to the vision and energy of businessmen throughout the ages.

Every time a human need has somewhere arisen, always somewhere there arose a businessman who made the satisfaction of that need his personal challenge. The history of commerce is the history of the successful acceptance of these challenges and the graph of progress is the graph charted by the constantly-improved standard of living thus made possible. The artisan of today, it cannot be denied, commands a better diet and more comforts than the feudal lord of three centuries ago.

I do not wish to exaggerate, but I am convinced that the mighty Pharaohs would have been delighted with a frigidaire, and Louis the Fourteenth thrilled with a television set.

Not only has trade, by making higher living standards possible, given vertical height to our civilization; it has also widened our view horizontally: our very continent owes its discovery to the search of a new trade-route....

As I speak of the ideal of Business, I do not wish to appear to be making an idol out of business. Into Industry, from realms beyond the boundaries of commerce, there enter those high precepts, those cherished values which are the very basis of our life. Man does not live by bread alone; but the value which he places upon that bread — whether he considers it the full meaning of life, or only a means toward higher appreciations, loftier reaches — is itself a revelation of his intellectual and religious outlook. Systems based upon a materialist conception of things consider that bread the be-all and end-all of existence. Our way of life, too, places importance upon the creature comforts, but considers them always as not exhausting the catalogue of comforts the Creator has bestowed.

It is because behind the routine operations of Industry there operate the laws of social obligation that I was prompted to state, in my preface to Dr. Stephen Leacock's *History of Canada*, that "the horizon of Industry does not terminate with the boundaries of its plants." It does, indeed, embrace the entire panorama of the society in which it lives and has its being. As a result its duties are many and its achievement by no means fully expressed by its balance-sheet....

To what does the fulfillment of these duties add up? It adds up to the creation by Industry of a large, yet intimate family, made up of Shareholder and Consumer, Management and Organization, Distributor and Retailer, each devoted to the entire operation, the entire operation redounding to the advantage of each, and constituting all together, now kith and kin, one of Industry's leading families....

written for Sam Bronfman (July 1950)

had been able to observe them together over a long period, reflected on the strength and complexity of their relationship:

It was a remarkable conjuncture of two very strong characters. Klein's imperial rhetoric harmonized with Bronfman's imperial position. At the same time, it was a rather delicate situation to have this already established and advanced poet spending much energy and time in anonymous hackwork that was to appear over the signature of another person. Bronfman was, I think, remarkably understanding and considerate of Klein in this situation.

Occasionally, noticing them in private conversation, I could sense an almost brotherly affection. It was an intimate and yet, after all, rather unequal relationship, which can be hard on both sides and can create peculiar tensions. I remember Klein speaking to me once about Sam Bronfman as a great and creative person. As he spoke I felt there was a confusion of identities, and I wasn't always sure when I was listening to Klein on Bronfman and when I was listening to Klein on Klein.

Working for the big organization men in the Jewish community, Klein found himself close to people of great weight and influence, aggressive people — and Klein wasn't a man to duck, he could be aggressive himself, especially with such people. Being subject to their personalities, including Bronfman's meaningful presence and weightiness, imposed a burden on him which an ivory-tower poet would not have had. Klein avoided hermitry. He could have had another life, as a poet and academic, but he was too, too much of the world.

Klein's dependence on Bronfman may, on a certain level, have afforded him the opportunity to act out vicariously the public and popular roles he had hoped to achieve in his own career. By the same token, though, was not Bronfman one of those very usurpers of the poet's identity that Klein had hinted at in his "Portrait of the Poet as a Nobody"?

> He thinks an impostor, having studied his personal biography,
> his gestures, his moods, now has come forward to pose
> in the shivering vacuums his absence leaves....
>
> Is it the local tycoon who for a hobby
> plays poet, he so epical in steel?
> The orator, making a pause?...
>
>   ... O lost impostor'd pride,
> it is another, another, whoever he is,
> who rides where he should ride.

DURING THE ONSET of his mental illness, Klein's frustrations as a writer, and above all his feelings of neglect and failure at winning wide public recognition, evolved into a morbid belief that all true artists are persecuted by those nearest them. This theme began to emerge in his writings as early as 1951, in an obituary for the Montreal-Jewish painter Alexander Bercovitch, who had collapsed and died in the street while on the way to attend the opening of his own one-man exhibition. What upset Klein terribly was that even as Bercovitch lay dead in the very heart of the Jewish district, none of the passers-by recognized the artist — his body had to be identified later at the city morgue. The incident bore ominous meaning to Klein. "What a parable we have here of the lot of the god-gifted man, creator of images! At the very moment when the audacity of his creativeness is about to be rewarded, the laurels by the jealous gods are snatched from him! And when he perishes, he perishes in the midst of the people, unknown and unrecognized!"

Klein's frightening, full-blown vision of the persecuted artist revealed itself most starkly in an essay he published in 1953 entitled "The Bible's Archetypical Poet." Following the same midrashic methods he had applied to Joyce, and no doubt influenced by Thomas Mann's *Joseph and His Brothers*, he read into the biblical tale an allegory on the fate of all poets in every generation. Klein's personal sense of identification with the character of Joseph probably ran deep — he too was the favorite child, the son of his parents' old age. Joseph's coat of many colors he took to be a symbol of the poetic imagination. Joseph is a dreamer; the dreamer is the poet. Seemingly arrogant and out of touch with things and with people, he is in reality the greatest lover of his brethren. This love, however, is returned by envy and malice. "And what they particularly abominate are those cursed dreams of his: How he preens himself on his imaginings; how he struts about after every inspired visitation! ... they resented even more the implication that upon the head of Joseph there rested some special kind of grace. They hated him."

Joseph's brothers conspire at first to murder him. In the end his life is spared, but he is stripped of his coat ("Now let it be seen how gloriously arrayed this poet is!") and flung into a pit ("he who in his mind had elevated himself to the highest of the sun and the moon now lay lower than the level of the earth"). Each stage of Joseph's downfall is symbolic in Klein's reading. "Him they leave in the pit, without water; themselves they sit down to eat bread. That bread tastes good — it is seasoned with revenge." Joseph is finally sold into slavery to a passing company of Ishmeelites. "To the motive of revenge," Klein acidly notes, "there is now added the motive of profit — the poet destroyed may yet be used."

The entire story, according to Klein, reveals the classic design of the relationship between the poet and his fellows. "It is a design which repeats itself down through the ages," he writes, "a design which, beginning with misunderstanding and envy, moves on towards conspiracy, suggests, at first, a mere humiliating of its victim, then, feeding upon its own thoughts, soon clamors for revenge, and thus, by its own clamorous blood encompassed, broods on the ultimate: murder."

Klein tried to draw some consolation from the tale's conclusion — Joseph's reunion with his brothers. "Joseph has suffered his trials and agonies. ... He has learned humility, not only with regard to his brothers, but also with regard to himself ... He has, despite antipathy, come to a closer understanding of his brothers." The ultimate reconciliation between the poet and his people is symbolized for Klein in the blessing bestowed on Joseph by his dying father Jacob: *Joseph is a fruitful bough, even a fruitful bough by a well; whose branches run over the wall.* Klein interprets:

Not isolated, not alone, not altogether self-sustained does the poet live; he lives hard by a refreshing and ever-renewed source of water; he lives and labors within a tradition .... Thus Jacob enjoins his favorite son from sundering himself from his brothers, themselves, in their way, the makers of a tradition. The bough is fruitful only near the well; removed therefrom, it thirsts, is parched, one withers away.

But to rest within a tradition, to remain content thereby, and not to seek to bring to it originality and innovation — this, too, would be a denial of the poet's devotion. ... The true poet is he who, nourished upon the ancestral heritage, yet — if only in the slightest — deviates therefrom. Rooted in the common soil, he turns his eyes to new directions. He is, indeed, a fruitful bough; he springs from earth fed secretly by a well, but his branches run over the wall. Thus are the ideas of convention and revolt, of tradition and innovation, conjured up in the single image of Jacob's benediction.

Here, as in many of his last writings, Klein's view is dialectical. The poet is not completely bound to his people, nor is he altogether sundered from them. He is poised, sometimes torn, between the two extremes, and out of this tension arises his creativity and the uniqueness of his art.

Now in his early forties, Klein was approaching the fullness of his literary powers during the very years that he was beginning to lose his hold on reality. His weekly columns for the *Canadian Jewish Chronicle,* which after almost fifteen years should have begun to sound wearily prosaic, still often sparkled with mordant wit. His editorials were edged at times with bitter pessimism, as he observed the resurgence of totalitarianism, the precarious situation of the State of Israel, brazen anti-Semitism in Soviet Europe, and the ever-present threat of an atomic holocaust. His dark mood was mirrored in a series of poems, mainly from the early forties, that he selected to reprint in the *Chronicle* in 1952 and 1953. Anxiety, despair, death, and the destruction of civilization were the recurring motifs of his selections; it was as if he were somehow reliving the nightmarish war years in which these poems had their origin.

Klein had virtually stopped writing poetry after the publication of *The Rocking Chair* in 1948. In 1951, when Lorne Pierce of the Ryerson Press invited him to submit a new manuscript, he replied that he hadn't enough material for another volume of poems and that he was confining himself largely to prose. Klein was pleased with the success of *The Rocking Chair* and may have felt no further inclination at the time to prove himself as a poet. Besides, the audience for poetry was too small ever to afford him the degree of recognition he was still seeking.

While he was not writing many new poems, Klein continually went back to his old ones, revising lines, rearranging sections, and weeding out the worst of his early work. It was thus that he began to form in his mind the outline for a volume of *Selected Poems*. The manuscript of thirty-nine poems that he finally gathered together, probably in the spring of 1954, would have been his last collection of verse, but was never published.

The work that Klein put into assembling his *Selected Poems* was clearly not in the writing — of the six unpublished pieces in the manuscript, two at most may have been written later than *The Rocking Chair.* His creative effort went rather into forming a complex symphonic pattern of poems that would, in its total effect, summarize his life and his vision of reality.

The formal key to the *Selected Poems* is the idea of the dialectic, the eternal cyclical progression from thesis to antithesis to synthesis. Klein's interest in this notion can be traced back to his reading of Karl Marx in the thirties — in fact, this seemed to be the only intellectual nugget that he ever cared to extract from communist theory. Later, working on Joyce, he became similarly engrossed in the cyclical theory of history expounded by the eighteenth-century Italian philosopher Giambattista Vico. Dialectical theories such as those of Marx and Vico confirmed on an abstract level Klein's intuitive belief in the eternal recurrence of ancient historical designs as well as his tragic sense of the contradictoriness of human experience.

It is the dialectic of personal life, and of his own life in particular, that concerns Klein in the *Selected Poems*. The collection is framed by two crucial poems, one an evocation of the poet's childhood and the other a portrait of the mature poet. As if to emphasize the circular interplay of these stages, "Portrait of the Poet as Landscape" is placed first in the collection and "Autobiographical" is placed last. Between these poles Klein presents the crucial moments and elements of his life.

Opening the cycle is a group of early Jewish poems meant to portray the culture he grew up in as a child. Even within the grouping there is a chronology: the fairy-tale world of boyhood ("Bestiary"), the market, whither he accompanied his mother ("Market Song"), the Talmud Torah ("Reb Simcha"), and the wedding canopy ("A Benediction"). There follow several transitional poems, leading up to "Basic English," an allusion to the English language which, after Jewish culture, is the second element in the triad of influences that shaped his character. The third of these influences is the French Canadian milieu, represented next by a selection of seven poems

Sestina on the Dialectic

Yes yeasts to No, and No is numinous with Yes. All is a hap, a haze, a hazard, a do-doubtful, a flight from, a travel to. Nothing will keep, but eases essence, — out! — outplots its plight. So westers east, and so each teaches an opposite: a nonce-thing still.

A law? Fact or flaw of the fiat, still — a law. It binds us, braided, wicker and withe. It stirs the seasons, it treads the tides, it so rests in our life there's nothing, there's not a sole thing that from its workings will not out.

The antics of the antonyms! From, to; stress, slack and stress, — a rhythm running to a reason, a double dance, a shivering still.

Even the heart's blood bursting in, bales out, an ebb and flow; and even the circuit within which its pulsebeat's beam — man's morse — is a something that grows, that grounds — treks, totters. So.

O dynasties and dominions downfall so! Flourish to flag and fail, are potent to a pause, a panic precipice, to a picked pit, and thence — rubble rebuilding, still rise resurrective, — and now see them, with new doers in dominion!

They, too, dim out.

World's sudden with somersault, updown, inout, overandunder. And, note well: also that other world, the two-chambered mind, goes with it, ever kaleidoscopic, one scape to another, suffering change that changes still, that focusses and fissions *the* to *a*.

When will there be arrest? Consensus? A marriage of the antipathies, and out of the vibrant deaths and rattles the life still? O just as the racked one hopes his ransom, so I hope it, name it, image it, the together-living, the together-with, the final synthesis. A stop.

But so it never will turn out, returning to the rack within, without. And no thing's still.

(1946)

from *The Rocking Chair*. The subsequent four poems bring us to the central historical experience of Klein's life, the destruction of European Jewry. From here the mood darkens: evil and death are man's fate. Only towards the end of the collection is the overwhelming sense of despair alleviated by a philosophical acceptance of the duality of human nature; man is part-animal, but also part-angel; he is composed of both matter and spirit.

Herein lies the great mystery of life for Klein — the coexistence of the mundane and the sublime. This strongly Judaic theme has its overture in the second poem of the collection, "Bread." Klein explained the symbolic significance this poem had for him when he introduced it as the keynote piece at a public reading in 1955:

"Bread" is concerned with a subject that binds all humanity together; it is a basic thing... humanity is concerned with basic things, with elementary things.... We are not angels; we must subsist upon matter; no one can exist without bread. This is our Achilles' heel. Those of us who would like to rise and mount and soar into the high altitudes empyrean and think of ourselves not only as lesser but almost close to the angels, always are brought back by this basic element, the element of our humanity, of our necessity to lean one upon the other.

Throughout the entire collection Klein swings constantly from hope and celebration, to anger and despair, and then back again. It is the movement of the pendulum, or of the rocking chair. The two penultimate poems, taken from the dark psalms of 1940, carry a sense of near-defeat and confusion, at which point the circle is closed with the serene nostalgia of "Autobiographical."

Similar themes run through Klein's last work of fiction, an unpublished novella entitled *The Bells of Sobor Spasitula*, which he completed in 1954. *The Bells* is cast in the form of a memoir set in Moscow around the time of the Bolshevik revolution. The narrator, Arkady Mikailovich, recalls his acquaintance with Vladimir Sergeivich Terpetoff, a celebrated composer of the pre-revolutionary period.

Reduced to its bare outline, Klein's tale is a simple one. Before the revolution, Terpetoff's new *Opus 13* is rehearsed in the presence of a small group of friends, among them the orchestra conductor Strynenko, who interprets the piece in Christian terms and renames it *Prelude to the Dormition of the Little Mother*. After the revolution, Terpetoff refuses to produce the Marxist program music demanded of him by the authorities. His friends finally persuade him to make a show of compliance, and he pretends to write his new *Overture Proletarian*, which in reality is nothing other than his old *Opus 13*. After the work has been performed and praised as a revolutionary masterpiece, the commissar of culture learns of how he has been duped. Terpetoff is threatened with blackmail and given one last chance to produce a composition "for the people." In defiance he breaks into the bell tower of the shut Cathedral of the Savior (*Sobor Spasitula*) and sounds the forbidden bells until he is silenced by rifle fire.

On a simple level the story deals with the conflict between the artist and political authority. Klein all his life had ridiculed Marxist attitudes to art.

His scorn turned to abhorrence in the early fifties when he read of Stalin's purges of Jewish writers in the Soviet Union.

But *The Bells* is also concerned with deeper philosophical issues. Terpetoff personifies, in part, the striving of the artist towards absolute purity in his work, exemplified by his indifference to programmatic, descriptive music, whether Christian or Marxist. At the same time Terpetoff is a complex, ironic individual, fully aware of the paradoxes in his life. "All my altitudes have no meaning without those depths," he tells Arkady Mikailovich.

It is just because of the depths that the altitudes are high.... Angels are the least worthy of God's creatures. They do not crawl, they need not climb, they only fly. But man can know both, both depth and height. He must know the depths, that's the way he's born, but height is not inaccessible. And the height has meaning only because of the depth, the ethereal only in relation to the palpable.

The cosmic duality of the earthly and the heavenly, the material and the spiritual, is reflected within Terpetoff's own soul. While he is, on the one hand, attracted to pure art and platonic love affairs, he draws his greatest inspiration from clandestine trips to the Russian countryside, living with the peasants and collecting their folk melodies.

Through Terpetoff's character Klein was probably alluding to his own dilemma as an artist, for he too felt torn between his attraction to the freedom of art and his basic dependence on and responsibility towards his folk. Terpetoff's reluctant submission to the political regime has its parallel in Klein's various forms of professional servitude, which clearly grew more and more oppressive to him in the early fifties. If the identification between author and hero went still deeper, then Terpetoff's glorious self-immolation may have been Klein's own last cry of despair.

Les Vespasiennes

Dropped privily below the crotch of squares —
its architecture is like the sets in dreams:
the wide slow staircase...the unknown loiterers...
the floor that would be counted...the mirrors' gleams
dancing with daffodils...and before their white niches
all effigies reversed:
precisely that mise-en-scène, that whiteness which
is seen as having been in dreams seen first:

an anxiety dream where fallen seraphims,
maimed by metabolism, like children of men,
do get their leeching, and rise above their limbs,
and think themselves the angels once again:
and thus, standing in that dream, I and its persons
know at the chemical core,
at the bubbling self, that which was built on and known
even by Vespasian the Emperor,

namely: that we are not God. Not God. Why, not,
not even angels, but something less than men,
creatures, sicknesses, whose pornoglot
identities swim up within our ken
from the *graffiti* behind the amputate door, —
(the wishful drawing and rhyme!)
creatures — the homo, the pervert, the voyeur,
all who grasp love and catch at pantomime.

See how they linger here, while the normal (Who?)
climb up from the subterranean dantesque
into the public square, the shine, the blue,
and don again their feathers and the mask
angelic, and are 'valiant again to cope
with all high enterprise
of true pure love and sweet spiritual hope,'
as if no privies were and only Paradise!

(late 1940s)

from THE GOLEM

Klein's fragment of a novel, The Golem, *is narrated by Sinai ben Issachar, scribe and secretary to Rabbi Judah Loew, the creator of the Golem. Sinai opens his account by telling his own life story, beginning with his youth in Venice.*

Though it was in the ghetto of Cuneo, inland, at the other side of the peninsula, that I first saw the light of day, Venice, whither my father had removed, was to me, from my second year on, the world and all its water. It was as if my father had brought me to some complicated toy, some glittering construct, gift of a mariner, tied in a ribbon of silver. Here, the years of my childhood, like some iridescence of blown glass, had tumbled and preened themselves beneath the changing sun. Here, when young, I sat by the wharf of the *Giudecca,* and Venice was a cloud of wonder, a city builded out of foam, pillar'd of shafts of sunlight — a shimmering vision resting half in the insubstantial air and half in the wavering water.

For hours I watched its horizons, entranced, as if they themselves were made of painted sail. Here, I dreamed conjurations of far-off places; and, because I learned Venice while I learned my Bible, these dreams seemed always to float down the reaches of the sea always to settle at last over the hills of Palestine.

It was a city out of the Scriptures, this Venice, a commentary on all that in the Scriptures pertains to the sea; it evoked for me, as I watched the unburdening of the strange cargoes of its galleasses, the apes and peacocks of Holy Writ; its mighty traffic and great navigation, its captains and its pilots, its mariners, its caulkers, its hustle and bustle — this was Tyre restored again; Venice made even the thirty-ninth of Job, that gloomy writer than whom none knew better the ways of waves and water-courses or the pitchings and rollings of leviathan, or the sweet influence of the Pleiades, it made even those whirlwind verses things local, known, diurnal. I sat by the Grand Canal and it was as that first river that comes out of Eden to compass a land of bdellium and onyx.

Once when I got lost on the Rialto, I caught a glimpse of the Doge, his brocaded robes covering, I was sure, his tail and hooves, his hood suppressing horns, and I thought that parchment face the face of Asmodeus who, with Solomon's seal, had brought into being these castles on these streams. The multitudinous and variegated hues of this maritime fabric dazzled me, and I imagined that Noah's rainbow had been drawn down from the heavens and carved into a city. Wonderful were the mounting coruscating facades of the Venice of my boyhood — I thought some Joshua had blown resurgent trumpets to raise by the sea the walls of this Jericho. And often I suspected that this city was no city at all, but a sorcery, a spell cast upon the waters which some sudden storm would one day shatter.

I moved through these years of my life, happy, without care, every day rich with weather. Nor did I breathe my days empty away, for soon, having acquired the Pentateuch and the Prophets, I was advanced to the study of Talmud. Venice is a metropolis of learning — are they not treasured abroad, the sacred books marked *Printed in Venezia the Renowned?* — and my father set me at the feet of rabbis the most learned. The Talmud, my father maintained, was the true discourse of our tradition, and, punctilio and proviso, it had been to us an investiture stronger than armor. Its was a lore, moreover, which had also uses profane; for it exercised the mind, and made one sharp. The tractates touching monetary transactions, *The Three Great Gates,* these he especially held to be of a proper apprenticing to business, for they taught one the custom of trade, helped in the interpretation of contracts, and, as commented upon by scholars, rendered one perspicacious to perceive trickery ere yet it was planned. They aided one towards the resolution of ambiguity; they gave one skill to forestall evasion. My father would go on in this way, belauding the shrewdness of the masters of the Talmud, men who, though dedicate to pursuits holy, lost not ever their touch with merchantry.

I betook myself to these studies with zeal and pride. At the same time I attended every day for several hours at my father's manufactory — he was a weaver of silks, employing about forty men of the craft, spinners, throwsters, dyers — and over those years, too, there shines the sheer and shimmer of my youth. I kept my father's ledgers, I conducted, that is to say, I penned, for I wrote a fine hand, his correspondence with our factors and merchants of the Levant; sometimes I oversaw the shuttling of our weavers. But they were the silkworms, in their well-lit rearing chambers, who were my constant delight.

Composers of delicate distich, they were my first *payttanim,* these silkworms. Gilgul and metamorphosis of the winged moth, in the orchards on the mainland, on the leaf of the mulberry, we fed them, coupling thus the earthy and the aerial; we watched their hatchings; we measured their changes; and when, in the fullness of time, their little heads, as each fashioned its cocoon, its stanza, began to whirl, and whirl unceasingly for three days, we uttered benediction. These were, indeed, vermicules of the true inspiration! From the head and inward they wrought; the memory of their several transmigrations entered into their reelings, as with the floss and blaze of filament they breathed forth the raiment of a princess. Then they perished. Like small pharaohs in their sheathes they lay there, until our skilled men, like pious priests, disrobed them, twisting and reeling and weaving and dying the spool of their mummification into something bright and quick.

From these labors we won our sustenance; by God's grace our lives were stablished upon the thread of a worm.

Thus I divided my days between my studies of the Talmud and my duties of commerce. My teachers were the erudites Azriel Bassolo, Hezekiah Galico, and Samuel Archevolto, pedagogues who greatly affected that manner of Talmudic explication which is known, for that it is pepper-sharp, as pilpul. Years later, as increased my appetency towards solid doctrine, I learned to scorn this juggling of sophistries, this tossing about of the quillets and quiddities of our Law, but then I followed in wonder the prestidigitations with which my Masters halved a hair, or brought together in casuistical connexity a passage out of the treatise *Betrothals* with a passage in the treatise *Stripes,* or elenchized into verity a palpable absurd.

My teacher Samuel Archevolto was particularly agile in the formulation of such amazements. Again and again he would take, for my pleasure and the honing of his wit, four far-flung ordinances, each hidden either in a piece of commentary or a Tosfoth, and would found them, like four cornerstones, for the erection of some ingenious syllogistical structure; then he would build, with forced parallels and subtle divagations, story upon specious story, the last topped with two towers of dilemma, and the whole tipped, triangled, and crowned with some conclusion, earlier announced, and now rendered irrefutable: in wonder would I gape at this perfection; then would my teacher, adding virtuosity to virtuosity, point out the fallacy, Here lies a fallacy: with a twist of reason he would withdraw, then, one of the buttresses of our palace of logic: down would it tumble, myself astonished again; whereupon he would add, smiling: But here is the flaw which pronounced our argument fallacious: and back flew the buttress; the structure once more stood. Invariably these illusions of rationality wrung a tribute from me; they also succeeded in sowing in my mind, then unaware of the bursting seed, what was later to grow both thorn and rose, a scepticism of the speculations of reason itself....

My studies, moreover, bore yet other fruit, for it was through them that I fell in and became fast friends with Leon da Modena, that sweet plant now grown to a wry culture. We attended upon the same learned instructors and our companionship left upon my mind, whether for good or for evil, indelible imprints....

My admiration of him was so great, in fact, that though I have learned to reject his manner of life as a whole, many of his notions, I fear, still oft-times trouble me. He it was who introduced me to the erotic poetry of Immanuel of Rome; through him I made acquaintance with many gentiles and their ways; we exchanged confidence one with the other; we clinked canakins together; poetry, the world, wine — these were ours, and, over all, that intoxicating foam, Doubt, wherein the imps of enzyme are always at their revels. Today, because of what I learned at Prague, I repudiate, I renounce, I abjure those empty and arrogant delights; they were wind, they were vanity; they were shadows that feign to have color but are only darkness. Still, often when I suspect them least, when I nod, when I slide back to juvenescence, up they come, here they are, the fatuities of my youth. They set an ambush for righteousness, they hang chainlets on the tongue, they crop out in the very midst of piety.

The curiosity and pride of youth — they are vices to make miserable old age. What subjects did we not descant upon in those palmy days — the wicked theories propounded by Machiavelli for the governance of polity and people; the lecherous writings of Pietro Aretino; what makes for beauty in a woman; why the circle is the ideal form; how the people of the earth, when their tongues were confounded, continued the construction of the Tower of Babel with gesture; of concoctions to be made out of manna; of how King Solomon remembered the names and persons of his concubines; of the devices Samson used to reduce his potency, seeing, as the Talmud avers, that his every issue floated both bed and bride away; of the moon and of how it effects neap and high tide in the inlets of the heart; of these matters and of a thousand other themes biblic, talmudic, midrashic; and always, but in especial when our spirits were exalted with wine, would we return to youth's major and most orgulous preoccupation, the search for perfection.... O, life was for us at its burgeoning best, and all things, the virtues and the vices, were objects for our inquiry, toys for the mind, trifles to be juggled on air, while we stood by, ourselves abiding firm....

(early 1950s)

203

A COPPER ANGEL ATOP THE CHURCH OF NOTRE DAME DE BONSECOURS IN OLD MONTREAL LOOKS OUT OVER THE HARBOR.

from Portrait of the Poet as Landscape

And now in imagination he has climbed
another planet, the better to look
with single camera view upon this earth —
its total scope, and each afflated tick,
its talk, its trick, its tracklessness — and this,
this he would like to write down in a book!

To find a new function for the declassé craft
archaic like the fletcher's; to make a new thing;
to say the word that will become sixth sense;
perhaps by necessity and indirection bring
new forms to life, anonymously, new creeds—
O, somehow pay back the daily larcenies of the lung!

These are not mean ambitions. It is already something
merely to entertain them. Meanwhile, he
makes of his status as zero a rich garland,
a halo of his anonymity,
and lives alone, and in his secret shines
like phosphorus. At the bottom of the sea.

(1945)

204

13

In That Drowning Instant

FROM AS EARLY AS 1952, Klein's increasingly irrational suspicions and unprovoked bouts of anger had been poisoning many of his social and professional relationships. His relative seclusion while convalescing in 1953 may have minimized the opportunities for such clashes but did not alter his disposition. Emotional flare-ups persisted at home and were beginning to have a traumatic effect on his family.

Klein's condition entered a critical phase in the spring of 1954 when he tried on several occasions to commit suicide. By this time, according to Colman's recollections, he was already visiting a psychiatrist and had begun to receive electroshock therapy. In mid-July, following what was to be his last suicide attempt, he was committed to a psychiatric hospital in the Montreal suburb of Verdun. He returned home in late September, but continued to undergo shock therapy for a while longer as an outpatient at the Jewish General Hospital. Following each of these sessions he showed the normal signs of extreme fatigue.

There were evidently very few people with whom he was willing to talk openly about his illness. In an unusually frank conversation with one friend, probably not long after his return from hospital, he spoke of the entire experience as of a passage through a terrible nightmare. He feared its recurrence, and seemed quietly and sadly resigned to the idea that a full recovery was unlikely.

He did, at first, make an effort to resume his former life, but with a fitful eagerness that seemed almost desperate. Through the Jewish Center Lecture Bureau in New York he set up a series of speaking engagements for the winter. In November he began planning an ambitious trip to Europe with Bessie. According to his notes, he was contemplating an itinerary that encompassed London, Paris, Amsterdam, Prague, Zurich, Rome, Venice, Trieste, Athens, Istanbul, Tel Aviv, Madrid, and Lisbon. A number of these

PASSPORT PHOTOS OF KLEIN AND HIS WIFE, LATE 1954.

places had to do with his research for *The Golem*; some of the others were cities Joyce had lived in. Hoping also to obtain entry to some Arab states on the way, he applied for a separate set of passports which would not bear the stamp of an Israeli visa. However, by the time the passports arrived in January 1955, he had already called off the entire trip. In late February he wrote wistfully to his friend Melech Ravitch, then sojourning in Tel Aviv: "As for my own next visit to Israel, I dream of it but I don't know when it will take place."

This reversal seemed to mark the beginning of Klein's steady and deliberate withdrawal from all public activity. Through 1955 he was careful to limit his obligations. In June he gave up his editorship of the *Canadian Jewish Chronicle*. He delivered only a few out-of-town lectures, and two poetry readings — one in May at the "Y" Poetry Center in New York, and another in November at McGill University. The reading at McGill drew a large crowd, including several of Klein's old colleagues from *Preview* and *First Statement*, who had been concerned about him and were happy to see his apparent return to health. Layton, Dudek, and a small group of other friends and students took Klein and Bessie out to a Bleury Street café afterwards to celebrate the event. Klein was in relatively good spirits that evening, but as things turned out, it was to be his last public reading.

He apparently wrote very little after his hospitalization. The last few dated manuscripts of poems and verse translations that have survived among his papers are from the summer of 1955. Towards the end of the year he

206

applied some final touches to his *Selected Poems* and his novella *The Bells of Sobor Spasitula* and submitted them to his editor at Knopf, Herbert Weinstock. Around the same time he sent a copy of his play, *Worse Visitors We Shouldn't Have*, to the New York theater director and critic Harold Clurman, whose interest in Jewish drama was well known. In January 1956 he received a polite letter of rejection from Weinstock. The play drew no reaction at all from Clurman. Discouraged by these rebuffs, Klein subsequently shied away from the approaches of any other publishers.

In March 1956, without even a hint of warning, he announced to his law partners that he was leaving his practice and resigning from the Bar immediately. That same day, he packed all his files and brought them home, to the shocked dismay of his family. Refusing to reconsider his decision, he permanently abandoned his last important connection with the world of affairs. From then on, his only official occupation was that of public relations consultant to Seagrams, and through the late fifties he continued working on several company projects.

His last public lecture, on the poetry of Hopkins, was given in October 1956 at Assumption College in Windsor, Ontario. In June 1957 he was absent from the ceremony in Ottawa at which he was awarded the Lorne Pierce medal by the Royal Society of Canada for his contribution to Canadian literature. Later that summer Pierce wrote to him to say that the Ryerson Press was interested in bringing out an edition of his collected or selected poems. Without mentioning the manuscript he had already prepared, Klein answered as graciously as he could that he was not quite ready: "There are so many things to consider — selection of poems, my obligations to my other publishers, addition of unpublished work, etc. — I shall certainly be thinking of your suggestion, and, should I find the project possible, shall write to you." Pierce never heard from him again.

Klein was now becoming more and more of a recluse. Most of the time he shut himself in his study upstairs. He continued to read, but evidently wrote nothing apart from the occasional speech for Bronfman. Whatever else he may have written he destroyed. He retained a great number of his early manuscripts in his file cabinet, but apparently threw out his voluminous notes on Joyce. His study was his private sanctum and whatever he was working on remained hidden from view. If Bessie or one of the children would knock at the door, he would hastily clear his desk and push away any books or papers he might have been handling.

AS THE YEARS PASSED, fewer and fewer visitors outside the family were able to see him. Sometimes an old literary friend would phone and ask permission to come by. Of the Montreal poets, Layton remained the closest, though as he later recalled:

June 1, 1955:

And, cornucopic, the unfathomable horn
It's musk of plenty toxic on the air.

        *   *   *

The nulls and zeros of the daylong hours
The wild laocöon cauchemar of the night.

July 28, 1955:

This globe, this world, this onion of humanity!
Unsheathe it, sheath by sheath
      mask after mask —
even the core is unsheathable! —
      pungency, bitterness, tears!

How was I to know, those months in my mother's womb,
that exit meant ambush?

July 29, 1955:

O tribune, tribune manqué, passed over in favor
of an unworthier one,
bear up, hold fast, political success
is a course in the callousing of disappointments.

After Abe's breakdown, communication became infrequent. It was diffidence on my part, shyness about intruding on what I felt was a personal tragedy. His friendliness towards me never altered, but I did detect an increasing irascibility in his demeanor. With the world and himself as much as anything. A sort of querulousness had crept into his voice and manner, an abruptness. But he was still capable of flashes of wit, though the timing and lambency were somewhat off. The topics were the familiar ones of politics, books, and gossip.

In his effort to understand Klein's illness, Layton fell back on some of his earliest impressions of the man. Klein, in his view, had never been able to face up to the evil realities of twentieth-century existence. In the end, "he found that modern life, Jewish or Gentile, could not support the spirit, the soul. Today there is a destructive element — a poison in the atmosphere — making it difficult for the writer to sustain himself, find nourishment ... the very

Jewish community he extolled and celebrated no longer gave him spiritual nourishment."

Layton suspected that there must have always been a tragic disparity between Klein's intellectual and emotional development. "Often I thought of him as the boy in knee-pants, very clever, and using his cleverness as a compensation for the fact that he can't play baseball on the lot with the boys or get into a fist-fight." It seemed to Layton that Klein simply could not open up emotionally. "For all his exuberance and seeming extroversion, he never unbuttoned himself, never dwelt on anything personal. For me, the symbol of Klein was always that buttoned-up collar and tight bow tie of his. I never saw him with an open collar." Layton, who in his own career was seeking to cultivate a fearless Nietzschean persona, saw Klein as just the opposite: a man who was basically evading reality and who in his writings therefore "romanticizes the Jew, presents him as quaint and vanishing. The emotions he exploits are the minor ones — sentiment, disappointment, heartache. There is a backward-looking quality in his poetry."

In the summer of 1958 Klein allowed himself to be interviewed over several days by Eli Palnick, a young Montrealer who had grown up a few doors away from him on Hutchison Street in the forties. Palnick was preparing a short biographical study of Klein as his Master's thesis for Hebrew Union College in Cincinnati, where he was being ordained as a Reform rabbi. Among several other people whom he interviewed were Irving Layton, and Dan Wolofsky, whose family published the *Canadian Jewish Chronicle*.

Palnick portrayed Klein's life as a devastating series of frustrations and failures. Wolofsky told him that Klein had felt used by the Jewish community, that he had been ignored by the wealthy Jews who admired his Zionism and social conscience but who prudently took their legal business elsewhere. Klein rejected such talk, saying he "never had any complaints" about his income. He admitted only to having made an unsuitable career choice: he had naively hoped that as a lawyer he would be able both to support his family and to be a poet. "In my law practice," he ruefully observed, "I had plenty of time for poetry." As for the Jewish community: "They owe me nothing. Whatever I did, I didn't do because I expected the Jewish community — I was part of the Jewish community." Layton told Palnick that Klein privately disparaged the rich bigwigs of the community but refused to show his true feelings publicly or in writing; he disguised and rationalized his contempt.

Palnick sent Klein a draft of his thesis early in 1959. Klein eventually conveyed his general disapproval of the manuscript, but was helpless to stand in the way of its submission, and in fact seemed rather indifferent to what was said or written about him.

After his meeting with Palnick he granted no more interviews. Word got around that he was receiving few visitors and wished to be left alone. Now and then an out-of-town writer passing through Montreal would still seek him out. The Israeli Yiddish poet Abraham Sutzkever managed to see him once in 1959. Klein was unusually receptive and conversed affably about Israel, Jewish literature, and Canadian literature. When talk faltered after a while, he took Sutzkever up to his study and showed him some books that he thought would be of interest. Sutzkever, discreetly avoiding any mention of Klein's illness, ventured to ask what he was working on most recently. In response, Klein simply nodded to his desk, which was completely bare.

A. J. M. Smith's last contact with Klein was in the summer of 1960, while on a visit to Montreal.

My *Oxford Book of Canadian Verse* was published that year, and I had dedicated it to Pratt and Klein. I'd sent a copy of it to Abe and never heard from him, so I called him on the phone and asked if he'd received it. I didn't know how ill he had been. There was a long pause and he said nothing. I said, "I dedicated it to you and Pratt." A pause again, and then he said, "Thank you." I asked if he would come out and have lunch. He said no, he didn't go out. I asked if I could come up to see him, and he said yes.

So I went with my wife to see him at his house. She and Bessie sat talking in the front parlor, and Abe took me into the library. He poured me a good stiff slug of Scotch, though he took nothing himself, and I talked to him. I asked if he was writing anything. He answered only in monosyllables, he said no. I said, "Did you see Steinberg's article on *The Second Scroll*?" — it had come out just a while before in *Canadian Literature*. He said, "No, I didn't read it." So after a few minutes of talking to him and getting polite but distant monosyllables, I decided that I had to go. It was very, very sad, and that was the last time I saw him. Our wives had made plans for all of us to go on a picnic the next day, but Klein phoned afterwards and said no, he couldn't go.

IN HIS REMAINING YEARS, Klein's circle of activity — the distances he would venture from home, the number of people he would see — grew progressively smaller. Very close friends and relatives continued to visit the house, never knowing whether he would speak to them that day or even just come down from his study.

By 1960 he was no longer answering his mail. At about that time he also stopped writing for Sam Bronfman, though he maintained his official position as a public relations consultant to the end of his life. Once each year he would dictate a birthday greeting to Bronfman — his only written communication of any kind with anyone.

The suicide of his psychiatrist in August 1961 may have influenced his decision to refuse any further medical treatment. His family physician pleaded with him to try new forms of drug therapy in the early sixties, but to no avail. Nor could Bessie persuade him to change his attitude. In Colman's view, a tacit if not explicit pact had been established between his parents: Klein would go on leading a tranquil existence as long as Bessie would refrain from any effort to have him treated. He curtly refused to discuss his illness with his children and gave them no sign of any self-awareness or insight into his own condition.

In the face of severe emotional and financial difficulties, Bessie struggled to maintain as normal a household as possible for her children. She refused to despair and spoke philosophically of the balance of good and bad years she had shared with Klein. Through the worst of times her family continued to rely on her warmth, her cheerful receptiveness, and her comforting ability to listen to them with openness and sympathy.

Klein's older son, Colman, married and left home in 1958, completed his architecture studies in 1961, and then spent several years away from Montreal during the sixties. Sandor lived with his parents through most of the decade while studying to become a lawyer and did not move out until after his marriage in 1968. In Colman's absence he gradually assumed the main position of responsibility at home and developed a close day-to-day relationship with his father. It was Klein's daughter, Sharon, who was most adversely affected by the trauma of his breakdown. Though gifted with superior intelligence, she dropped out of high school in her final year and went through a long period of emotional turmoil in the sixties.

Towards the end, Klein's conversations with his own family were usually limited to very short responses. Sometimes he would remain completely silent for days at a stretch, although even then he was clearly able to understand everything that was being spoken around him. Intellectually he remained quite alert. He followed news stories with interest, read constantly, played Scrabble with Bessie and the children, and watched a good deal of television. He liked to listen to Sandor talk about his law studies and his first experiences as a practicing lawyer. He rarely spoke of his own past, but there was no evidence that he had forgotten it.

His paranoia persisted and would sometimes give rise to visible fits of anguish. For the most part it resolved itself into a general habit of suspicion about any unfamiliar item that was brought into the house from the outside. Despite everything, he remained capable of getting around on his own. In the earlier years of his illness he would often take a streetcar or bus downtown, though he would never enter an automobile or ride in an elevator. In later years he would just go for short walks in his own neighborhood.

Until the late sixties he was somehow able to work up the presence required to discuss a loan with his bank manager. He was particularly fussy about shaving daily and having his hair cut regularly, but refused to give up his old clothes until they were completely tattered. He refused to be seen by

COLMAN'S MARRIAGE TO ALICE EVELSON IN 1958 WAS THE LAST PUBLIC FUNCTION THAT KLEIN ATTENDED. TEN YEARS LATER, SANDOR MARRIED MONA GARMAISE, THE YOUNGER DAUGHTER OF MAX GARMAISE, KLEIN'S FIRST LAW PARTNER.

any doctors and fortunately never suffered from any physical illness during all his years of seclusion. Only a painful toothache would ever bring him to a dentist's office.

Strolling near his home, he would cut a striking figure with his still-distinguished gait and slightly outmoded attire. Sometimes he would be greeted by old friends along the way, but would usually pretend not to have seen them or heard their hello. To neighbors he was generally more polite. He disliked being recognized in bookstores, whether by the owner or other patrons. In the late sixties, to avoid such encounters, he began confining his visits to just one French bookstore on Laurier Avenue a few blocks from his home. French books were virtually all he bought in his last years.

As long as the children were around, the household itself remained a fairly lively place. Sharon had a large number of friends who often came over, and Bessie in particular always made them feel welcome. Klein was generally unperturbed by young visitors — in fact, the younger they were, the more harmless and innocent they seemed to be in his eyes. When his first grandchildren were born he delighted in joining their make-believe games and reading to them in his study.

Young children from the surrounding neighborhood would often play in front of the house while Klein sat silently for hours on the porch. They thought of him as mute. Once he spotted a group of French-speaking children running into the street while cars were passing by and shouted a brusque warning to them to stay on the sidewalk. Amazed at this "miracle," they reported to Bessie later, "Non seulement qu'il parle, il parle français!"

Small royalties on his books continued to trickle in, but Klein refused to endorse any checks from his publishers. It seemed his way of saying that he was no longer worthy, no longer the same man he once was. Similarly he would never acknowledge requests for permission to publish various of his uncollected and out-of-print works. His stubbornness in this exasperated Bessie, who was most aware of how badly they needed even these negligible earnings.

In 1969 Bessie's health began to deteriorate rapidly, following a bout of influenza. She suffered a heart attack in January 1971 and after several weeks in hospital died on February 26, just two weeks after the thirty-fifth anniversary of her wedding.

Klein's grief momentarily shook him out of his emotional isolation. Bessie had become virtually the only person in his world and he mourned her loss deeply. Though he would not attend the funeral, he allowed himself, for the first time in many years, to be taken out in a car to pay his last respects at the funeral parlor the night before. He sat *shiva* alone at home while the rest of the family gathered for the week of mourning at Sandor's.

Sharon continued to live with him, though for the most part he managed to look after himself with surprisingly little difficulty. His health seemed generally normal. On August 20, 1972, he died quietly in his sleep, apparently of a heart attack.

The funeral was small and traditional. Some of the Montreal writers who attended were surprised and even upset that no tribute was paid to Klein as a poet. His longtime neighbor and respected friend Rabbi Pinchos Hirschprung delivered a pious eulogy entirely in Yiddish. Struck by the stark simplicity of the occasion, Melech Ravitch described it afterwards as a funeral such as one might have witnessed in Ratno itself, in the days when Ratno was.

A spirit passed before me

(Translated from the Hebrew of Chaim Nachman Bialik)

A spirit passed before my face, it dazzled me; for an instant your fingertip,
O Lord, quivered the strings of my heart.
I stood there humbled, hushed, all ardor quelled. My heart curled within me;
my mouth could not muster a psalm.
And, in truth, with what was I to come into the Temple? And how could
my prayer ever be pure?

For my speech, O Lord, is altogether abhorrent, has become a broth
of abomination.
There is not a word in it that has not been infected to the root; not a phrase but
heard and it is mocked, not a locution but it has boarded in a house of shame.

My doves, my pure doves, that I had sent forth at dawn towards the sky, at dusk
they came back, and, behold, they were crows!
From their throats there issued the rooks' cawing; their beaks stank of carcasses;
naturalized of the dungheaps, my doves!

It encompasses me, this cluttering rampage of language, it surrounds me, like a
wreathing of harlots gone out on the town.
They glitter their gewgaws and gauds, they preen themselves, their eyes are
fucus'd red, rot is in their bones.
This is their grace.

And at their skirts there trail the imps of incest, bastards of the pen, the get of
fancy, words monstrous, arrogant, loathsome, a flux from empty-cockled hearts.
As the wildgrass they grow, they multiply like the thistle, there is no escape
from them.

Daily, as the gutters are swept and the urinals emptied, their fetor, too, rises and
corrupts the air, penetrates even to the man shut solitary in his room, unsabbaths
his peace.

Where shall I run from this stench? Where shall I hide from this jangle?
Where is the seraph and his gleed shall cauterize my lips?

Only in the twittering of the birds, twittering at sunrise, or in the company of
little children, playing in the street their simple games, only there may I be cleansed.
I will go, therefore, I will mingle with them, I will join in the *aleph-bais* of their
talk and their lessons; and in that clean breath feel clean again.

(early 1950s)

214

from Journal, 1945

I am at my oldest sister's funeral ... she is lying now, in a box, here in front of the pulpit of Applebaum's Funeral Chapel. On the mourners' bench sit her children, some red-eyed with weeping, and some pensive with thoughts of their own future....My sister Bessie stands beside the coffin and addresses the board under which she supposes the deceased's head lies, attentive. She begs forgiveness for the offences which she, and all of us, may have committed, wittingly or unwittingly, against the honor and dignity of the departed. She begs her to greet my father in his heavenly home, and there together with him to intercede for all our family and for all of Israel here below. At these words my brother begins to sob....

As for myself, I don't weep. Tears are not for the dead. Another's pain, another's prospect of death — there is subject for sympathy, and the balm of salt-water. But not for the dead this chemical tribute.

Nonetheless, as I listen to the women moaning their great sorrow, moaning and repeating to themselves the little gracious acts of her days that are no more — some of which I recognize to be true and of my own experience — it is memory and not death that brings the tears to my eyes.

They are big tears, bubbled by restraint. The whole room is blurred and foggy, and I can no longer clearly identify any of the people about me. Around the coffin stand several members of the family, but I do not, any longer, perceive them in their individuality; through the haze of my tears, they have become a conglomerate family blur, a single large shadow hovering over the black-draped box.

And suddenly it is I who lie there in that box. I am the one whom all have come to mourn. My mother, clasping her fingers and breaking them backwards, weeps that her crown has fallen. My sisters' eyes can no longer be seen, they have been crying so much, and particularly my sister Dora who sobs how helpless she is now without me. She makes a scene — she was always forthright — and she shouts that there are others who should have died before me. Supported by friends, my wife, my poor wife — she has already fainted several times....

The rabbi mounts the pulpit to make the obituary laudation. He tells of my scholarship, of my lectures, of my articles, of my contribution to the intellectual life of my community. He speaks of my honesty, and makes a contrast between public reaction at my passing and that upon the passing of a mere rich man. He tells of how I was good to my mother, how I honored my father, and how I brought up my children in the spirit and according to the traditions of my race....At this stage, the rabbi cannot continue, for my kith and kin have abandoned their respectful and sobbing silence. They wail; they tear their hair; they faint. Strangers rush forward to console them. The rabbi finishes his speech with some biblical verses.

From behind my tears, I watch the entire ceremony, a stranger at my own funeral. Among the dead, I am beyond pain and pity, and am unmoved by the ululation which I have so unintentionally caused. But I feel a certain glow of mild satisfaction. Here, my whole biography has been recounted, but nobody mentioned the fact that I was a poet.

I have kept the secret well. Now, no one will ever know of what I died.

Spinoza: on Man, on the Rainbow

All flowers that in seven ways bright
Make gay the common earth,
All jewels that in their tunneled night
Enkindle and flash forth

All these, now in the sky up-thrust,
To dazzle human sight
Do hang but on a speck of dust,
But dust suffused by light.

(early 1950s)

14

The Nth Adam

Klein's death released an unexpectedly strong current of affection and interest that had been pent up for nearly two decades. It was as if the obscurity into which he had retreated had, against all intentions, enlarged his legend. In various Canadian and American cities, and across the ocean as far away as Jerusalem, memorial gatherings were held, where friends and admirers shared reminiscences and read from his poems. Deeply-felt tributes in both prose and verse cropped up in literary magazines and Jewish periodicals.

His reputation at the end was based mainly on a small number of poems that reappeared frequently in Canadian anthologies. Of his own books, only *The Rocking Chair* and a paperback edition of *The Second Scroll* were in print during his last years. After his death, however, his children were able to authorize the republication of his writings. In 1974 McGraw-Hill Ryerson of Toronto issued Klein's *Collected Poems,* bringing together his four books of verse and virtually all of his other published poems from the late twenties to the early fifties. Miriam Waddington, a Canadian poet who had written a short study of his work several years earlier, was assigned to compile and introduce the volume.

Klein's daughter, Sharon, who was perhaps the most literary of his three children and the closest of all to his artistic temperament, unhappily did not live to see the publication of the *Collected Poems.* She died suddenly of a heart attack on May 30, 1973, and it was to her memory that Waddington dedicated the volume.

The publication of the *Collected Poems* coincided with a growing interest in Klein among Canadian literary scholars. In the spring of 1974 a Klein symposium was held at the University of Ottawa, organized by a member of its English department, the poet Seymour Mayne. Among the gathered guests were many of Klein's old friends, including David Lewis, F.R. Scott, A.J.M. Smith, Leo Kennedy, Leon Edel, Max Garmaise, Irving Layton, Louis Dudek, and P.K. Page. The academic atmosphere of the proceedings was balanced by a mood of fond personal recollection. It was only at the last session, after two days of tributes and learned presentations, that Layton felt compelled to articulate the unuttered question still hanging in the air: "Why the silence of those seventeen or eighteen years at the end? Why did Klein not fulfill the greatness and the promise of his youth?" Layton held to his theory that Klein was a trapped man, who at a certain point had faltered and failed to maintain the freedom and absolute independence required of a true artist. Lewis, Garmaise, and others present forcefully resisted Layton's arguments by insisting that it was simply impossible to guess the causes of Klein's illness. Edel commented: "We are here to judge Klein, but not to sit in judgement. We can't tell him to have lived another kind of life."

The symposium provided the occasion for the first meeting of a group of scholars interested in editing Klein's unpublished and uncollected writings. Work has since begun on several volumes due to be published over the coming years by the University of Toronto Press, including a selection of Klein's newspaper articles and editorials, the complete short fiction, literary essays, and notebooks. Among other volumes planned for the future are the complete poems, selected letters, and the spy novel.

Klein's unpublished writings, which will make up a significant part of this series, are mostly to be found in the collection of private papers discovered after his death in a four-drawer filing cabinet that he kept in his study. Early in 1973 a strong bid for the papers was made by the University of Texas at Austin. Klein's children preferred, however, to keep the collection in Canada, and in the summer of 1973 the papers were sold to the Public Archives in Ottawa.

Klein evidently had little interest in saving his manuscripts for posterity and no concept of their potential value. The collection, therefore, consists mainly of the working files of an active writer at a particular moment in his career — in this case, the moment at which it was about to end. Among the papers are quite a number of unfinished and unpublished works from the forties and early fifties, some of which Klein probably intended to revise or to incorporate into larger structures. Many of the things one would have hoped to find in the collection are simply not there. From a practical standpoint, there was no need for him to save the manuscript of a completed and published work, such as *The Second Scroll*. Joyce scholars who had hoped to see the text of his long-awaited commentary on *Ulysses* were similarly disappointed. Klein's unfinished study of Joyce is the most obviously missing part of the collection and probably the only major part that he deliberately destroyed. All that has survived of it are some scanty notes, a few tattered, marked up copies of *Ulysses,* and a small library of copiously annotated books on Joyce.

Klein's poetry manuscripts, many of which he fortunately saved, constitute an especially rich part of the collection. Altogether there are over a hundred unpublished poems, mostly from the late twenties and early thirties. In handwritten form there are unfinished verse fragments as well as early drafts of some of the more familiar published works. Of particular interest are the numerous handwritten revisions that Klein was in the habit of adding to typed and printed copies of his earlier poems.

KLEIN'S POSTHUMOUS REPUTATION, which has been growing steadily in recent years, is something that he himself could hardly have foreseen. The popularity of Jewish literature in North America came too late for him; had he continued writing into the sixties and beyond, he surely would have found the Jewish audience he deserved. In Canada, as well, he would have been able to enjoy the literary flowering of the last fifteen years.

The qualities that make him so fascinating to a later generation are as various as the conflicting elements of his life. He will probably always be regarded as a poet's poet, and yet he was never really certain that poetry was the highest good. He was a word-intoxicated man, and his abiding respect for formal excellence and technical virtuosity often brought him close to a pure "art for art's sake" attitude. But as a Jew, and as a humanitarian, he could not put art above people. It is of himself that he speaks when he has someone say of Uncle Melech, in *The Second Scroll,* that "he greatly loves the right word, but he loves righteousness more."

His hesitancy about playing the poet was noticeable even in his most confident moments. When asked by A.J.M. Smith to describe his literary credo for *The Book of Canadian Poetry,* he replied:

I do not intend to give you "a brief statement of my attitude towards my art, etc." I am surprised that you ask it. You know that such questions elicit only the sheerest of arrogant balderdash. What shall I say in reply: "I sing because I must!" — How phoney! Or that I wish to improve the world with my rhyme! — How ridiculous! Or that I seek to express the standards of my age, etc. Me, I will have none of that cant. Simply expressed, I write poetry only to reveal my civilization, my sensitivities, my craftsmanship. This, however, is not to be quoted.

He was most comfortable with Judaic models of the poet's vocation. In the line of David and Isaiah, the poet is psalmist and prophet. Like the scribe, copyist of the Torah scroll, he is a holy vessel, the transmitter of a venerable heritage. Like Adam, he is the archetypal namegiver and partner in creation

> ... taking a green inventory
> in world but scarcely uttered, naming, praising,
> ... Until it has been praised, that part
> has not been.

Even like God, the supreme Creator, he aspires through the use of language to "make a new thing... bring new forms to life."

His brief career was a brilliant and original experiment in the mingling of cultures. At a time when ethnicity was shunned by intellectuals and assimilation the order of the day, he reveled in his Jewishness, all the while remaining as open as anyone could be to the English and French influences around him. In his last creative years he continued growing and seemed to be moving into even wider spheres, exploring Irish, Russian, Arabic, and other cultures.

A large part of the mystique that now surrounds Klein undoubtedly stems from the fact of his breakdown. The self-destructive element in his character seemed to emerge out of some deeply-rooted messiah complex. In his endless search for models of Jewish heroism, he continually fell back on images of martyrdom. The suicide attempts, and then his permanent silence — his non-physical suicide, as Colman saw it — rounded his life with the completeness of some ancient legend: the hero achieving immortal fame by choosing a premature death.

Yet the enduring fascination lies elsewhere. What is finally most appealing in Klein is not his sad end, but the strength that he projected in his best moments — the frank pride of race, the sense of justice, the love of tradition. His traditionalism harked back to a lost world — for him the immortal days of his own childhood.

> All days thereafter are a dying-off,
> A wandering away
> From home and the familiar. The years doff
> Their innocence.
> No other day is ever like that day.

The nostalgia that informs so much of Klein's poetry evokes a universal longing for an earlier age and its certainties that have vanished. Now he himself has entered the tradition, and it is we who seek his "fabled city," that sentimental dream world out of which he built, "in Space's vapors and Time's haze," his lasting monument.

Photo Credits

Audrey Aikman, 98 right
Concordia University, 100
Louis Dudek, 98 left
Leon Edel, 52
Jewish Agency (New York), 166
Jewish Public Library of Montreal, 85, 171, 176, 190
David Kaufman, 27, 28, 31, 44, 59, 145, 148, 162, 204, 216
Colman and Sandor Klein, 6, 19, 37 left, 63, 66, 70, 73, 80, 94, 103, 143, 169, 180, 212
Library of Congress (Washington, D.C.), 78
Montreal Municipal Archives, 21
Ottawa Jewish Historical Society, 49

P. K. Page, 97
Public Archives of Canada, 2 (C58352), 33, 37 right (C64042), 38 (C64044), 50 (C70429), 58 (PA87776), 60 (C64035), 69 (C64033), 75 (PA107943), 86 (MG30, D167, vol. 22), 88 (C58355), 92, 97 left (PA116395), 111 (PA107910), 122 (C58356), 125 (MG30, D167, vol. 17, p.8839), 134 (C58339), 137 (C58344), 138, 158 (MG30, D167, vol. 18), 159 (MG30, D167, vol. 16), 173 (C58349), 183 (MG30, D167, vol. 13), 206
Quebec National Archives, 16, 118
F. R. Scott, 52
Peter Smith, 52
YIVO Institute (New York), 108, 116, 120

Index